ULTIMATE IRON MAN

ULTIMATE IRON MAN

WRITER:
ORSON SCOTT CARD

PENCILS:
ANDY KUBERT AND MARK BAGLEY

INKS: DANNY MIKI
WITH BATT, JESSE DELPERDANG, JOHN DELL & SCOTT KOBLISH
COLORS: RICHARD ISANOVE
WITH DAVE MCCAIG & LAURA MARTIN
LETTERS: CHRIS ELIOPOULOS
ASSISTANT EDITOR: SEAN RYAN
EDITOR: NICK LOWE
CONSULTING EDITORS: RALPH MACCHIO & MIKE MARTS

COLLECTION EDITOR: JENNIFER GRÜNWALD
ASSISTANT EDITOR: MICHAEL SHORT
SENIOR EDITOR, SPECIAL PROJECTS: JEFF YOUNGQUIST
VICE PRESIDENT OF SALES: DAVID GABRIEL
PRODUCTION: JERRY KALINOWSKI
BOOK DESIGNER: JEOF VITA
VICE PRESIDENT OF CREATIVE: TOM MARVELLI

EDITOR IN CHIEF: JOE QUESADA
PUBLISHER: DAN BUCKLEY

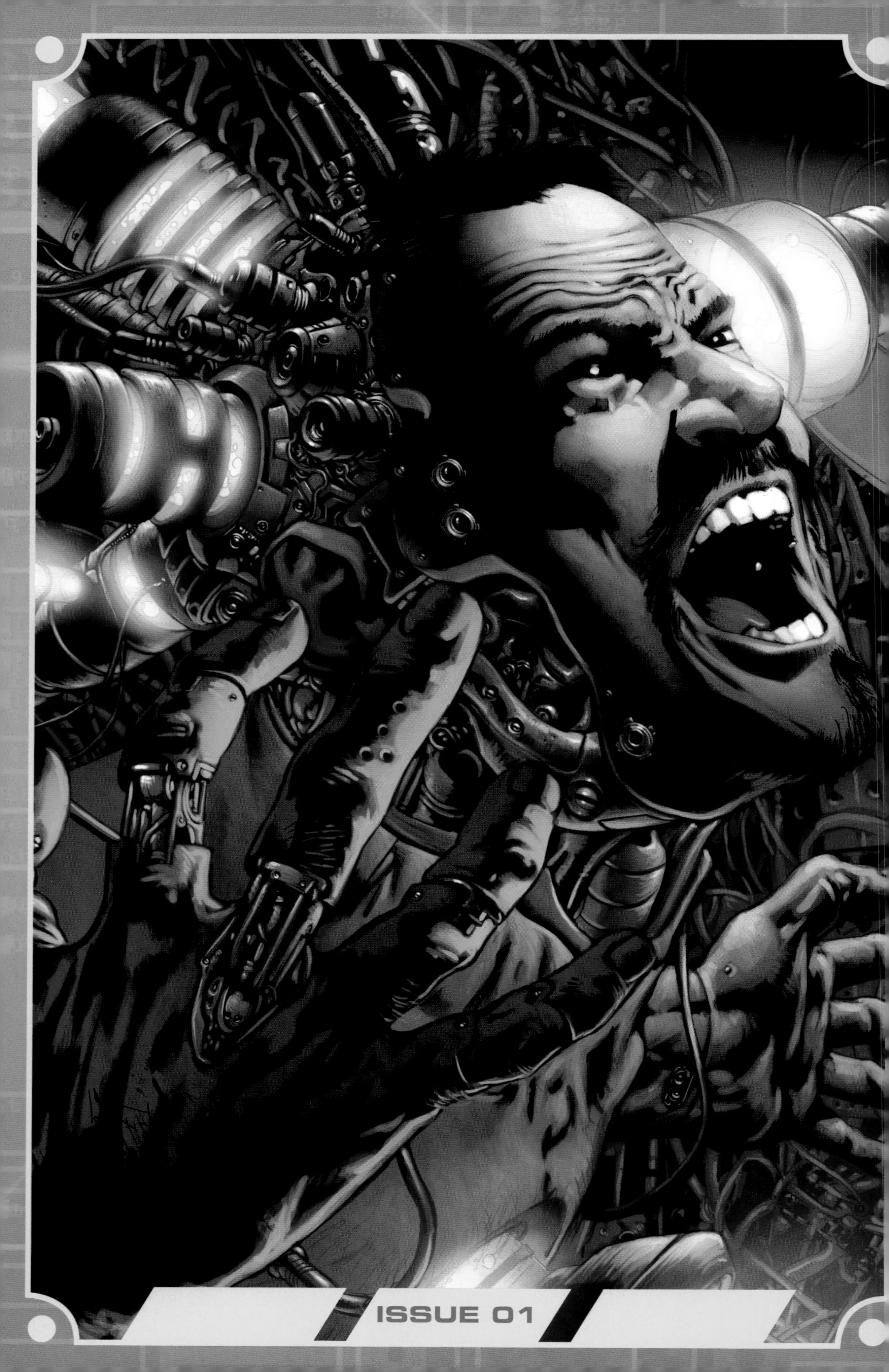
ISSUE 01

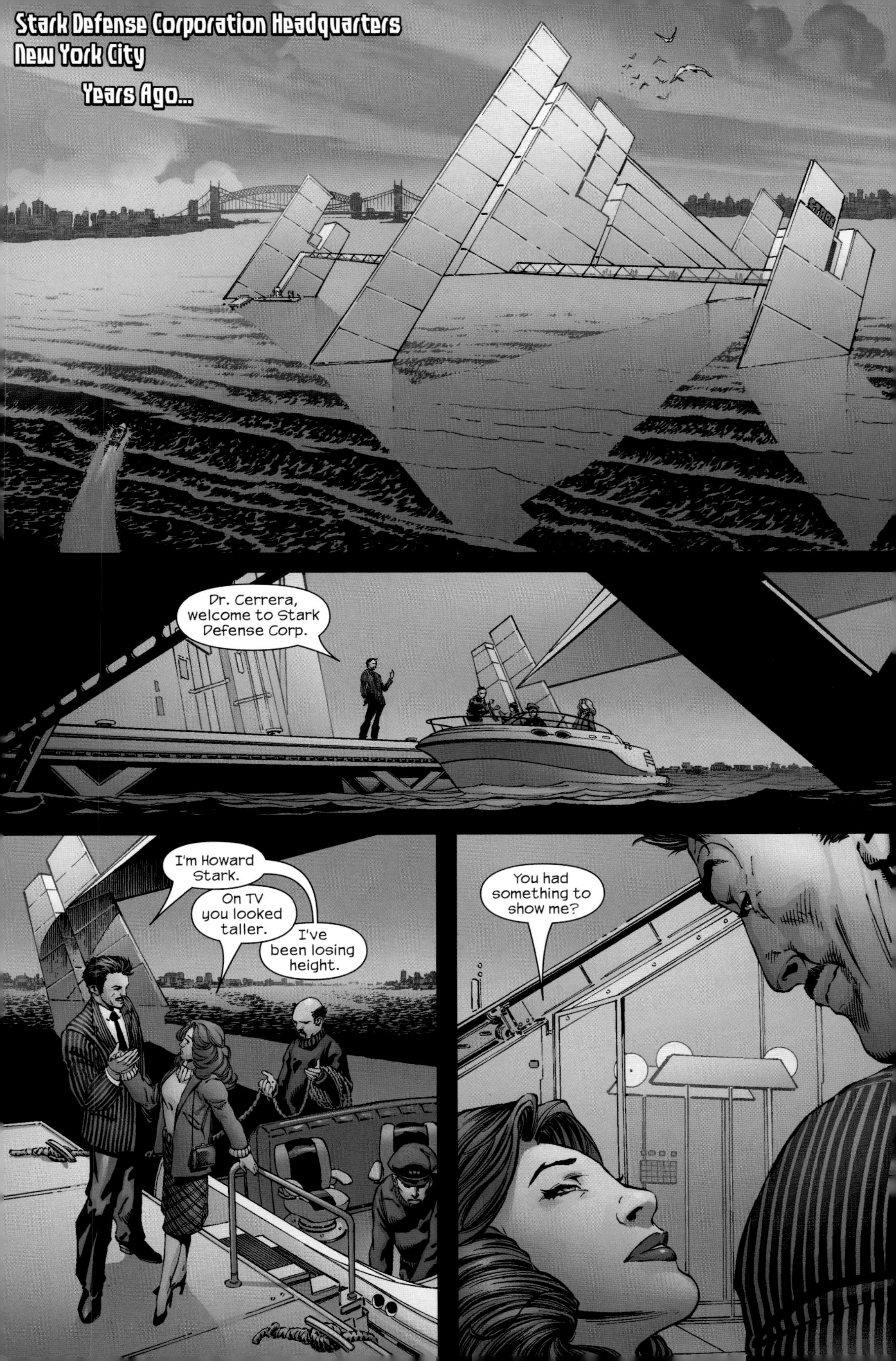

Stark Defense Corporation Headquarters
New York City
Years Ago...
STARK
Dr. Cerrera, welcome to Stark Defense Corp.
I'm Howard Stark.
On TV you looked taller.
I've been losing height.
You had something to show me?

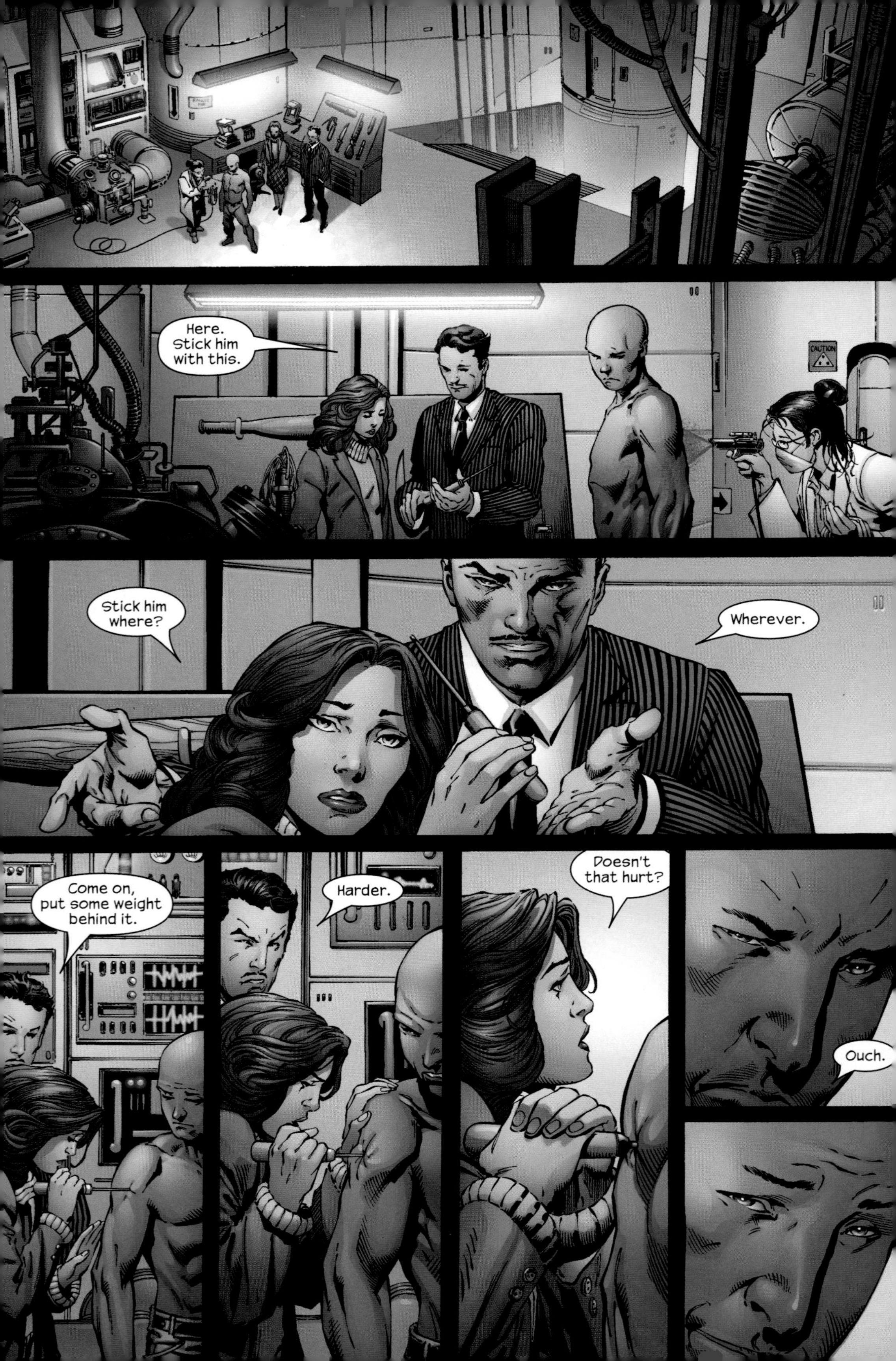
Here. Stick him with this.
Stick him where?
Wherever.
Come on, put some weight behind it.
Harder.
Doesn't that hurt?
Ouch.

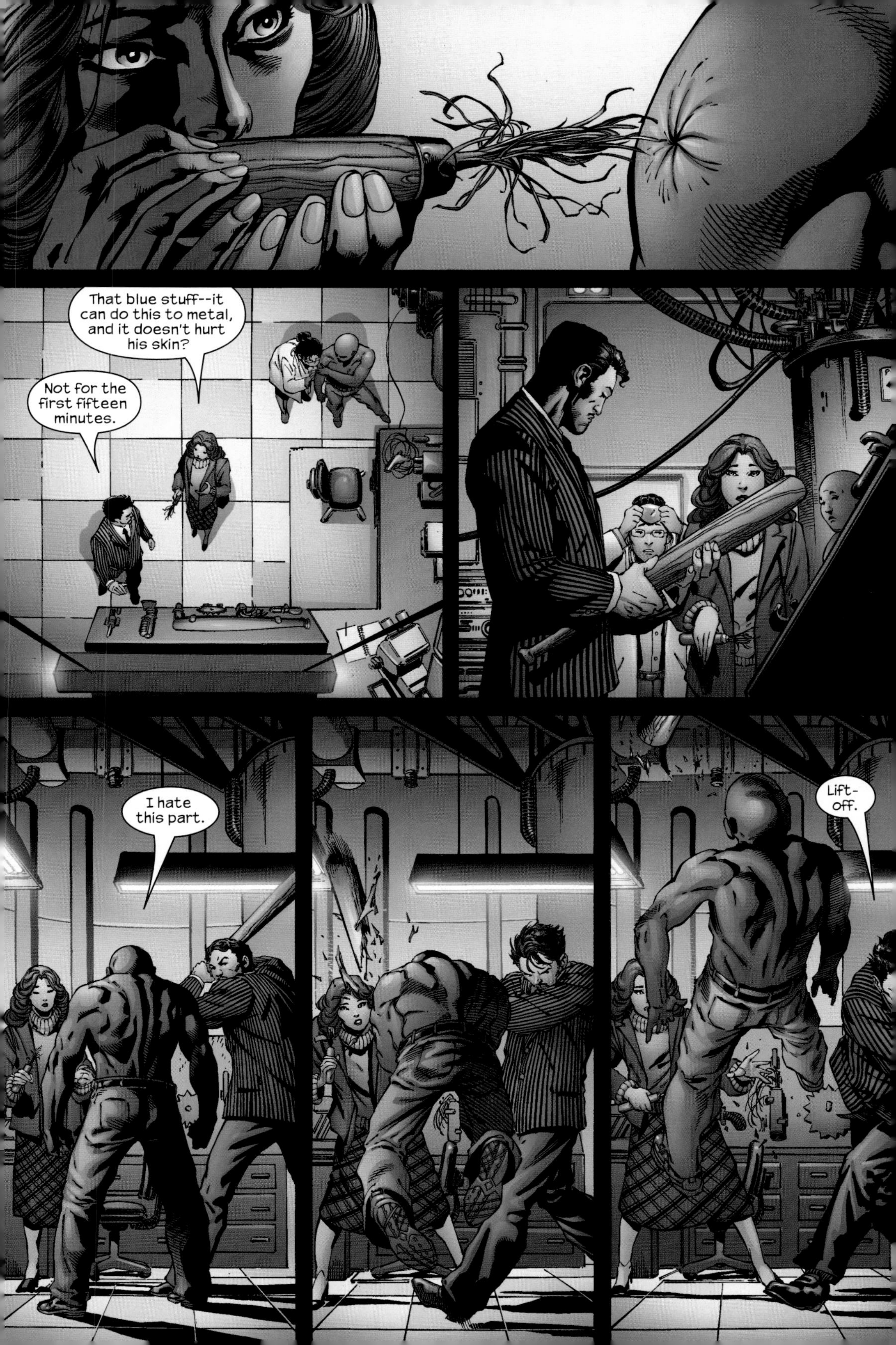

That blue stuff--it can do this to metal, and it doesn't hurt his skin?
Not for the first fifteen minutes.
I hate this part.
Lift-off.

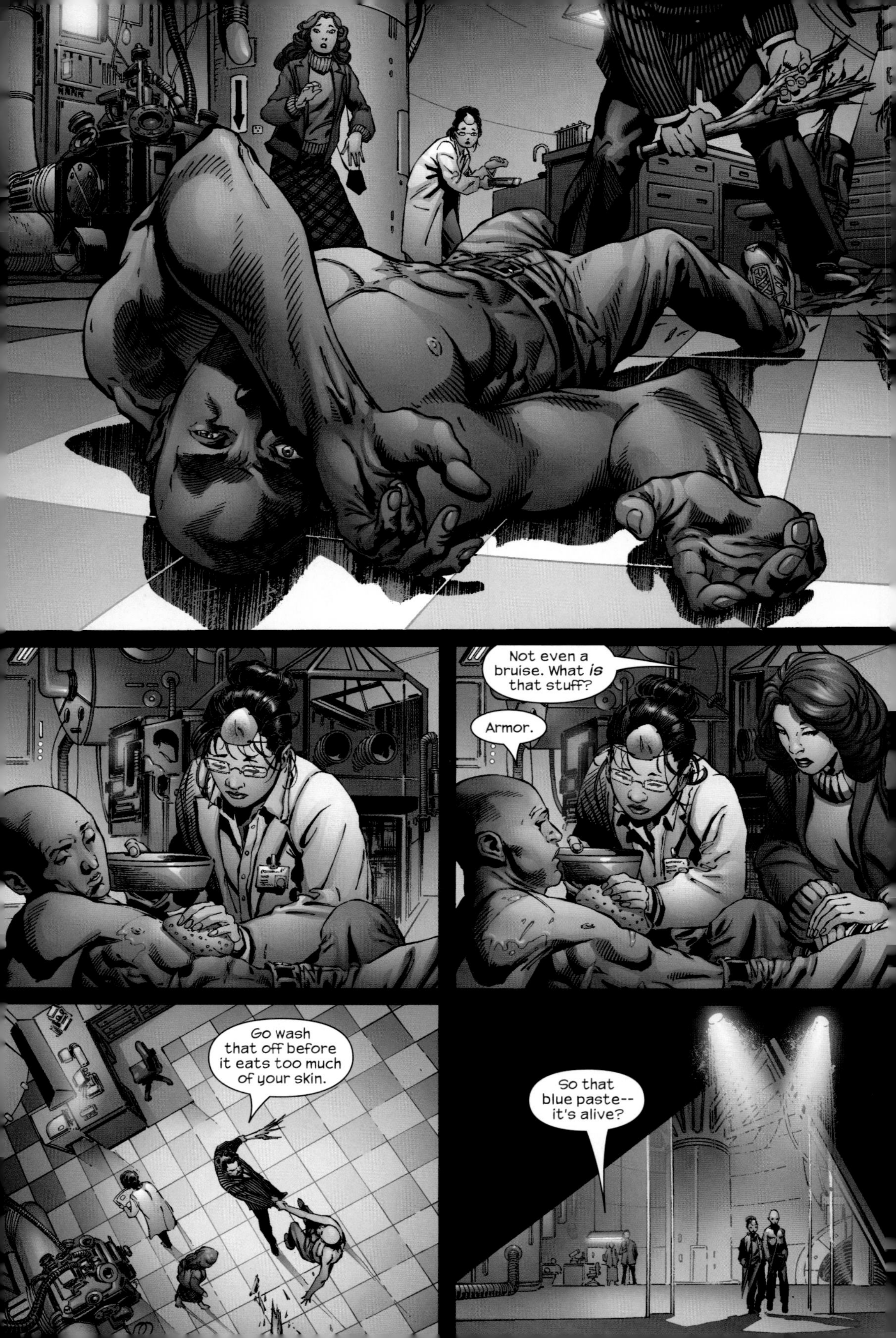
Not even a bruise. What *is* that stuff?
Armor.
Go wash that off before it eats too much of your skin.
So that blue paste-- it's alive?

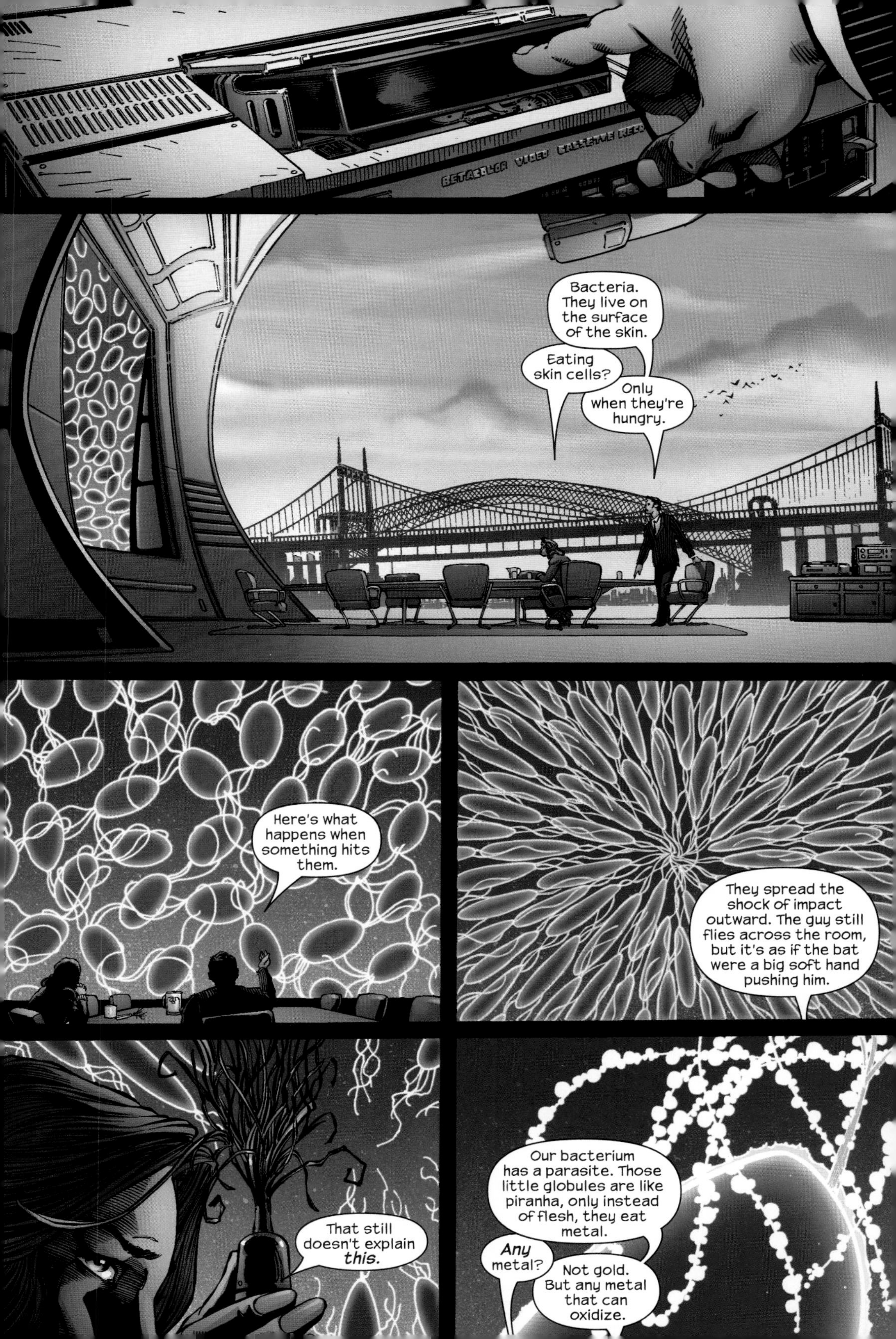
Bacteria. They live on the surface of the skin.
Eating skin cells?
Only when they're hungry.
Here's what happens when something hits them.
They spread the shock of impact outward. The guy still flies across the room, but it's as if the bat were a big soft hand pushing him.
That still doesn't explain *this.*
Our bacterium has a parasite. Those little globules are like piranha, only instead of flesh, they eat metal.
Any metal?
Not gold. But any metal that can oxidize.

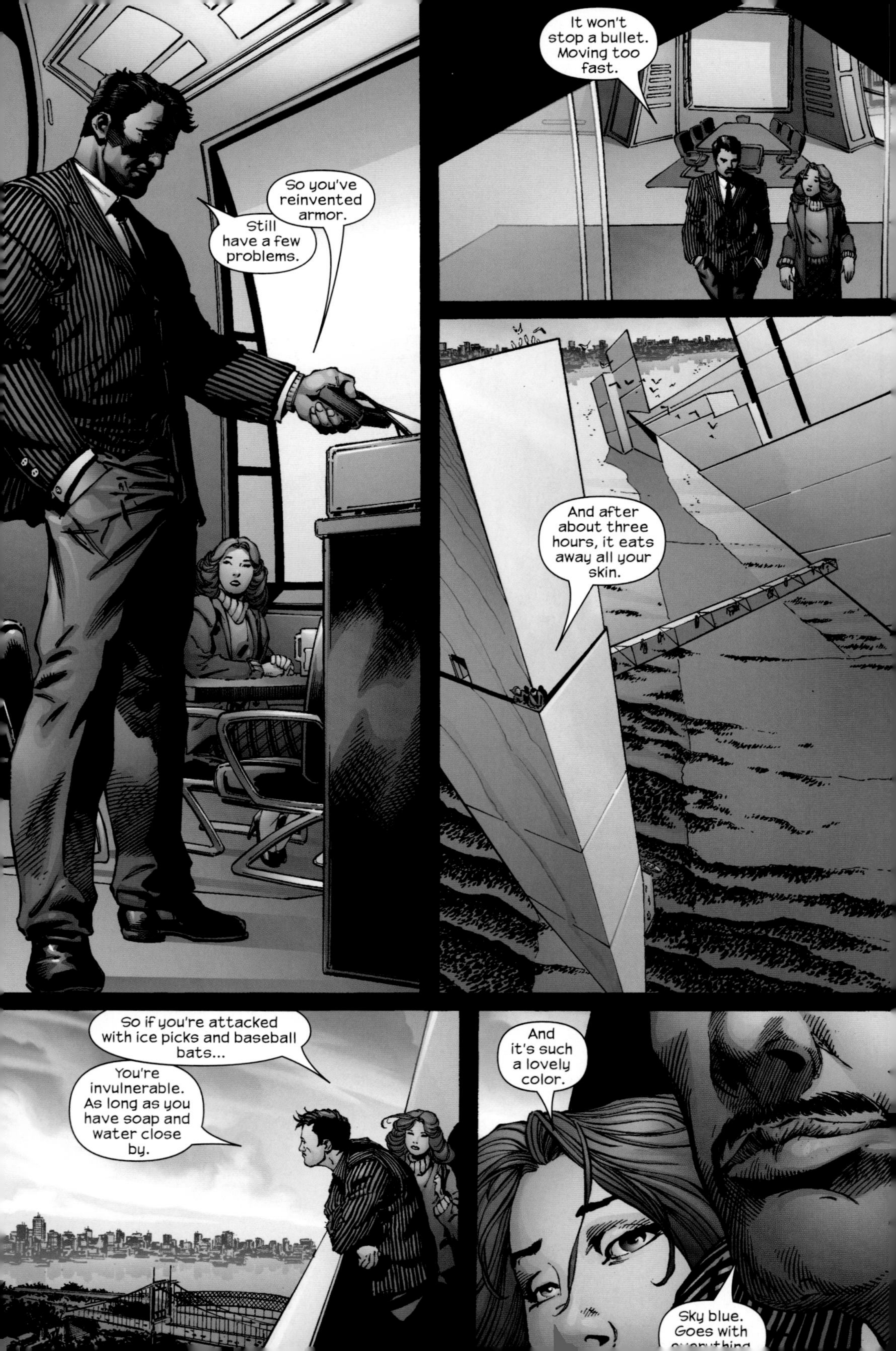
So you've reinvented armor.
Still have a few problems.
It won't stop a bullet. Moving too fast.
And after about three hours, it eats away all your skin.
So if you're attacked with ice picks and baseball bats...
You're invulnerable. As long as you have soap and water close by.
And it's such a lovely color.
Sky blue. Goes with

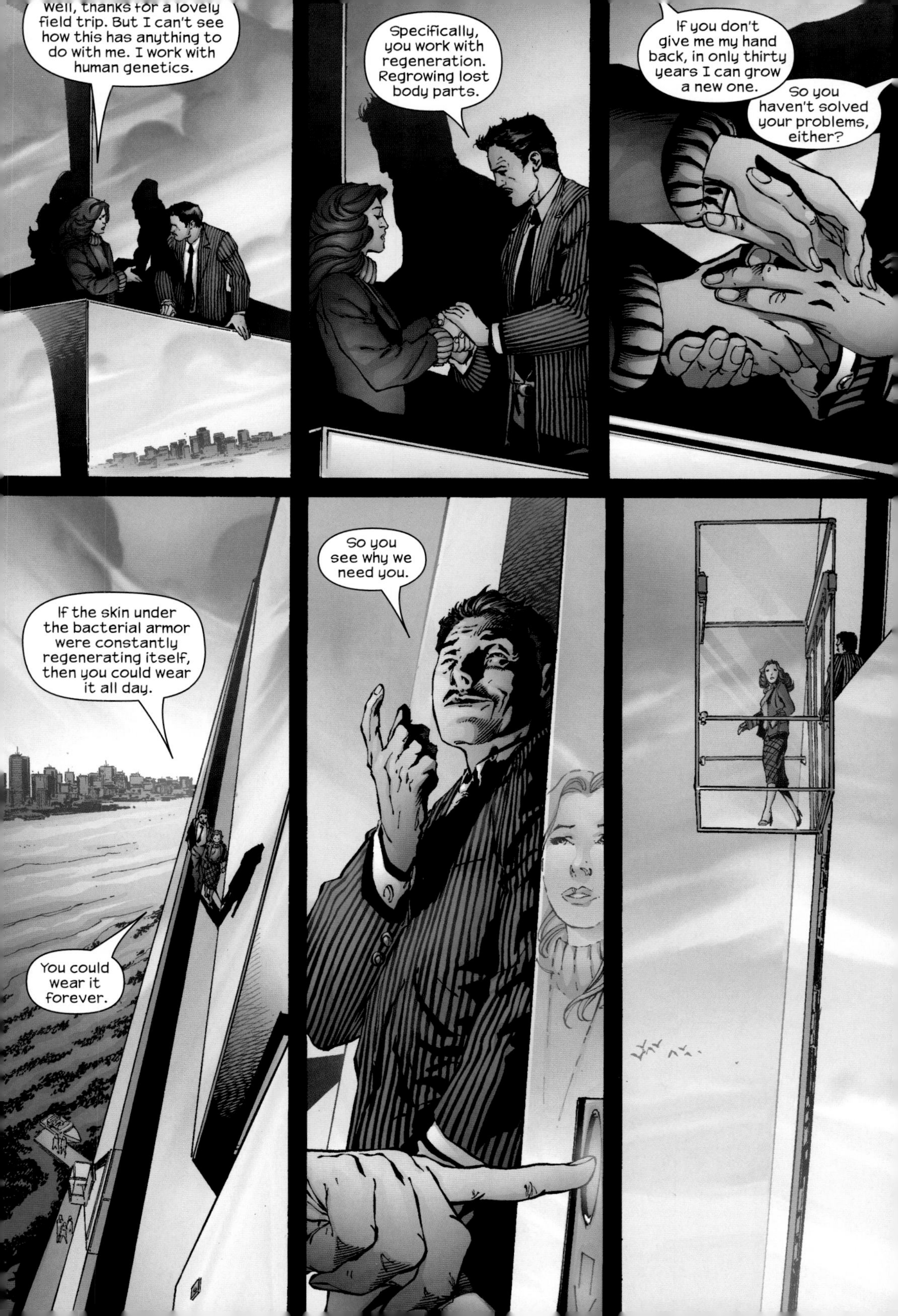
Well, thanks for a lovely field trip. But I can't see how this has anything to do with me. I work with human genetics.
Specifically, you work with regeneration. Regrowing lost body parts.
If you don't give me my hand back, in only thirty years I can grow a new one.
So you haven't solved your problems, either?
If the skin under the bacterial armor were constantly regenerating itself, then you could wear it all day.
You could wear it forever.
So you see why we need you.

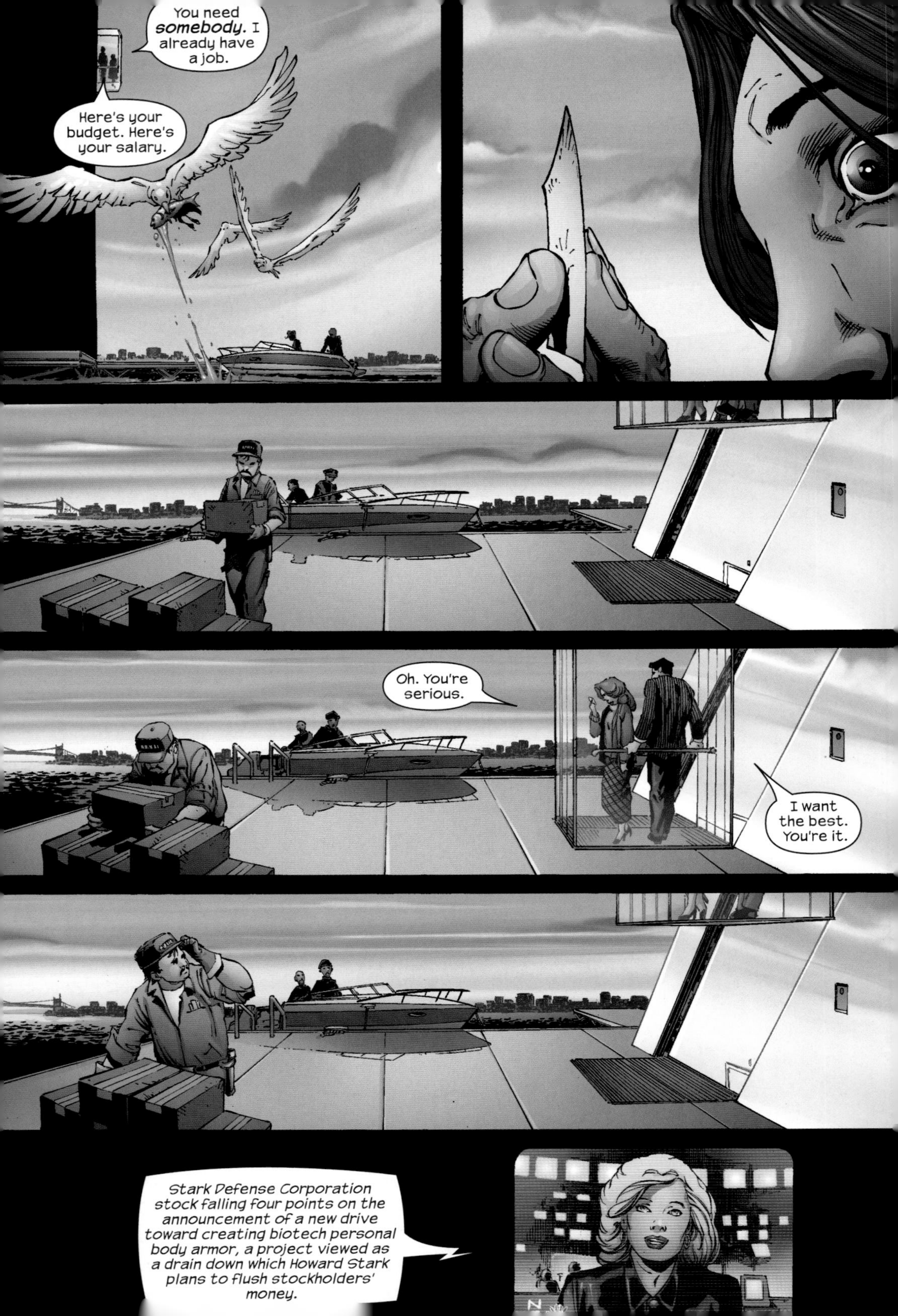
You need somebody. I already have a job.
Here's your budget. Here's your salary.
Oh. You're serious.
I want the best. You're it.
Stark Defense Corporation stock falling four points on the announcement of a new drive toward creating biotech personal body armor, a project viewed as a drain down which Howard Stark plans to flush stockholders' money.

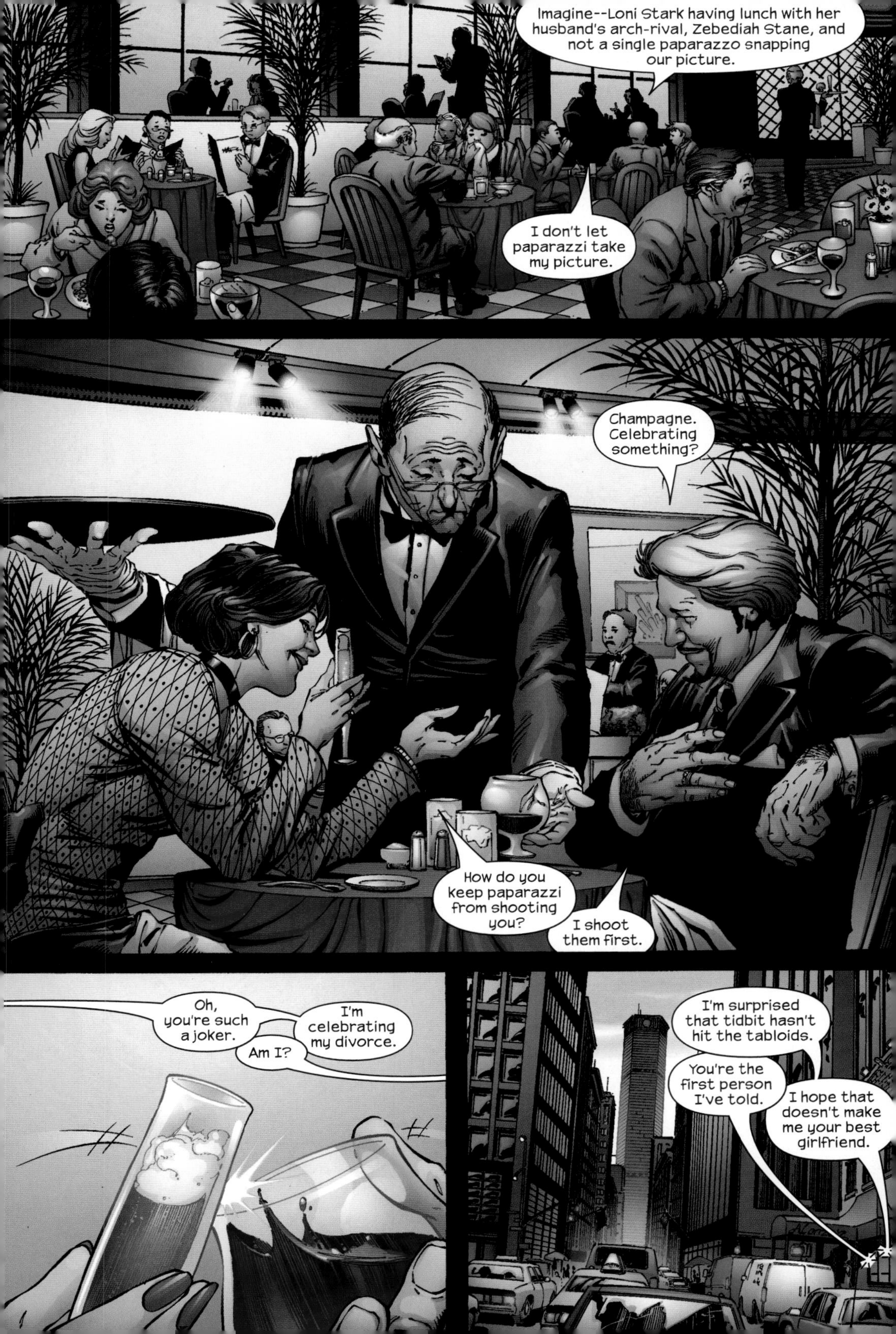
Imagine--Loni Stark having lunch with her husband's arch-rival, Zebediah Stane, and not a single paparazzo snapping our picture.
I don't let paparazzi take my picture.
Champagne. Celebrating something?
How do you keep paparazzi from shooting you?
I shoot them first.
Oh, you're such a joker.
I'm celebrating my divorce.
Am I?
I'm surprised that tidbit hasn't hit the tabloids.
You're the first person I've told.
I hope that doesn't make me your best girlfriend.

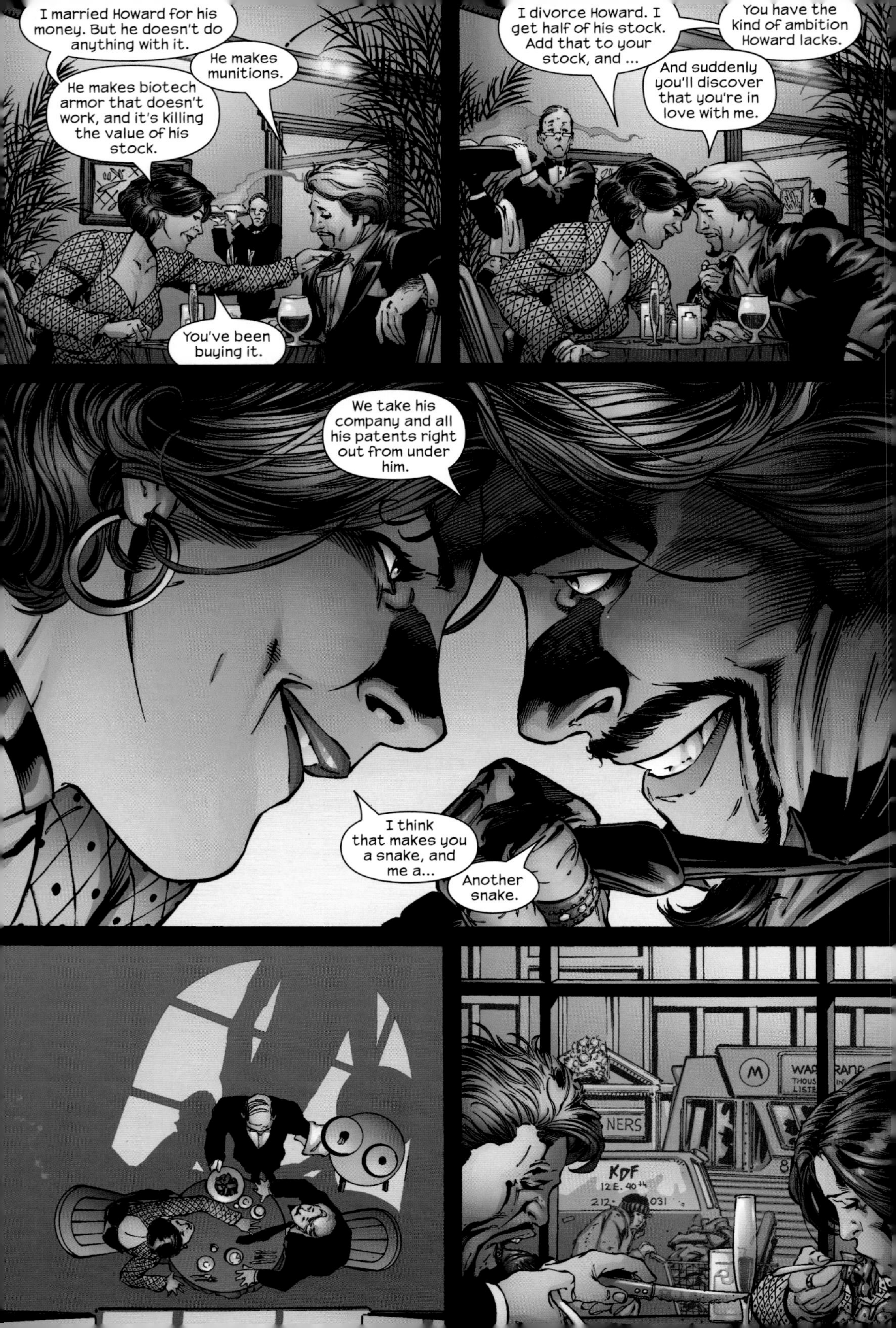
I married Howard for his money. But he doesn't do anything with it.
He makes munitions.
He makes biotech armor that doesn't work, and it's killing the value of his stock.
You've been buying it.
I divorce Howard. I get half of his stock. Add that to your stock, and ...
You have the kind of ambition Howard lacks.
And suddenly you'll discover that you're in love with me.
We take his company and all his patents right out from under him.
I think that makes you a snake, and me a...
Another snake.
NERS
KDF
12 E. 40th

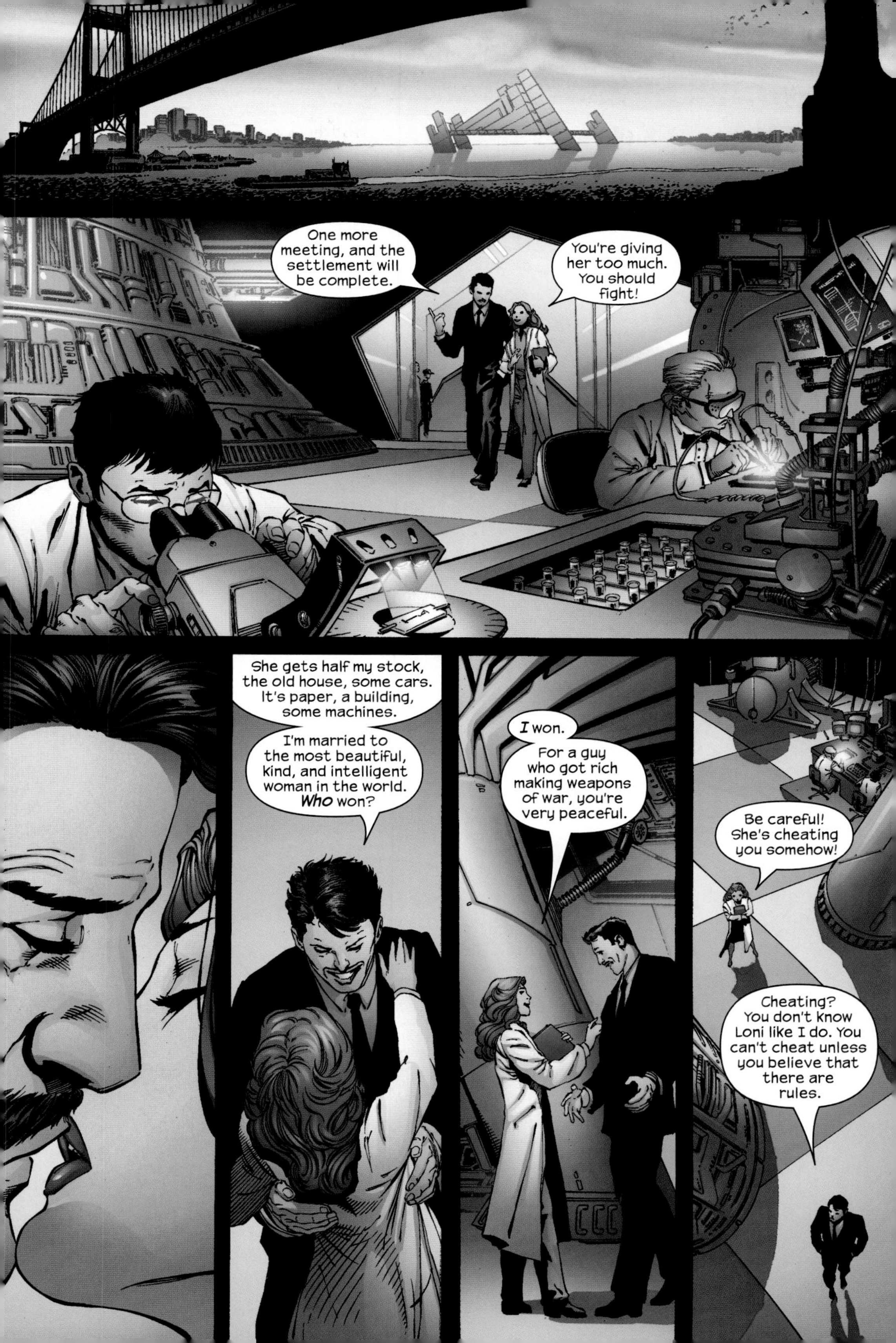
One more meeting, and the settlement will be complete.
You're giving her too much. You should fight!
She gets half my stock, the old house, some cars. It's paper, a building, some machines.
I'm married to the most beautiful, kind, and intelligent woman in the world. *Who* won?
I won.
For a guy who got rich making weapons of war, you're very peaceful.
Be careful! She's cheating you somehow!
Cheating? You don't know Loni like I do. You can't cheat unless you believe that there are rules.

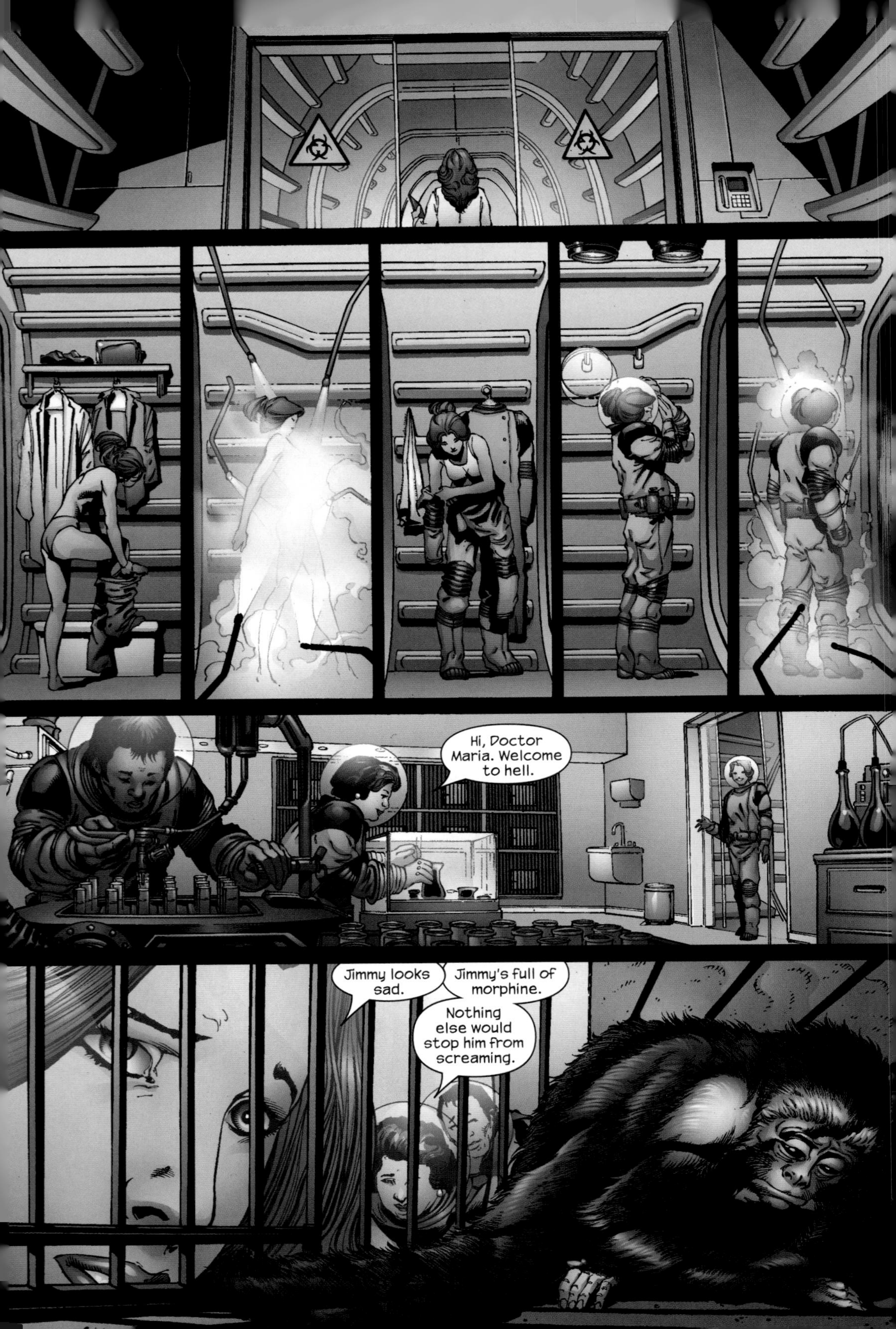
Hi, Doctor Maria. Welcome to hell.
Jimmy looks sad.
Jimmy's full of morphine.
Nothing else would stop him from screaming.

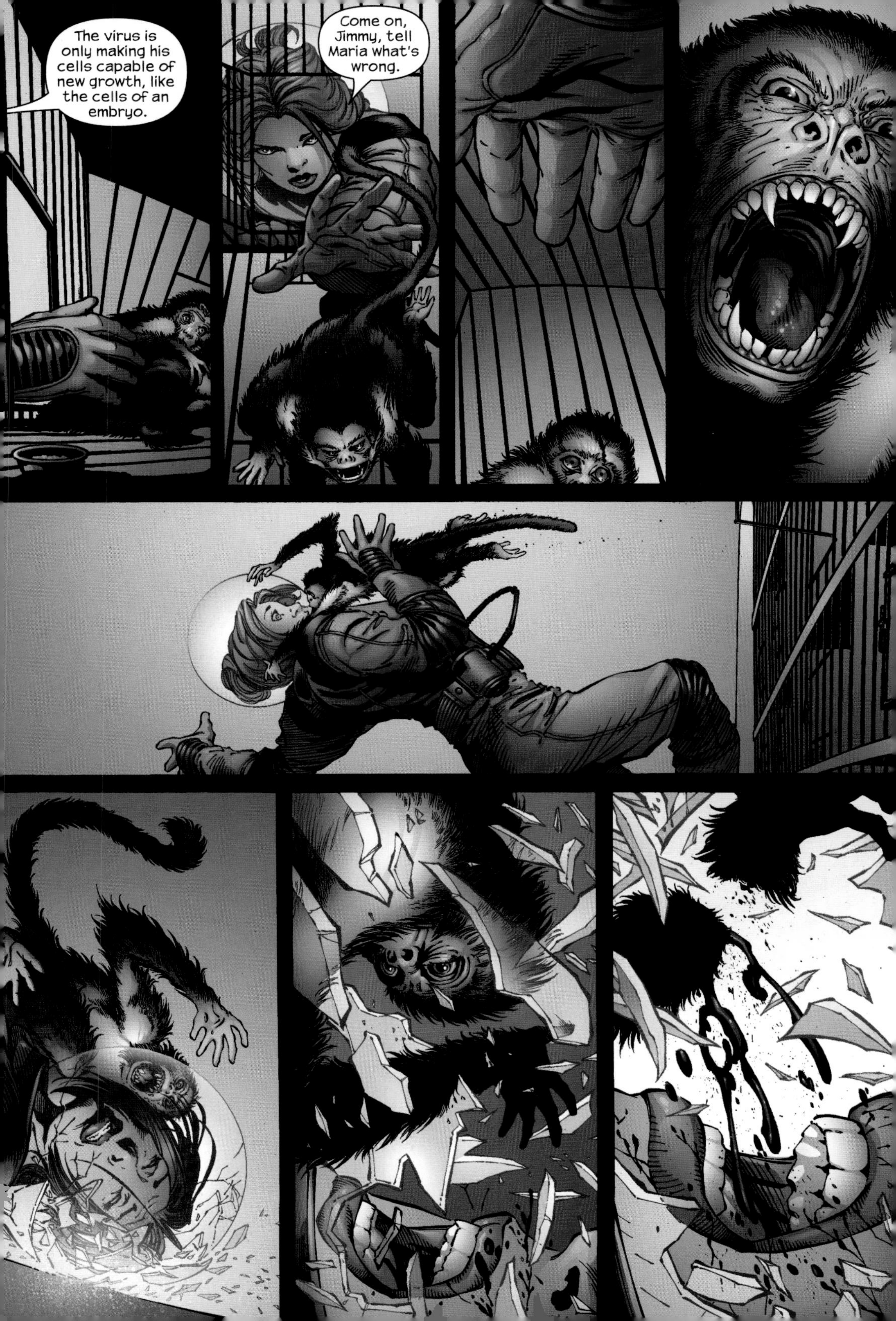
The virus is only making his cells capable of new growth, like the cells of an embryo.
Come on, Jimmy, tell Maria what's wrong.

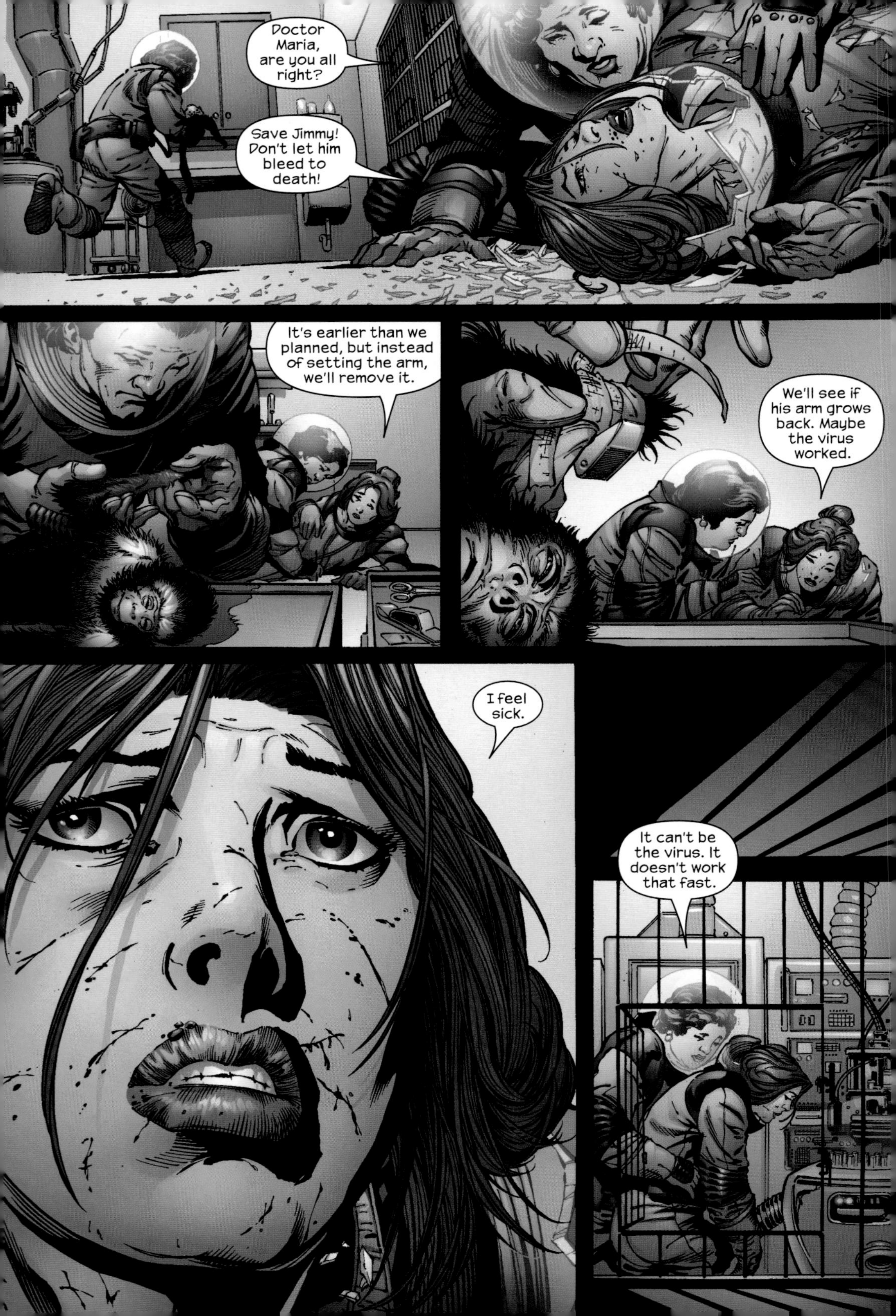

Doctor Maria, are you all right?
Save Jimmy! Don't let him bleed to death!
It's earlier than we planned, but instead of setting the arm, we'll remove it.
We'll see if his arm grows back. Maybe the virus worked.
I feel sick.
It can't be the virus. It doesn't work that fast.

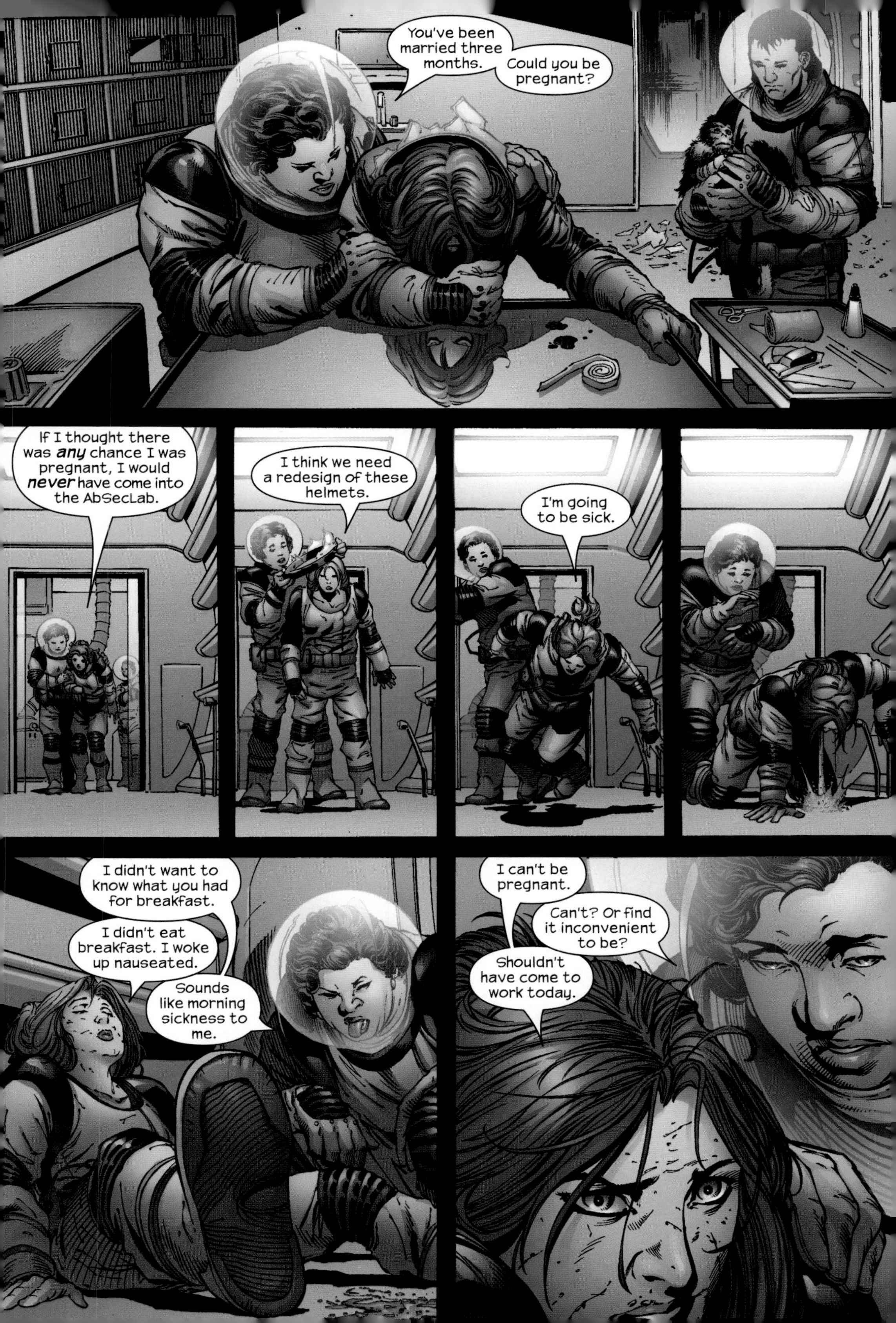
You've been married three months.
Could you be pregnant?
If I thought there was *any* chance I was pregnant, I would *never* have come into the AbSecLab.
I think we need a redesign of these helmets.
I'm going to be sick.
I didn't want to know what you had for breakfast.
I didn't eat breakfast. I woke up nauseated.
Sounds like morning sickness to me.
I can't be pregnant.
Can't? Or find it inconvenient to be?
Shouldn't have come to work today.

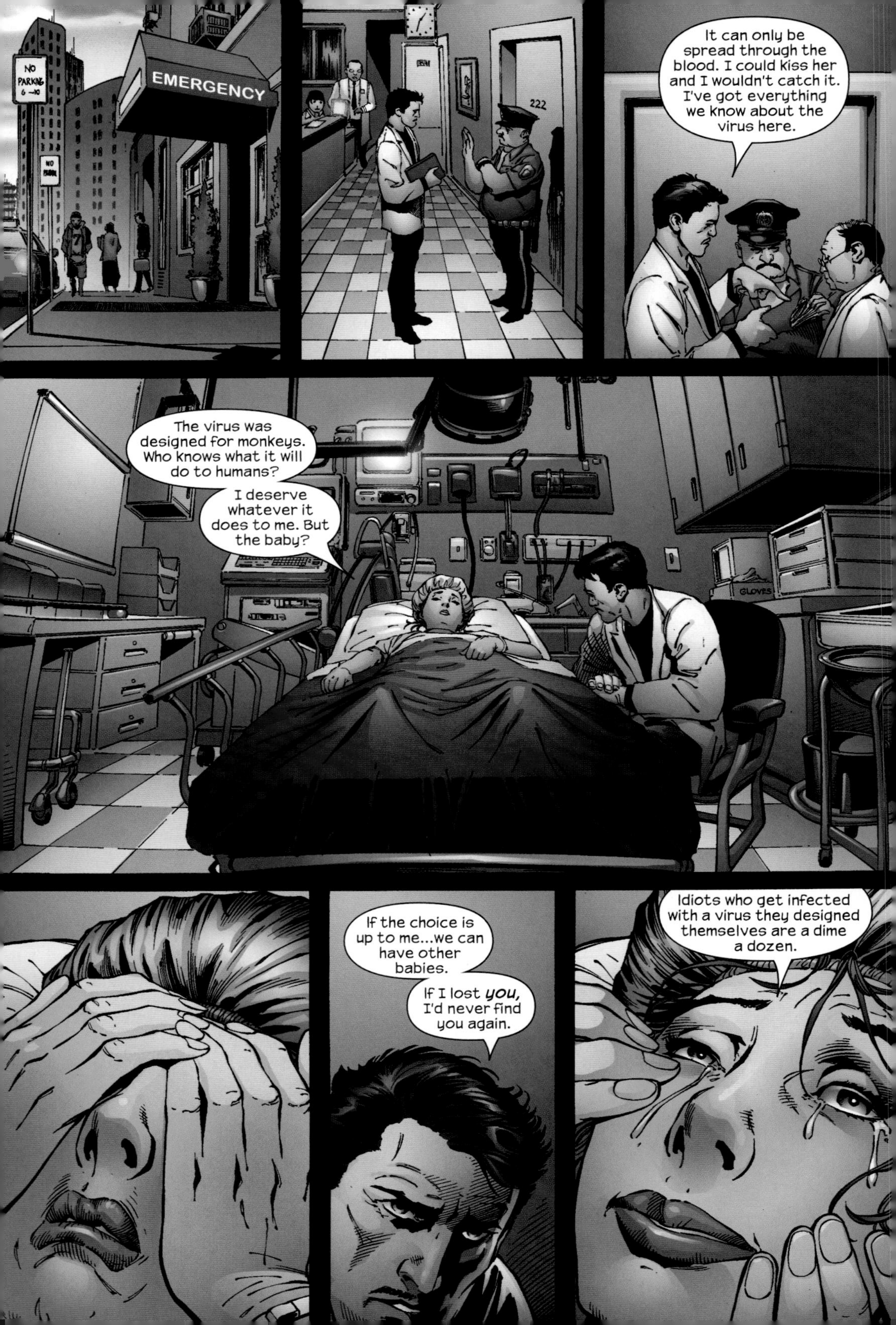
NO PARKING 6 —10
EMERGENCY
NO PARKING
222
It can only be spread through the blood. I could kiss her and I wouldn't catch it. I've got everything we know about the virus here.
The virus was designed for monkeys. Who knows what it will do to humans?
I deserve whatever it does to me. But the baby?
GLOVES
If the choice is up to me...we can have other babies.
If I lost *you,* I'd never find you again.
Idiots who get infected with a virus they designed themselves are a dime a dozen.

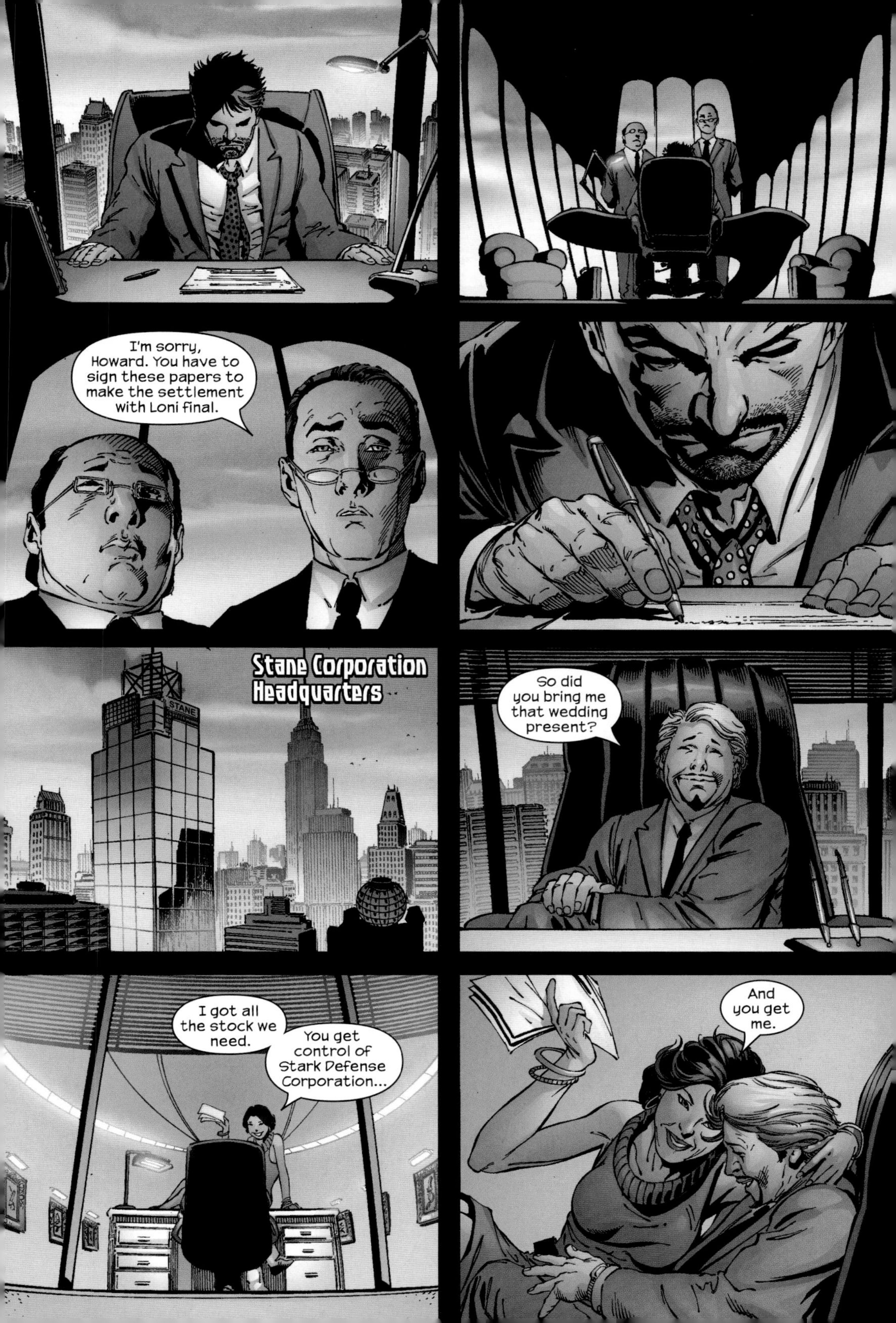
I'm sorry, Howard. You have to sign these papers to make the settlement with Loni final.
Stane Corporation Headquarters
STANE
So did you bring me that wedding present?
I got all the stock we need.
You get control of Stark Defense Corporation...
And you get me.

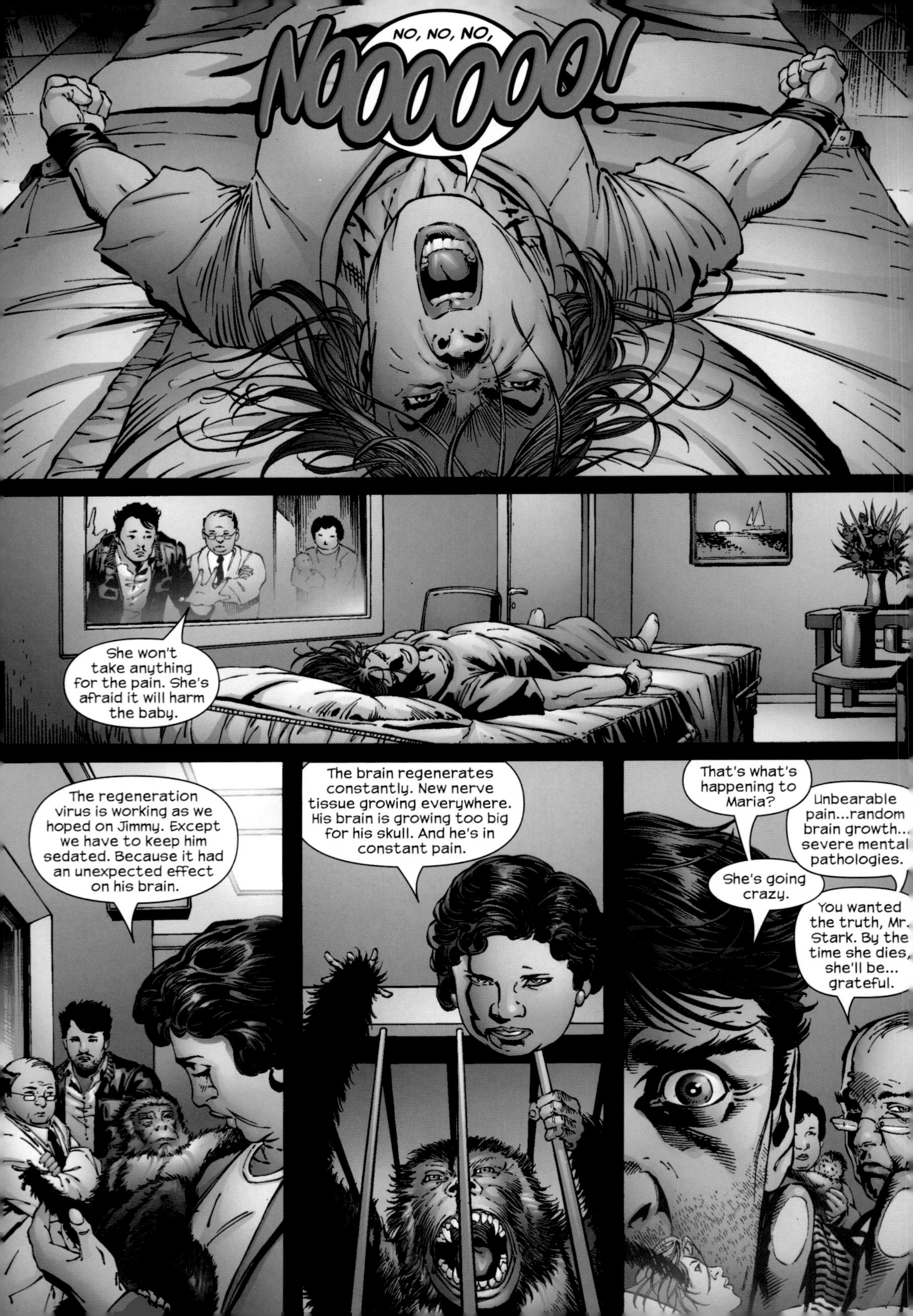
NO, NO, NO,
NOOOOOO!
She won't take anything for the pain. She's afraid it will harm the baby.
The regeneration virus is working as we hoped on Jimmy. Except we have to keep him sedated. Because it had an unexpected effect on his brain.
The brain regenerates constantly. New nerve tissue growing everywhere. His brain is growing too big for his skull. And he's in constant pain.
That's what's happening to Maria?
Unbearable pain...random brain growth... severe mental pathologies.
She's going crazy.
You wanted the truth, Mr. Stark. By the time she dies, she'll be... grateful.

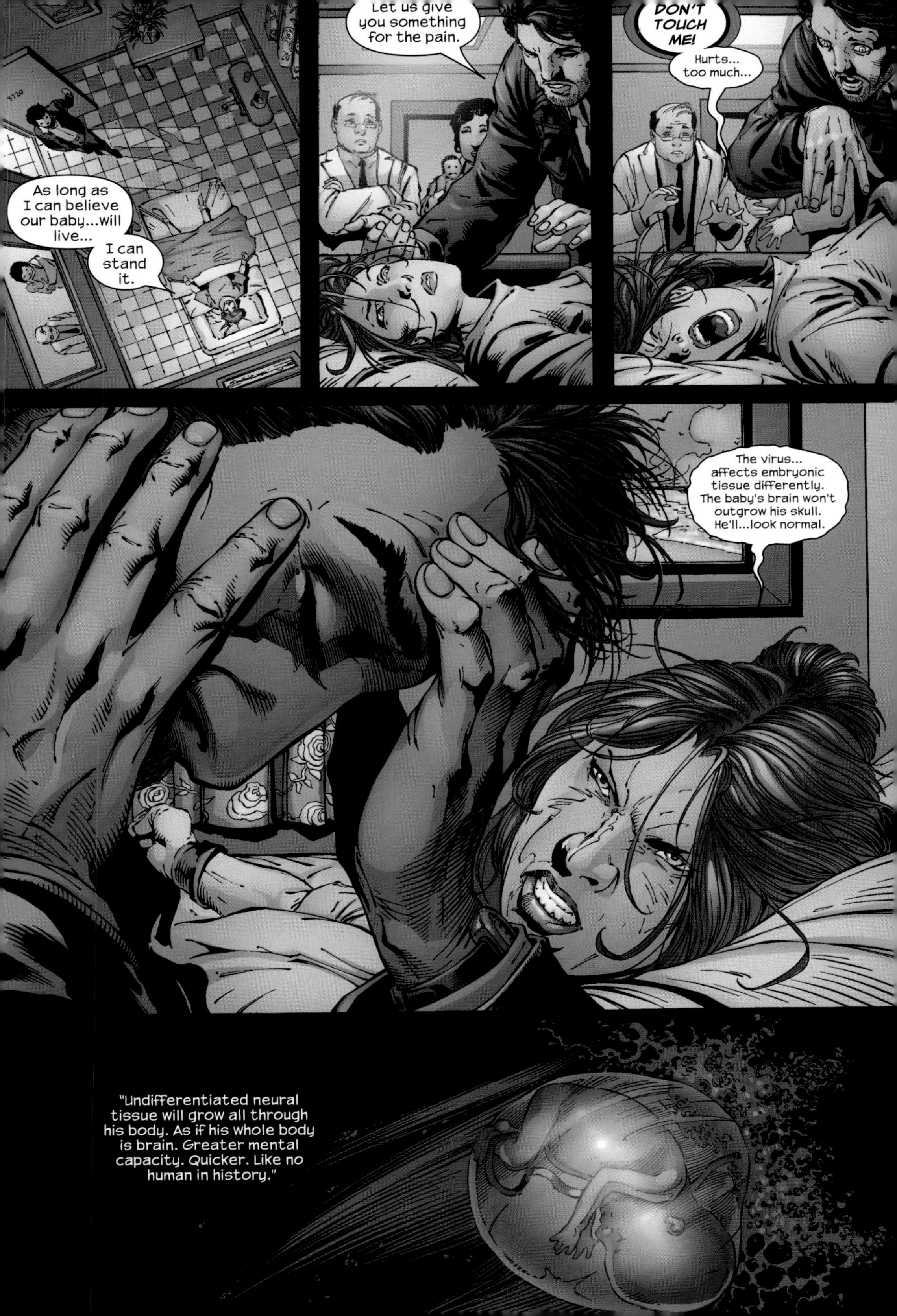

As long as I can believe our baby...will live...
I can stand it.
Let us give you something for the pain.
DON'T TOUCH ME!
Hurts... too much...
The virus... affects embryonic tissue differently. The baby's brain won't outgrow his skull. He'll...look normal.
"Undifferentiated neural tissue will grow all through his body. As if his whole body is brain. Greater mental capacity. Quicker. Like no human in history."

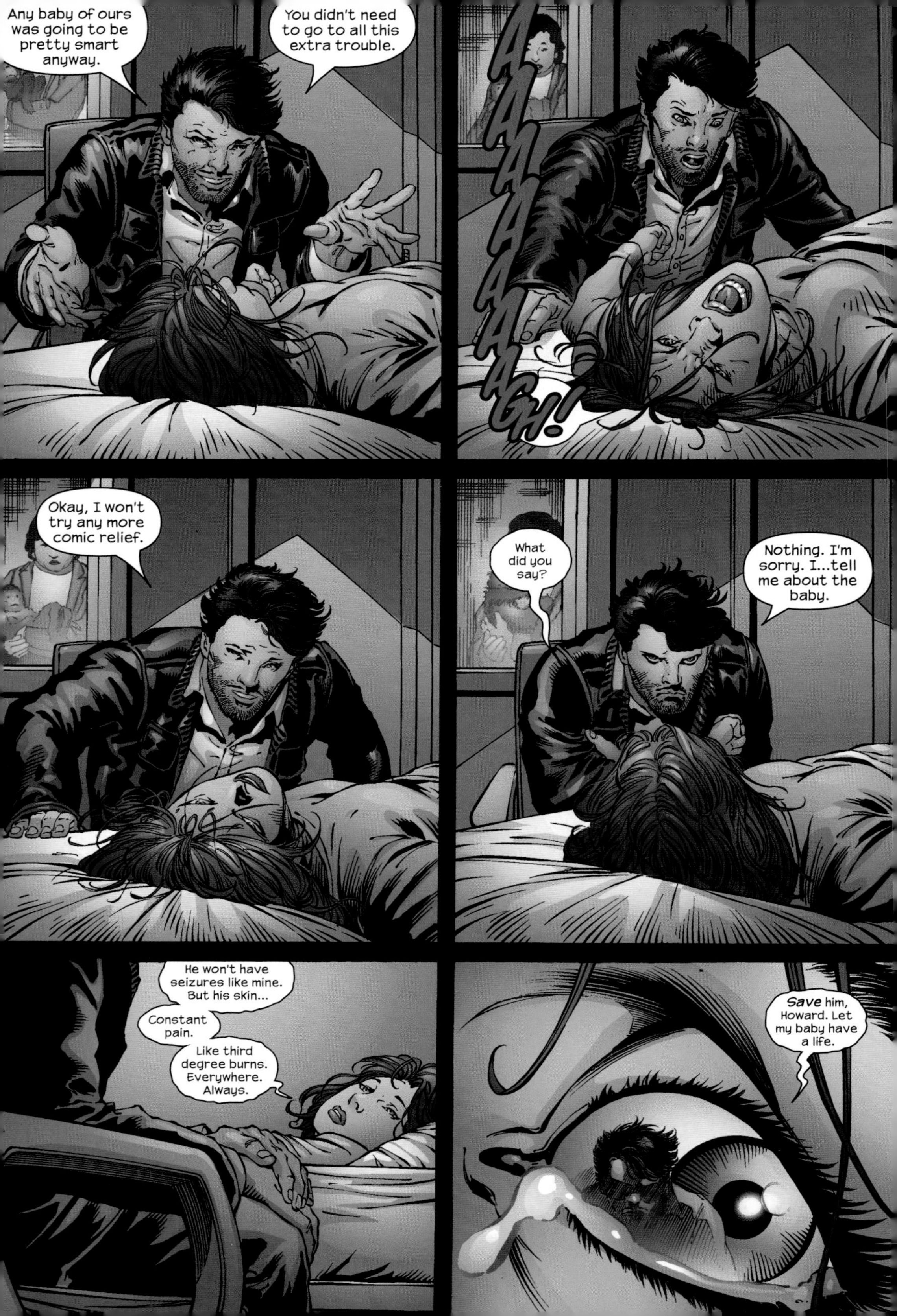
Any baby of ours was going to be pretty smart anyway.
You didn't need to go to all this extra trouble.
AAAAAAAAAAGH!
Okay, I won't try any more comic relief.
What did you say?
Nothing. I'm sorry. I...tell me about the baby.
He won't have seizures like mine. But his skin...
Constant pain.
Like third degree burns. Everywhere. Always.
Save him, Howard. Let my baby have a life.

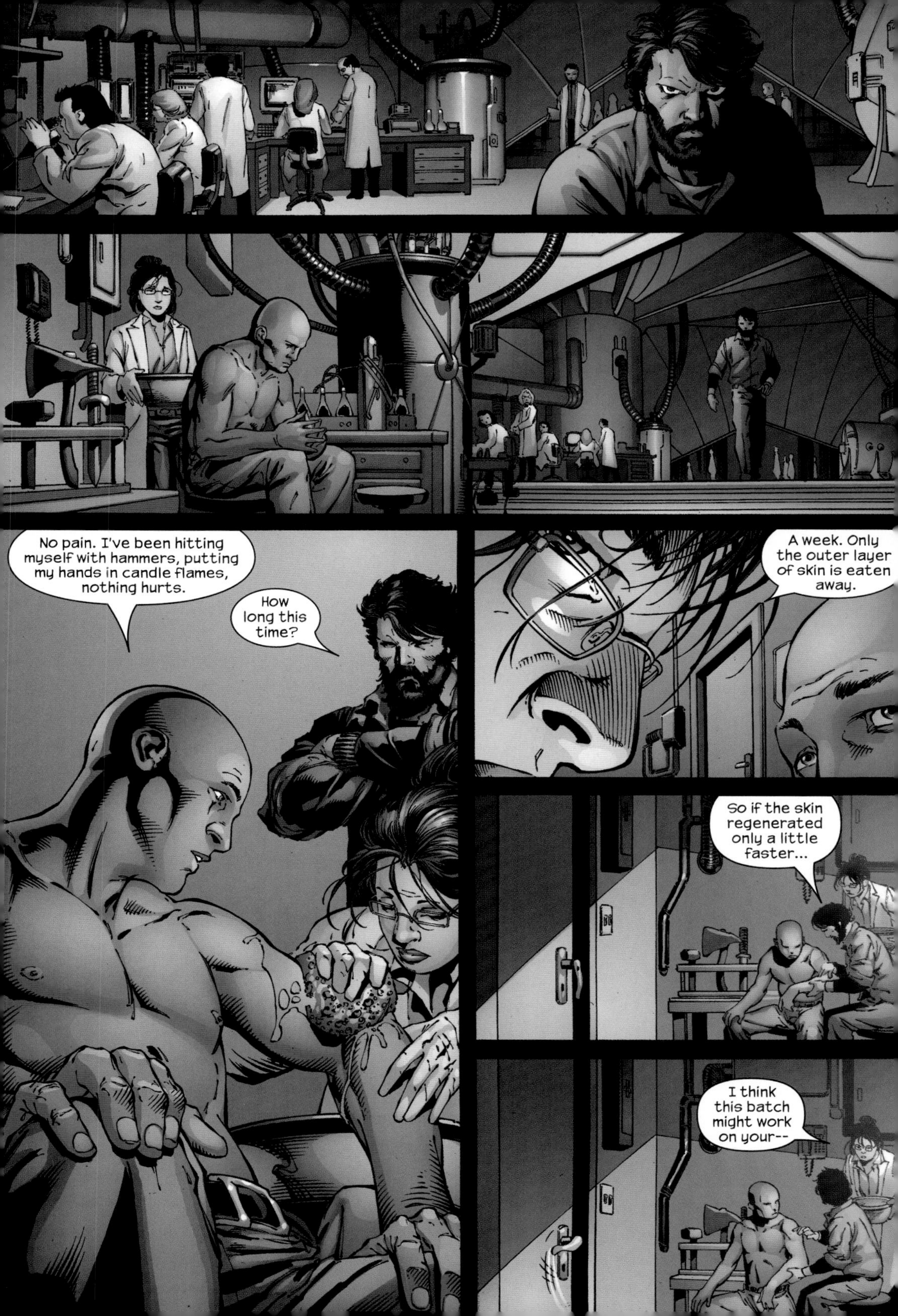
No pain. I've been hitting myself with hammers, putting my hands in candle flames, nothing hurts.
How long this time?
A week. Only the outer layer of skin is eaten away.
So if the skin regenerated only a little faster...
I think this batch might work on your--

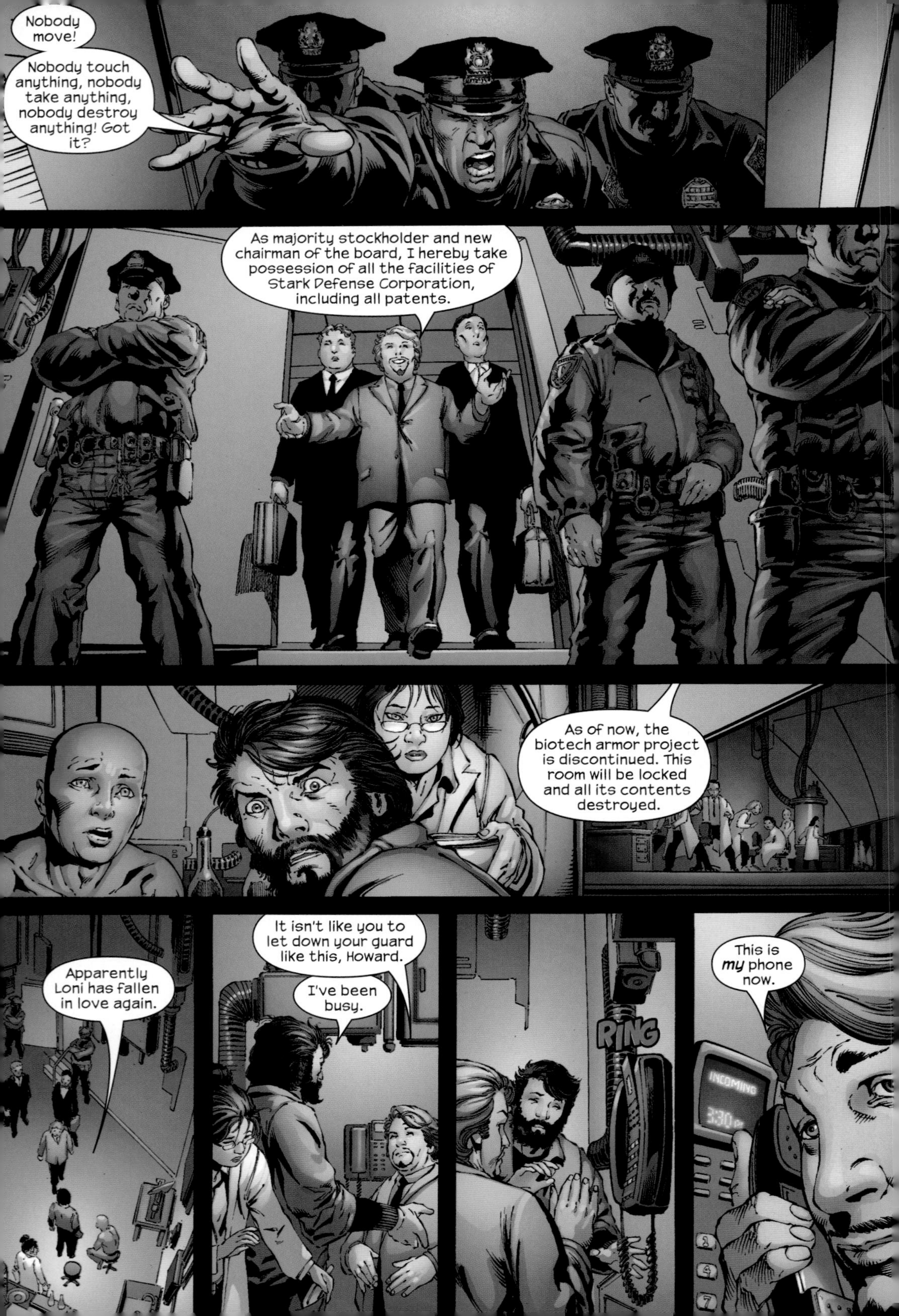
Nobody move!
Nobody touch anything, nobody take anything, nobody destroy anything! Got it?
As majority stockholder and new chairman of the board, I hereby take possession of all the facilities of Stark Defense Corporation, including all patents.
As of now, the biotech armor project is discontinued. This room will be locked and all its contents destroyed.
Apparently Loni has fallen in love again.
It isn't like you to let down your guard like this, Howard.
I've been busy.
RING
INCOMING
This is *my* phone now.

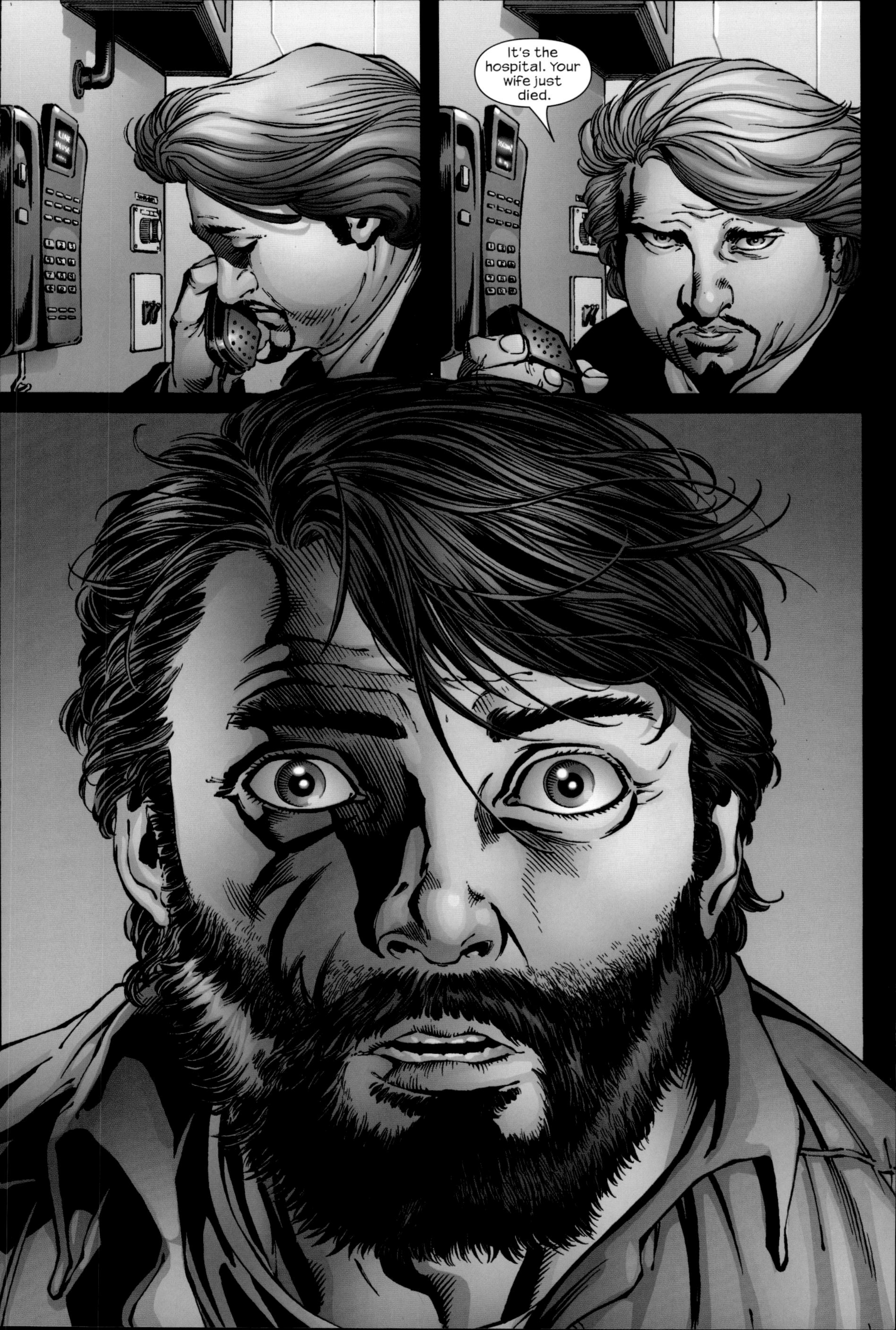
It's the hospital. Your wife just died.

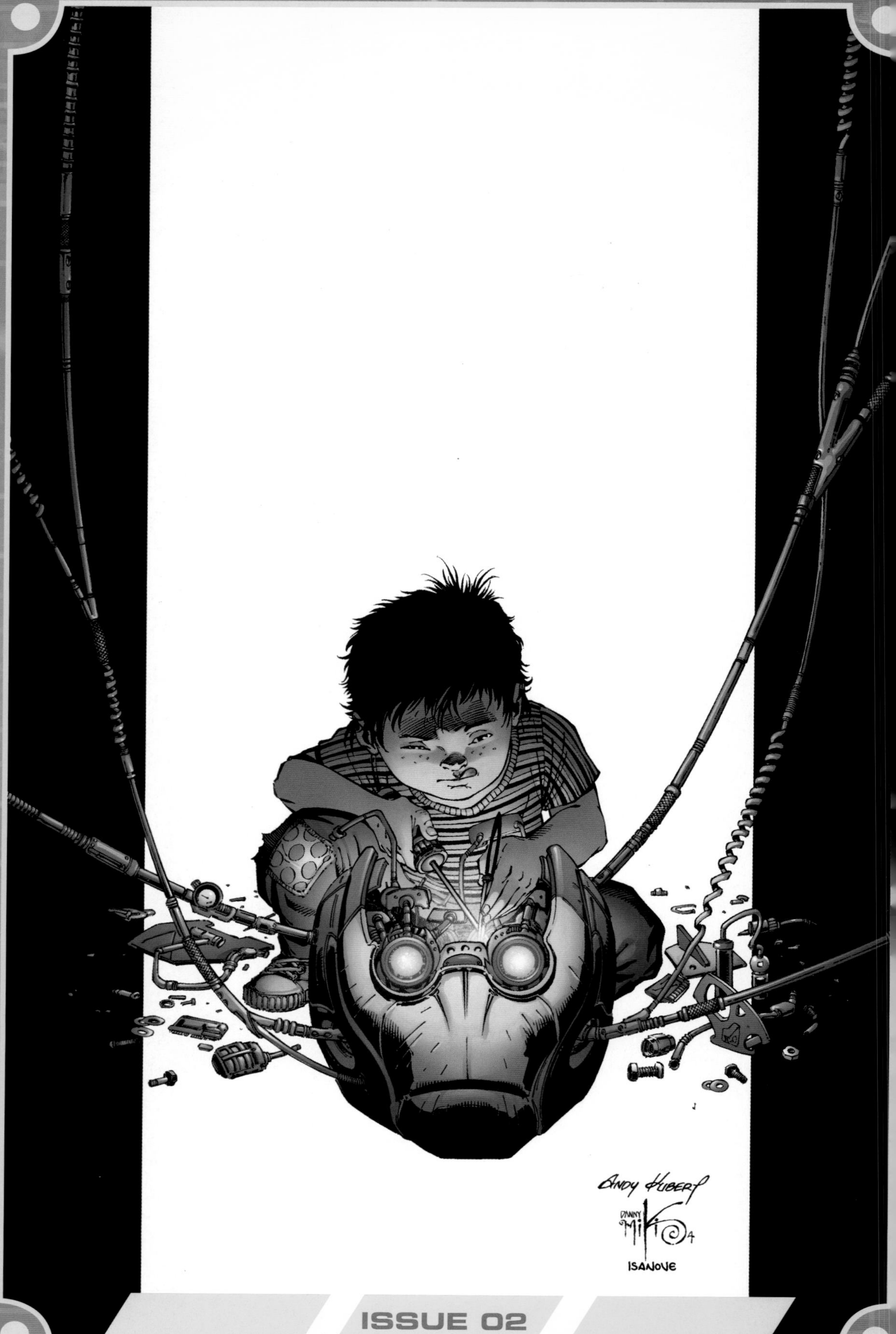
ANDY KUBERT
DANNY MIKI 04
ISANOVE

ISSUE 02

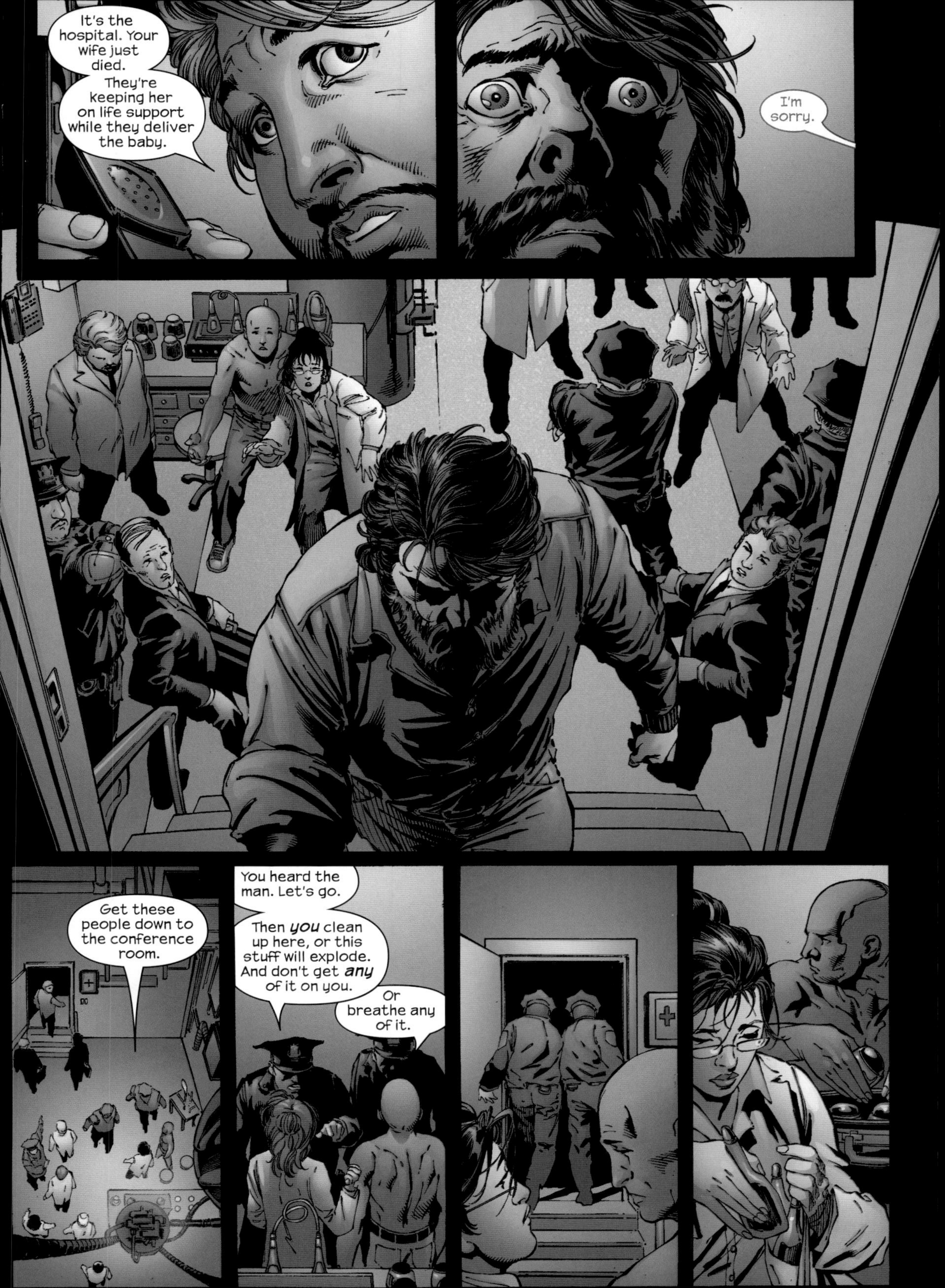
It's the hospital. Your wife just died.
They're keeping her on life support while they deliver the baby.
I'm sorry.
Get these people down to the conference room.
You heard the man. Let's go.
Then *you* clean up here, or this stuff will explode. And don't get *any* of it on you.
Or breathe any of it.

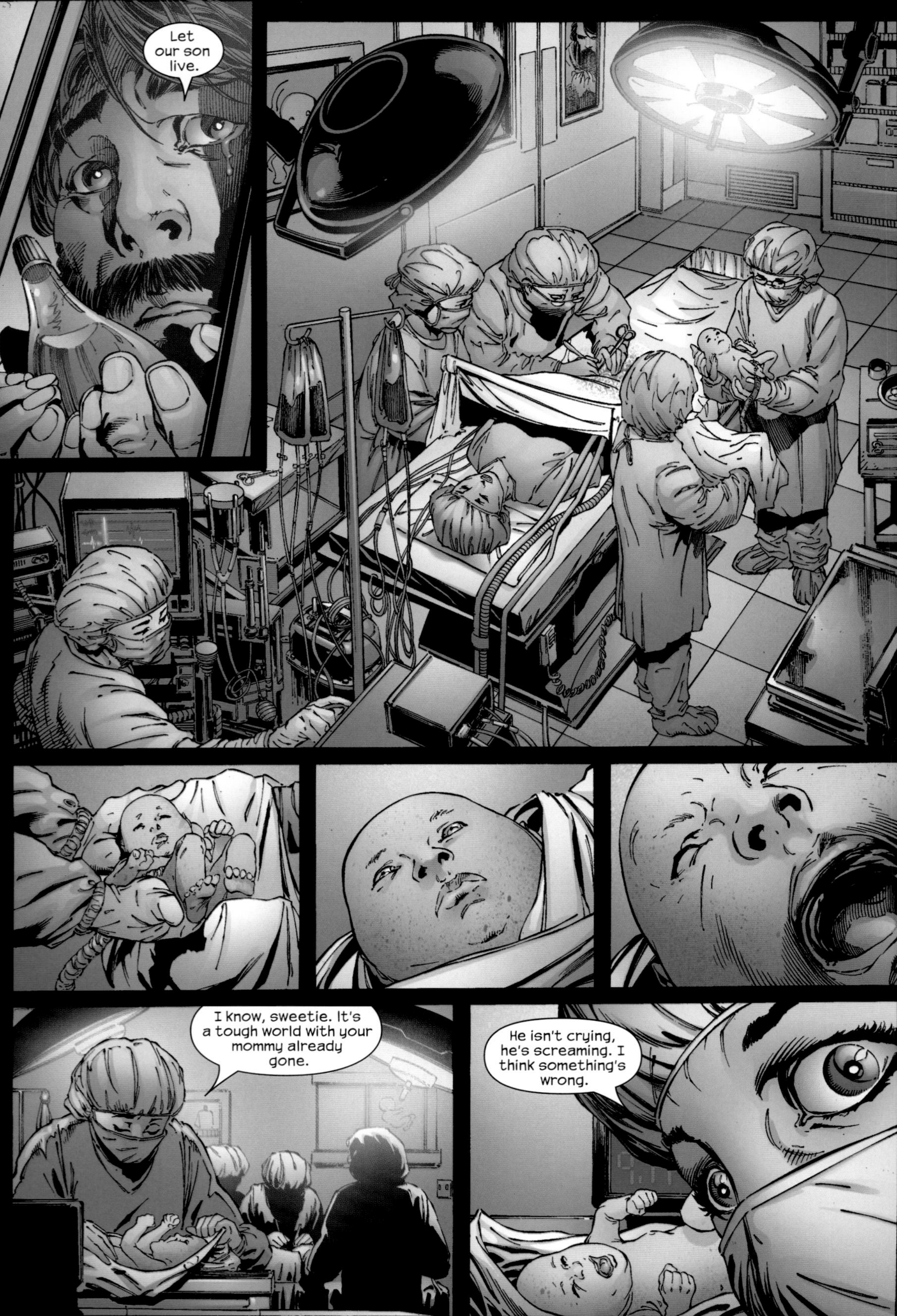
Let our son live.
I know, sweetie. It's a tough world with your mommy already gone.
He isn't crying, he's screaming. I think something's wrong.

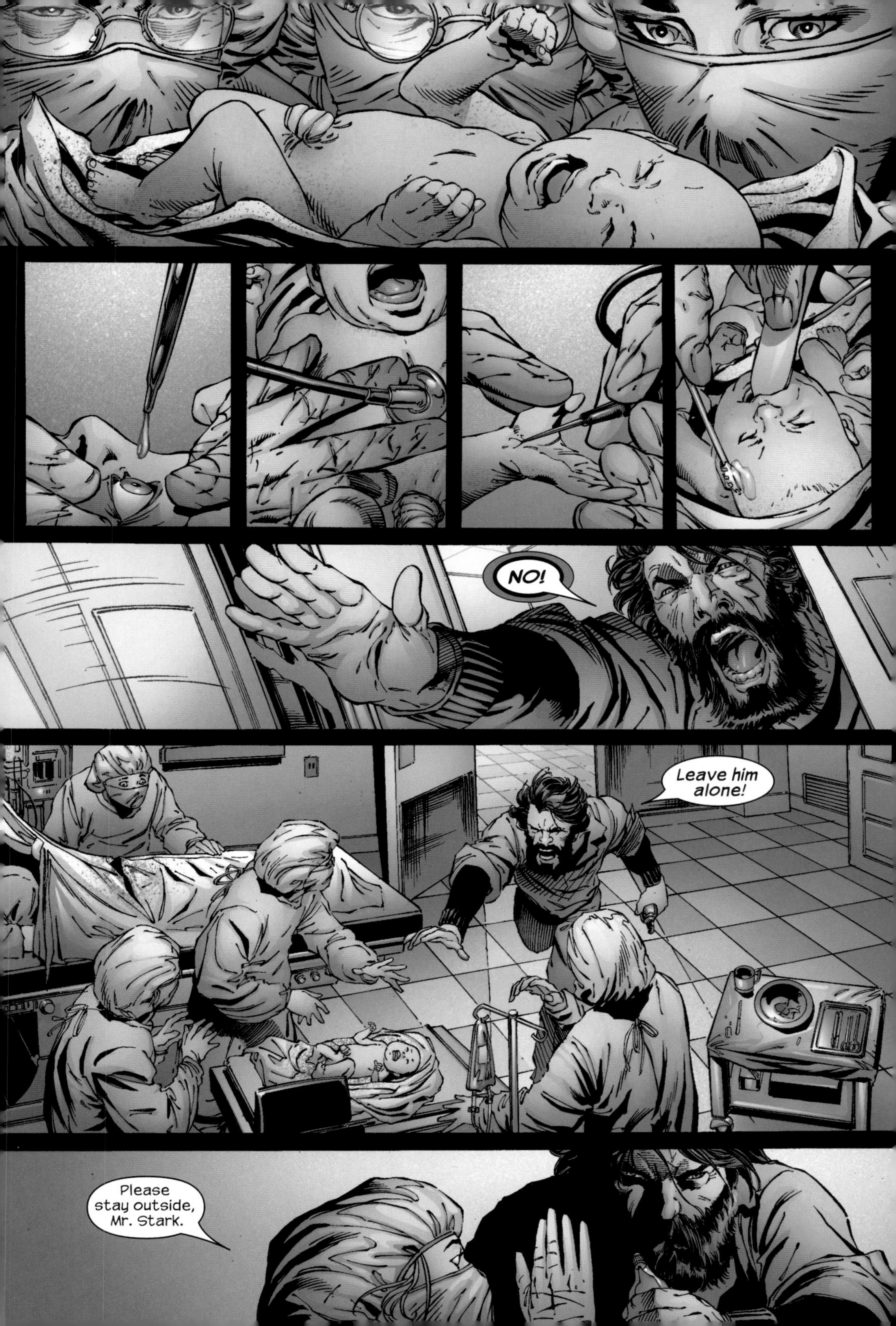
NO!
Leave him alone!
Please stay outside, Mr. Stark.

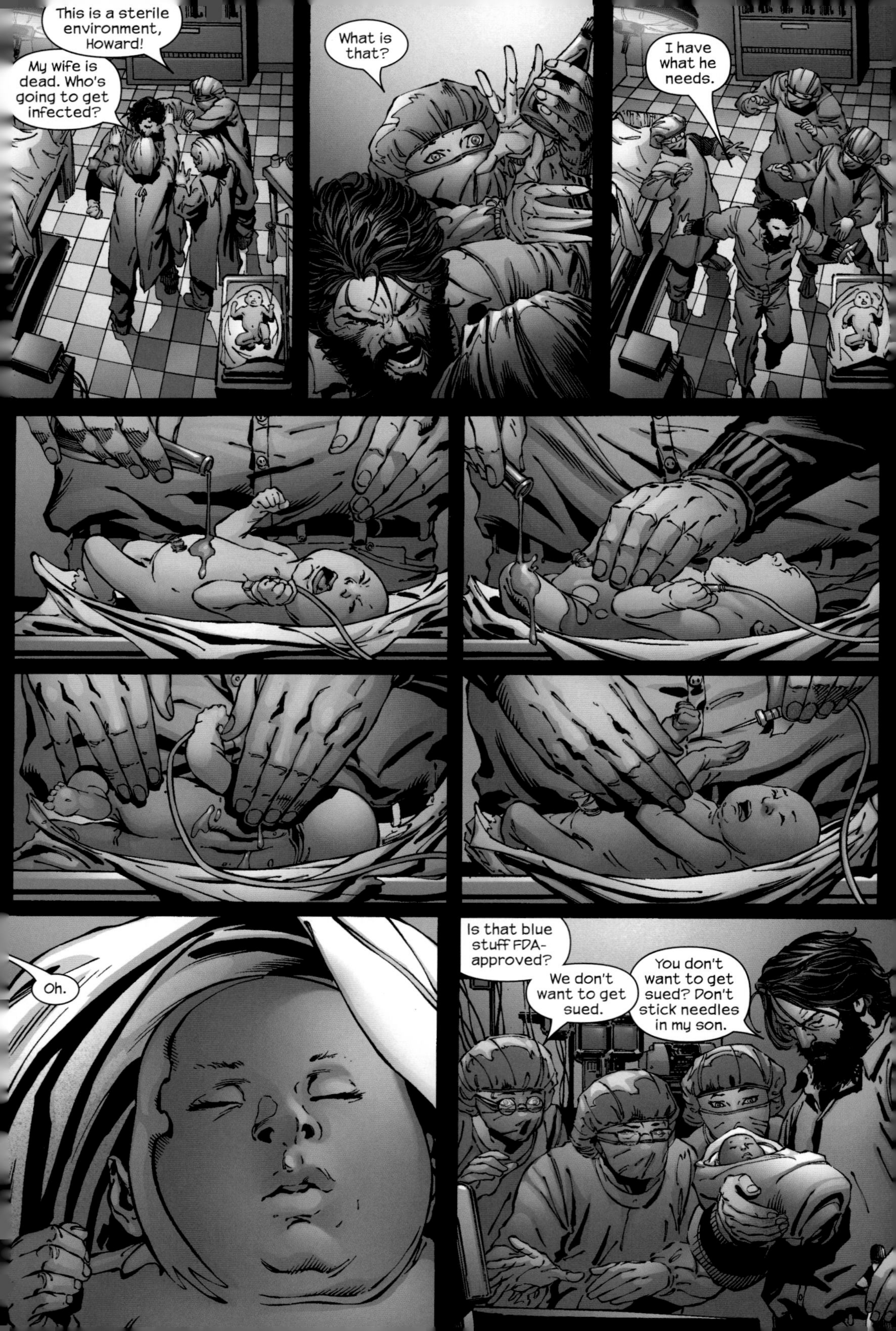
This is a sterile environment, Howard!
My wife is dead. Who's going to get infected?
What is that?
I have what he needs.
Oh.
Is that blue stuff FDA-approved?
We don't want to get sued.
You don't want to get sued? Don't stick needles in my son.

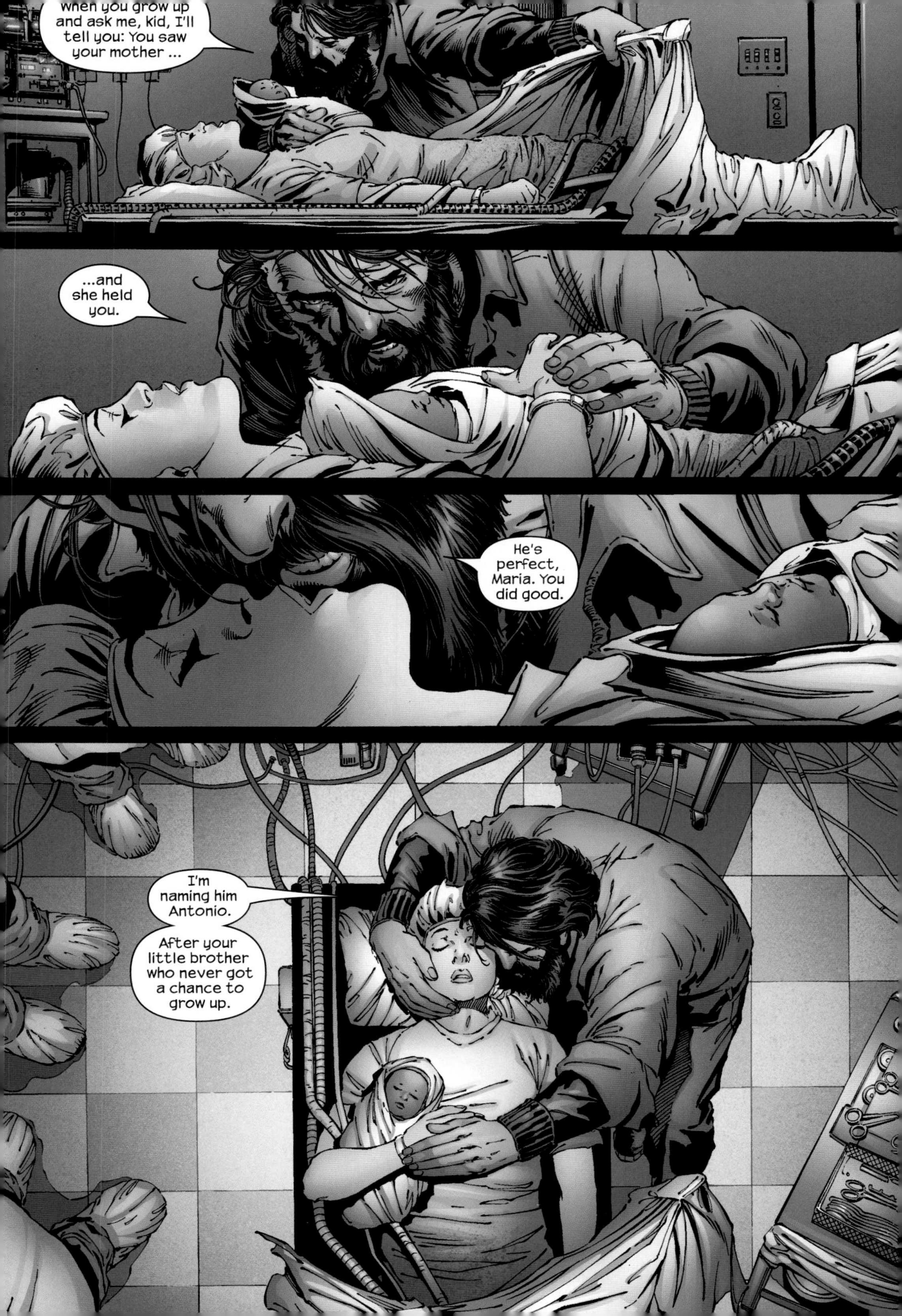
when you grow up and ask me, kid, I'll tell you: You saw your mother ...
...and she held you.
He's perfect, Maria. You did good.
I'm naming him Antonio.
After your little brother who never got a chance to grow up.

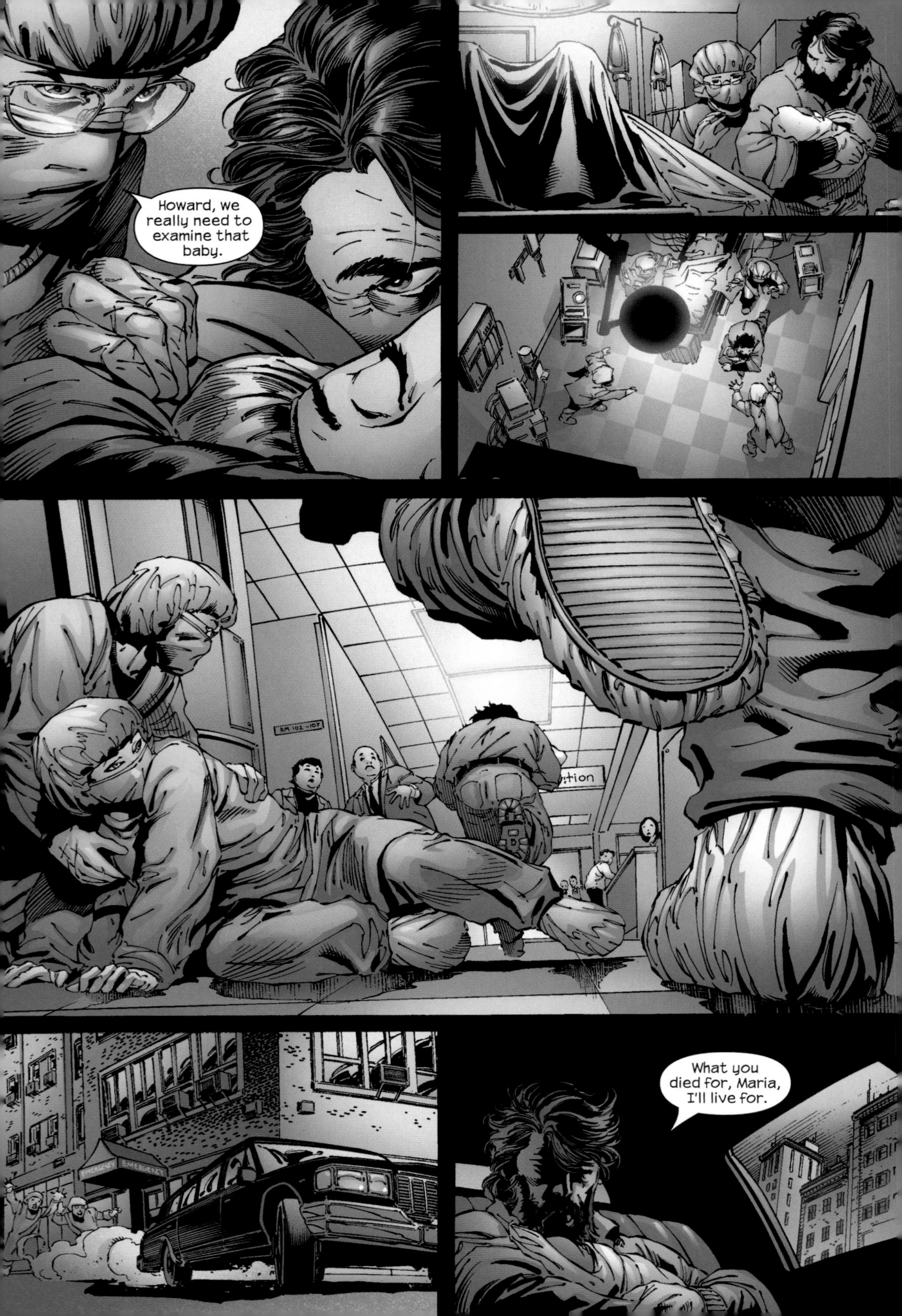
Howard, we really need to examine that baby.
RM 102-107
EMERGENCY
What you died for, Maria, I'll live for.

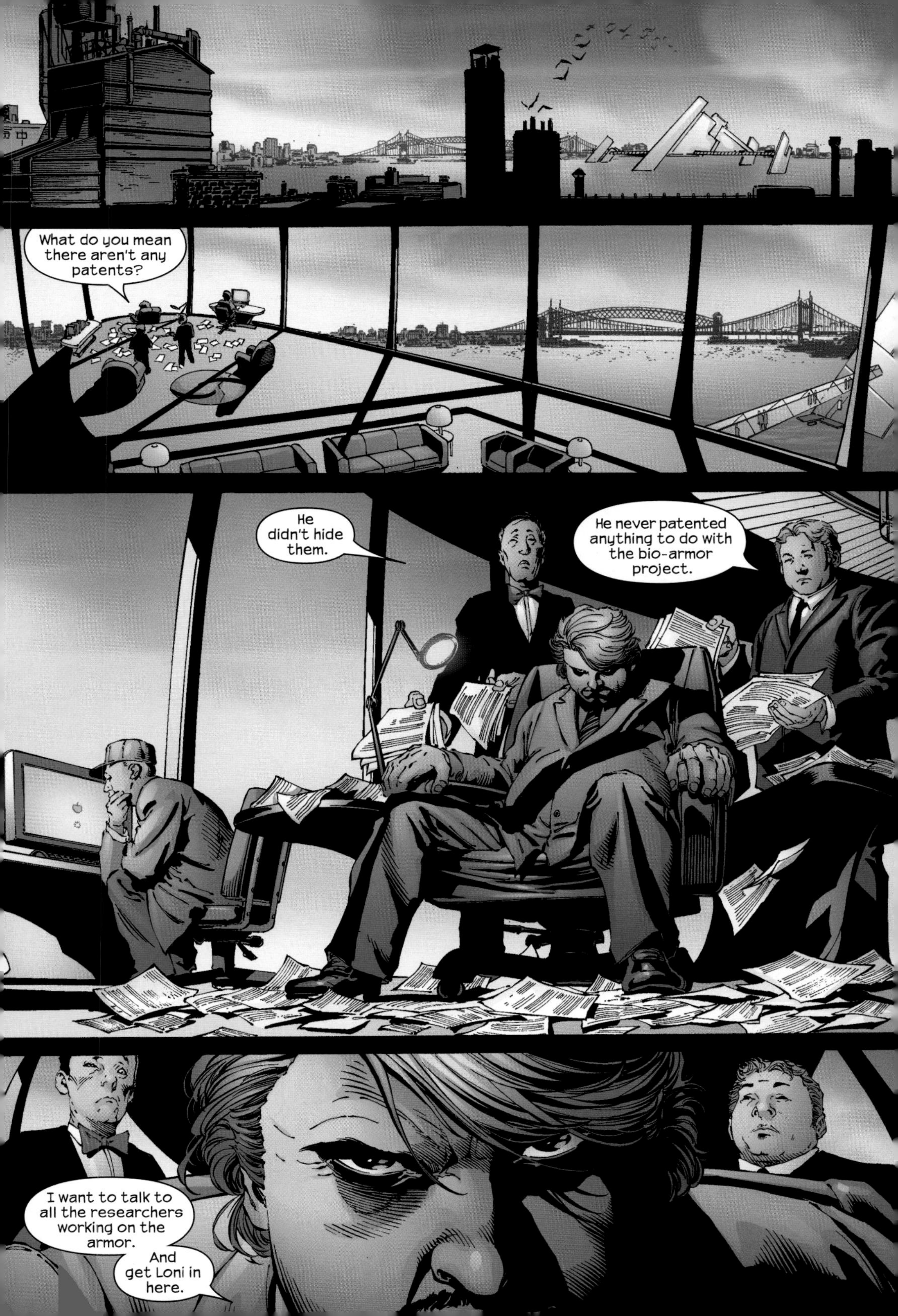
What do you mean there aren't any patents?
He didn't hide them.
He never patented anything to do with the bio-armor project.
I want to talk to all the researchers working on the armor.
And get Loni in here.

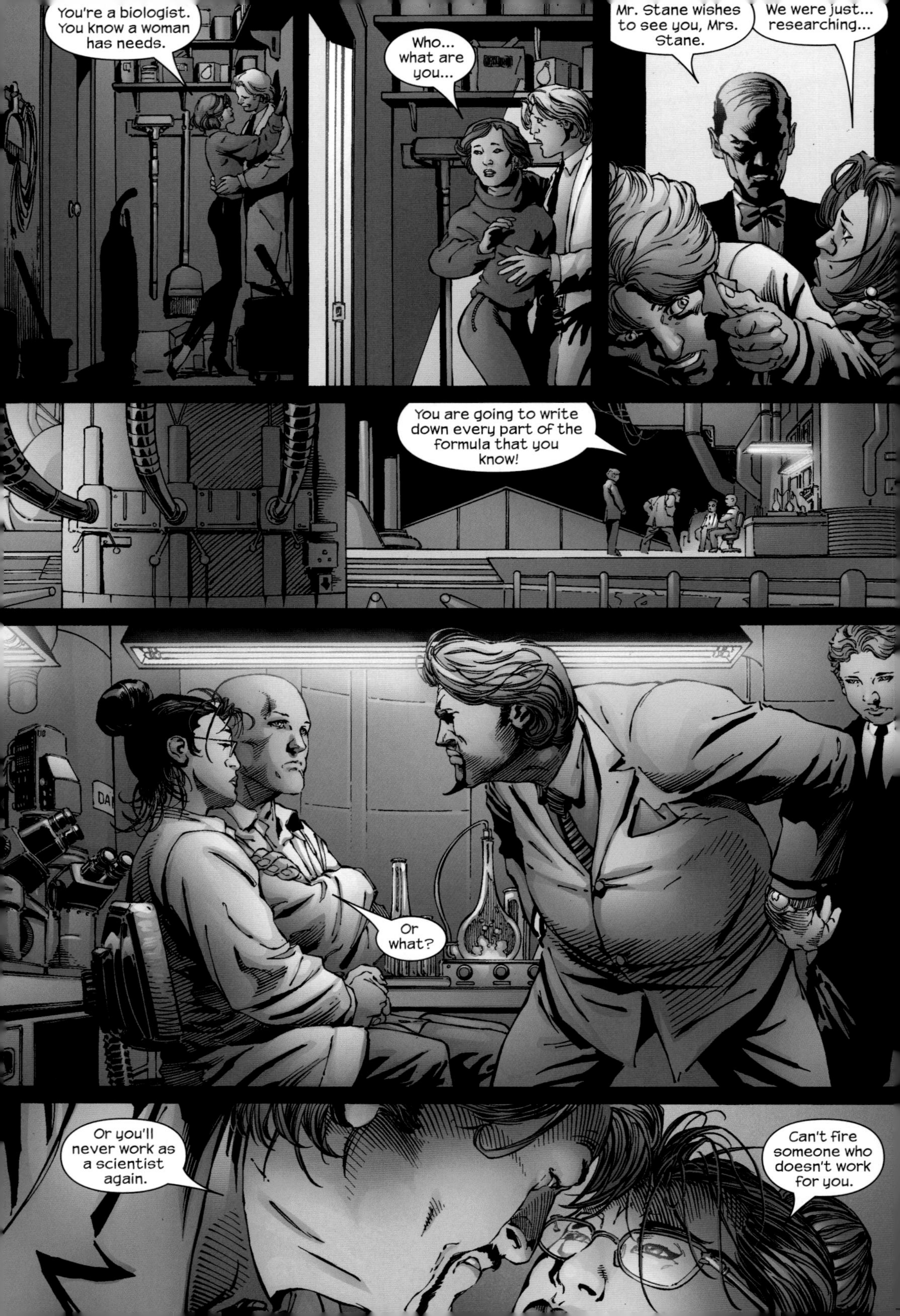

You're a biologist. You know a woman has needs.
Who... what are you...
Mr. Stane wishes to see you, Mrs. Stane.
We were just... researching...
You are going to write down every part of the formula that you know!
Or what?
Or you'll never work as a scientist again.
Can't fire someone who doesn't work for you.

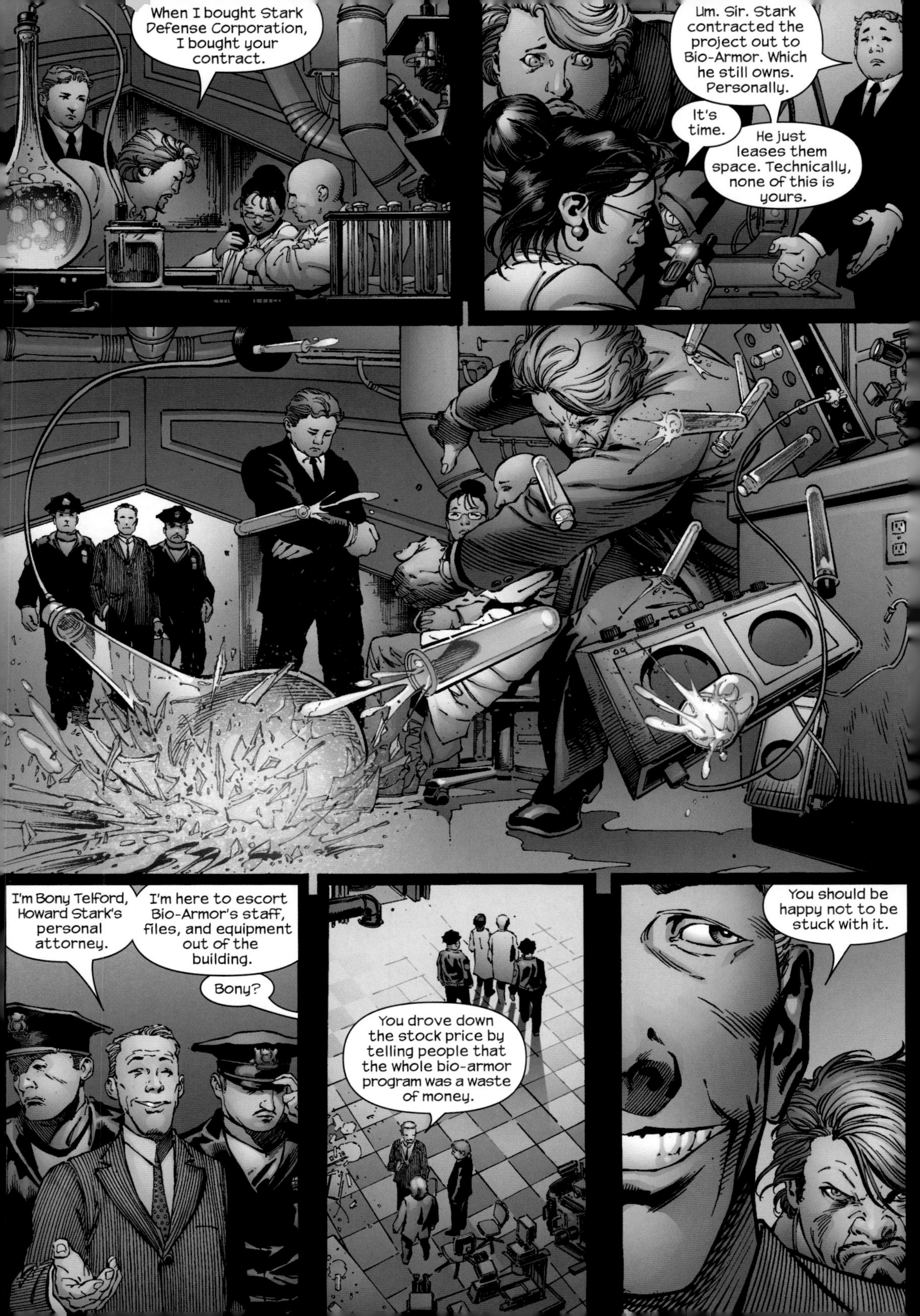
When I bought Stark Defense Corporation, I bought your contract.
Um. Sir. Stark contracted the project out to Bio-Armor. Which he still owns. Personally.
It's time.
He just leases them space. Technically, none of this is yours.
I'm Bony Telford, Howard Stark's personal attorney.
I'm here to escort Bio-Armor's staff, files, and equipment out of the building.
Bony?
You drove down the stock price by telling people that the whole bio-armor program was a waste of money.
You should be happy not to be stuck with it.

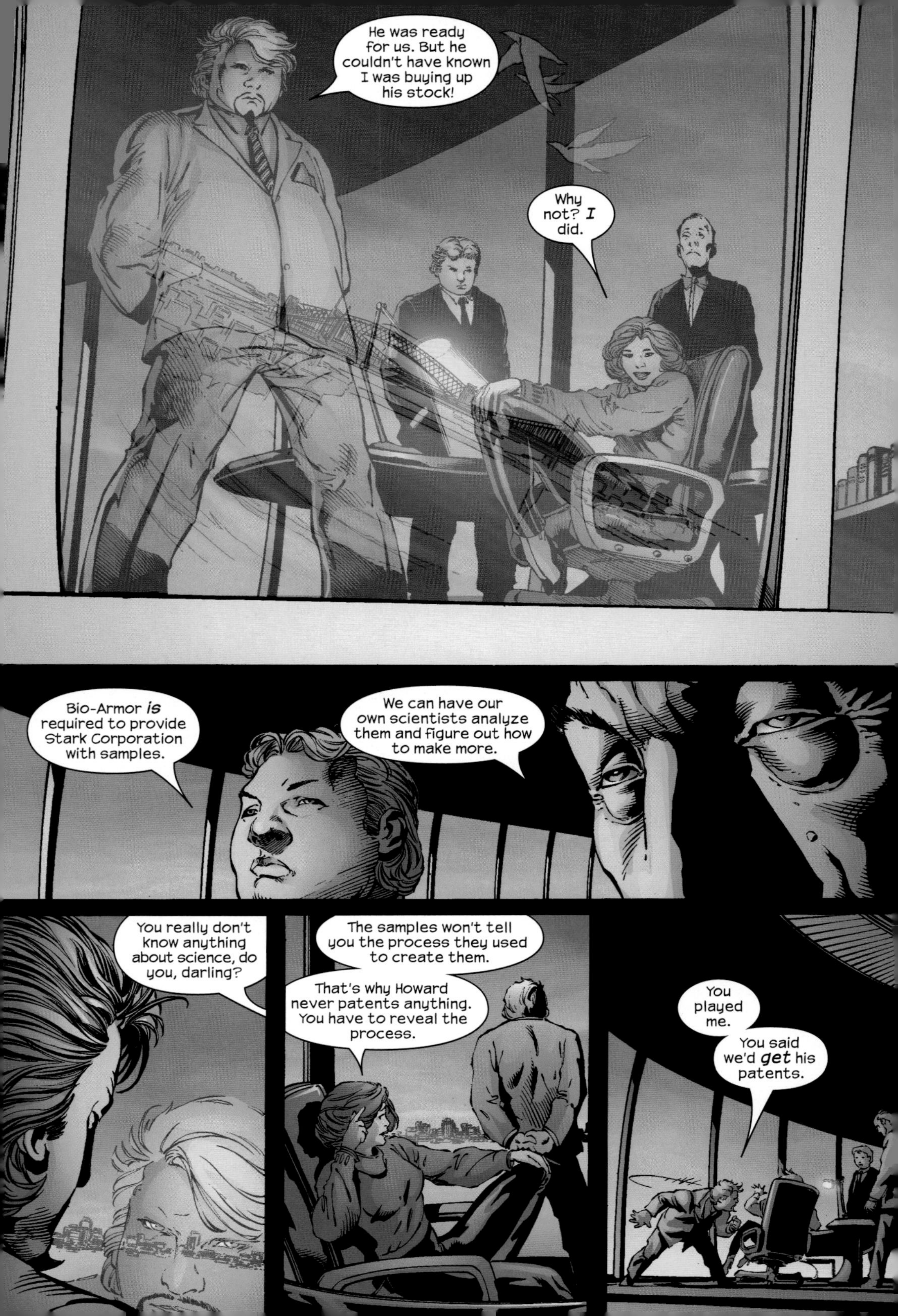
He was ready for us. But he couldn't have known I was buying up his stock!
Why not? *I* did.
Bio-Armor *is* required to provide Stark Corporation with samples.
We can have our own scientists analyze them and figure out how to make more.
You really don't know anything about science, do you, darling?
The samples won't tell you the process they used to create them.
That's why Howard never patents anything. You have to reveal the process.
You played me.
You said we'd *get* his patents.

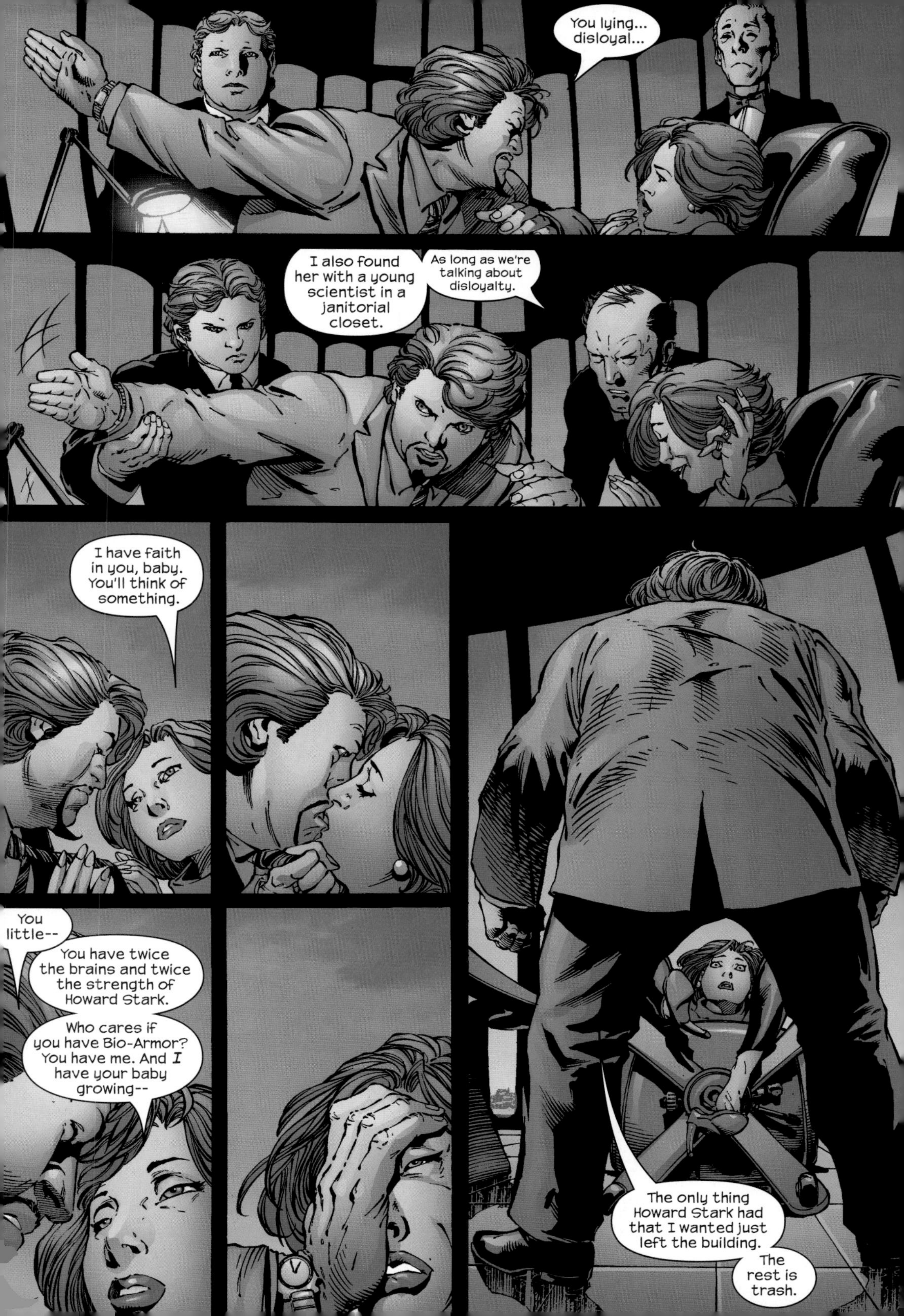
You lying... disloyal...
I also found her with a young scientist in a janitorial closet.
As long as we're talking about disloyalty.
I have faith in you, baby. You'll think of something.
You little--
You have twice the brains and twice the strength of Howard Stark.
Who cares if you have Bio-Armor? You have me. And I have your baby growing--
The only thing Howard Stark had that I wanted just left the building.
The rest is trash.

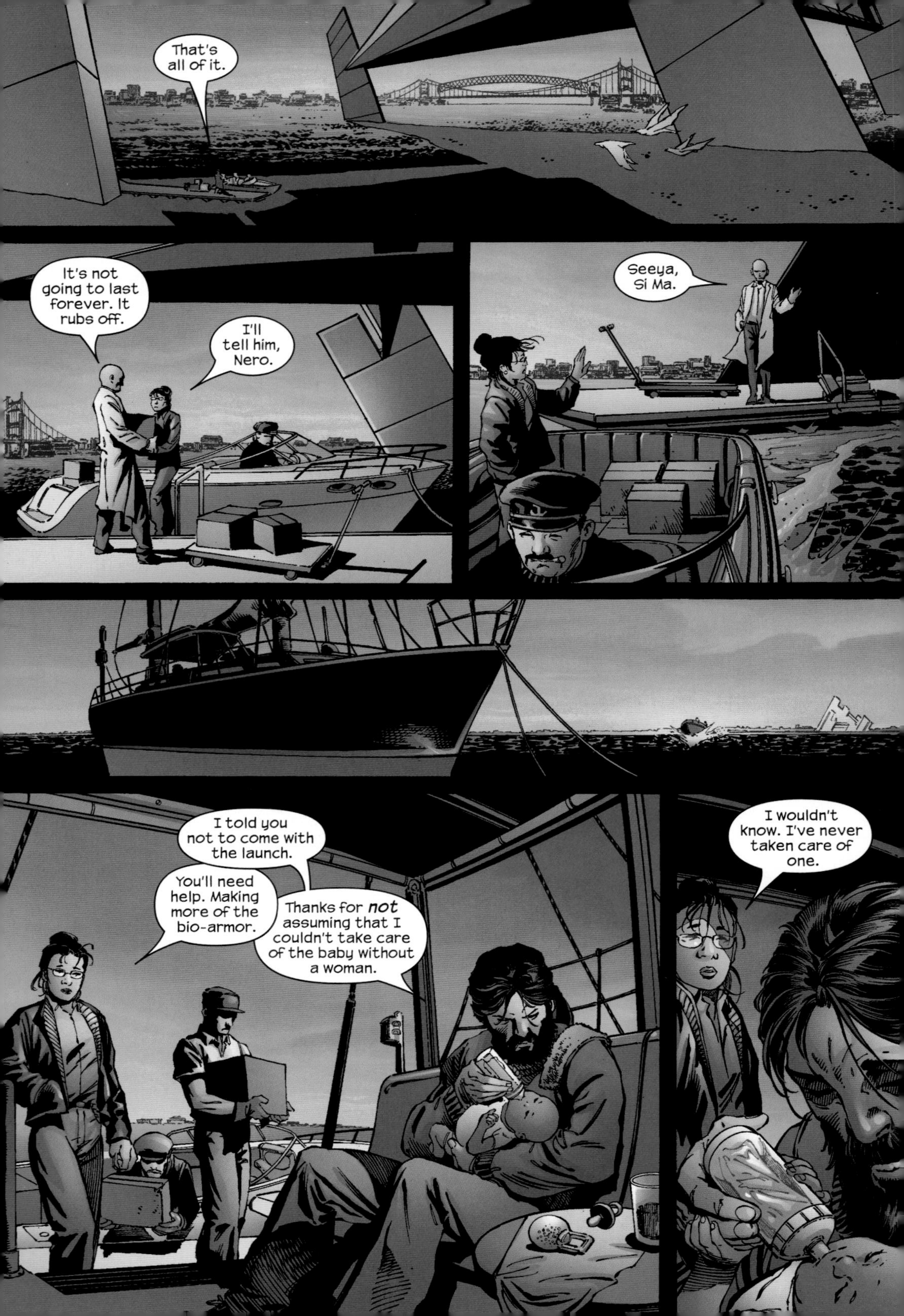
That's all of it.
It's not going to last forever. It rubs off.
I'll tell him, Nero.
Seeya, Si Ma.
I told you not to come with the launch.
You'll need help. Making more of the bio-armor.
Thanks for *not* assuming that I couldn't take care of the baby without a woman.
I wouldn't know. I've never taken care of one.

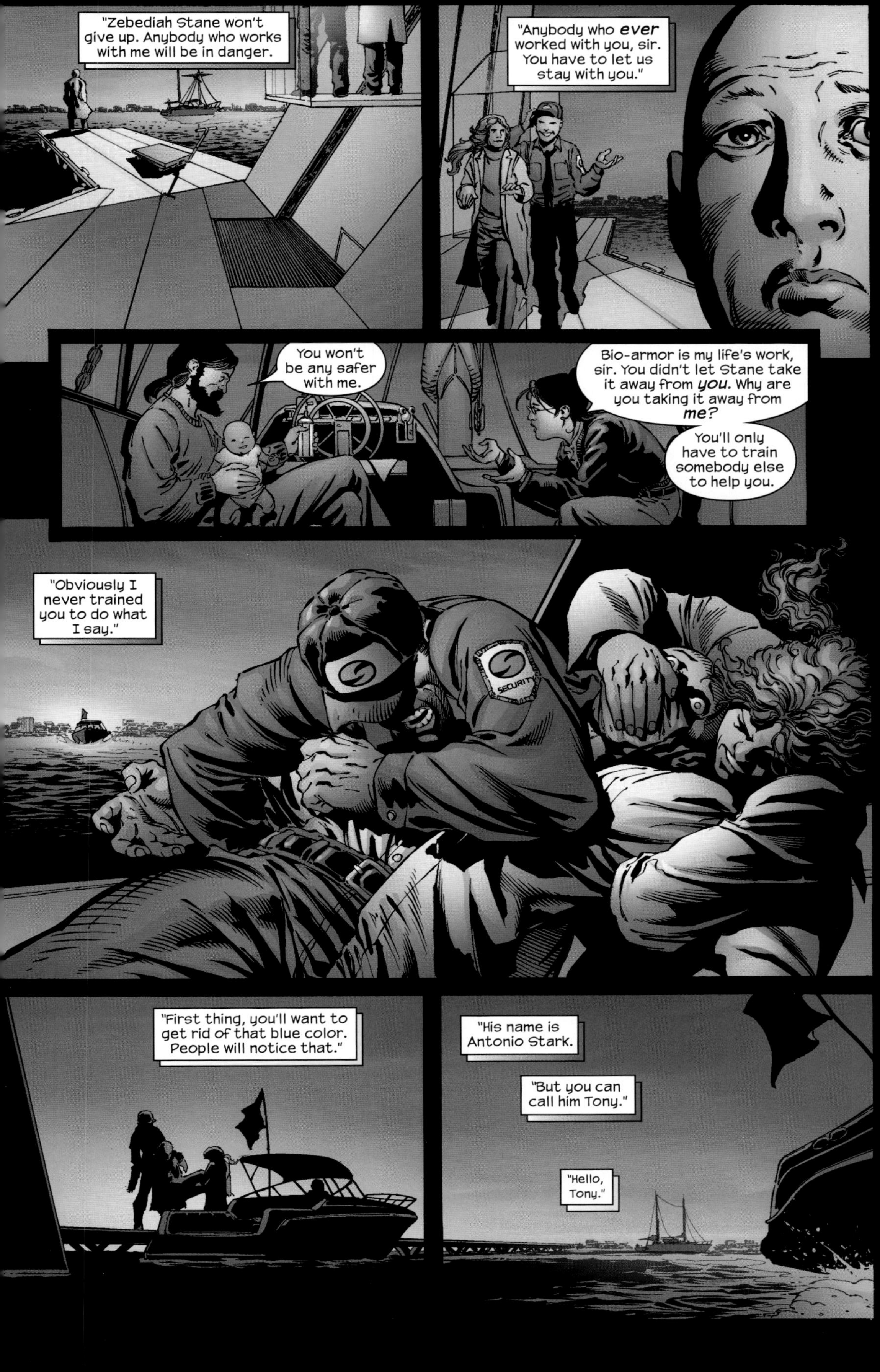
"Zebediah Stane won't give up. Anybody who works with me will be in danger.
"Anybody who ever worked with you, sir. You have to let us stay with you."
You won't be any safer with me.
Bio-armor is my life's work, sir. You didn't let Stane take it away from you. Why are you taking it away from me?
You'll only have to train somebody else to help you.
"Obviously I never trained you to do what I say."
SECURITY
"First thing, you'll want to get rid of that blue color. People will notice that."
"His name is Antonio Stark.
"But you can call him Tony."
"Hello, Tony."

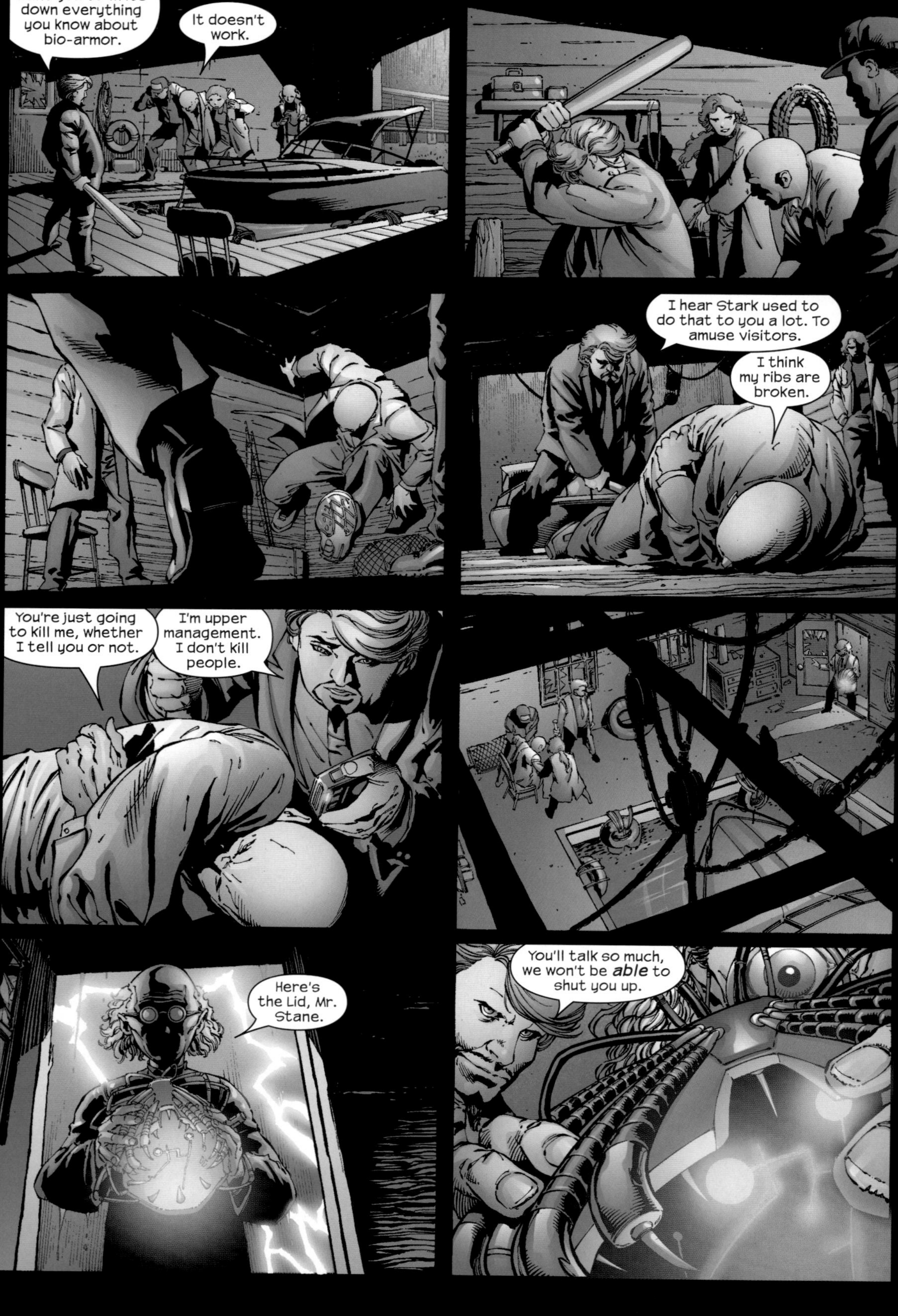
As I told you, I want you to write down everything you know about bio-armor.
It doesn't work.
I hear Stark used to do that to you a lot. To amuse visitors.
I think my ribs are broken.
You're just going to kill me, whether I tell you or not.
I'm upper management. I don't kill people.
Here's the Lid, Mr. Stane.
You'll talk so much, we won't be *able* to shut you up.

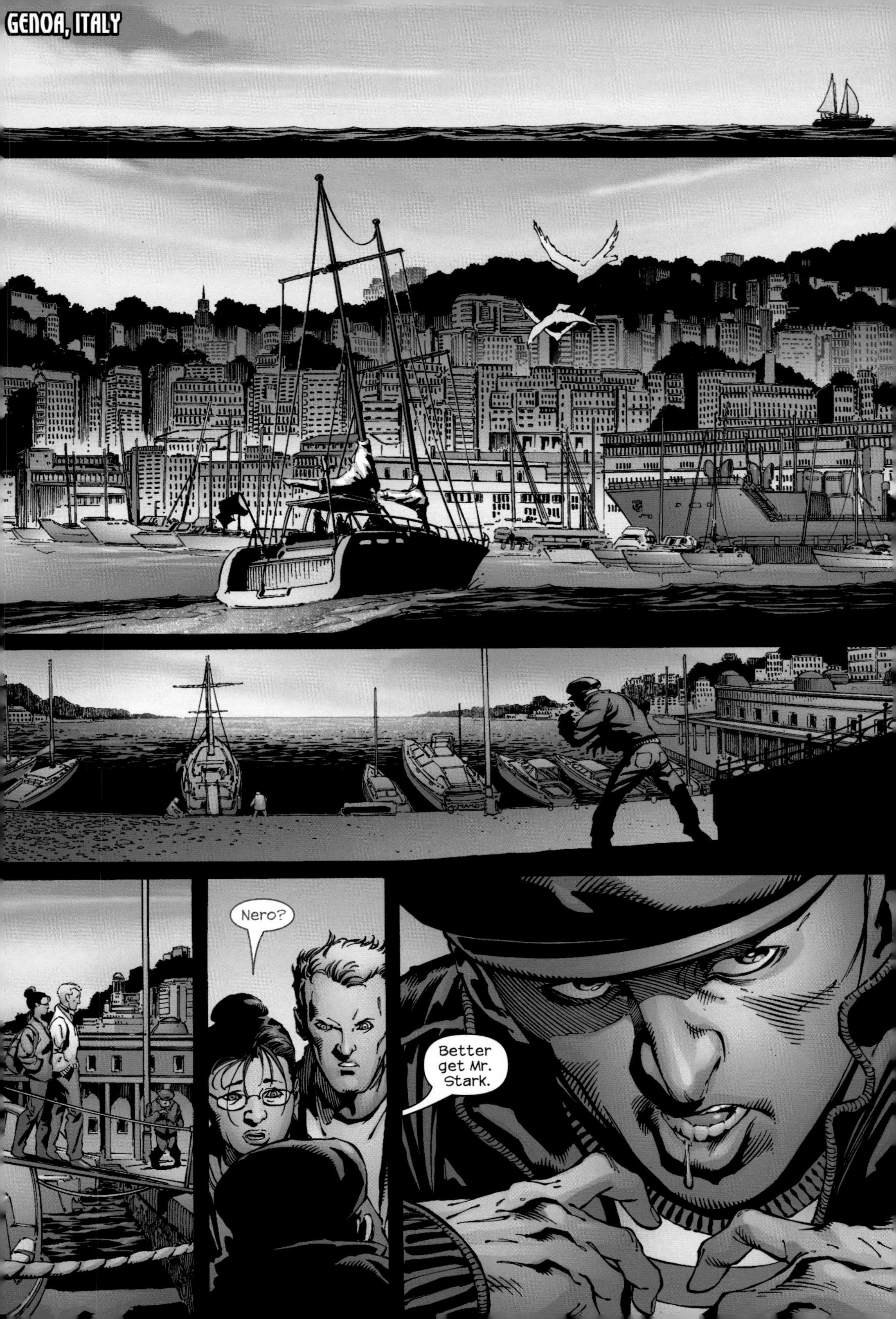
GENOA, ITALY
Nero?
Better get Mr. Stark.

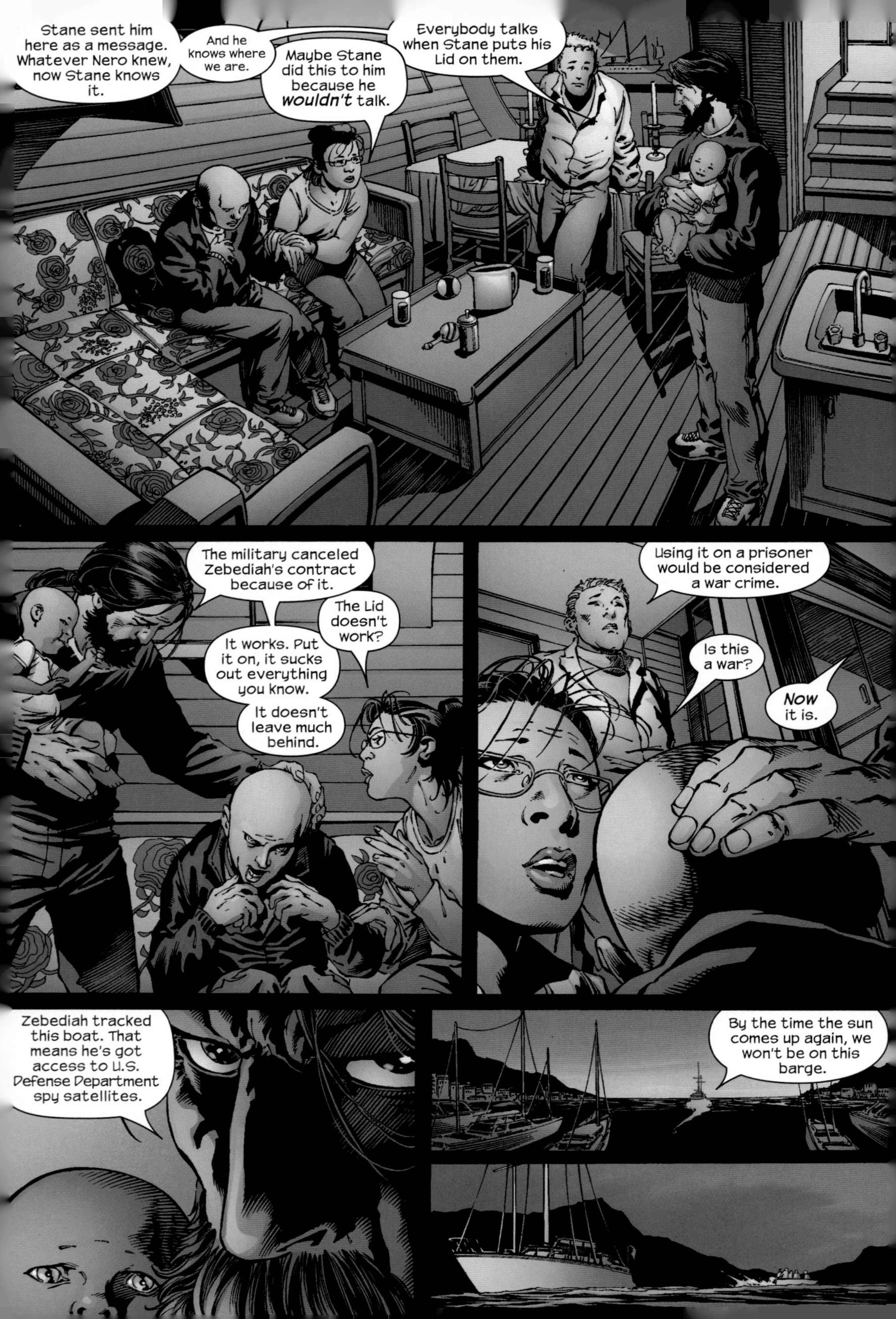
Stane sent him here as a message. Whatever Nero knew, now Stane knows it.
And he knows where we are.
Maybe Stane did this to him because he ***wouldn't*** talk.
Everybody talks when Stane puts his Lid on them.
The military canceled Zebediah's contract because of it.
The Lid doesn't work?
It works. Put it on, it sucks out everything you know.
It doesn't leave much behind.
Using it on a prisoner would be considered a war crime.
Is this a war?
Now it is.
Zebediah tracked this boat. That means he's got access to U.S. Defense Department spy satellites.
By the time the sun comes up again, we won't be on this barge.

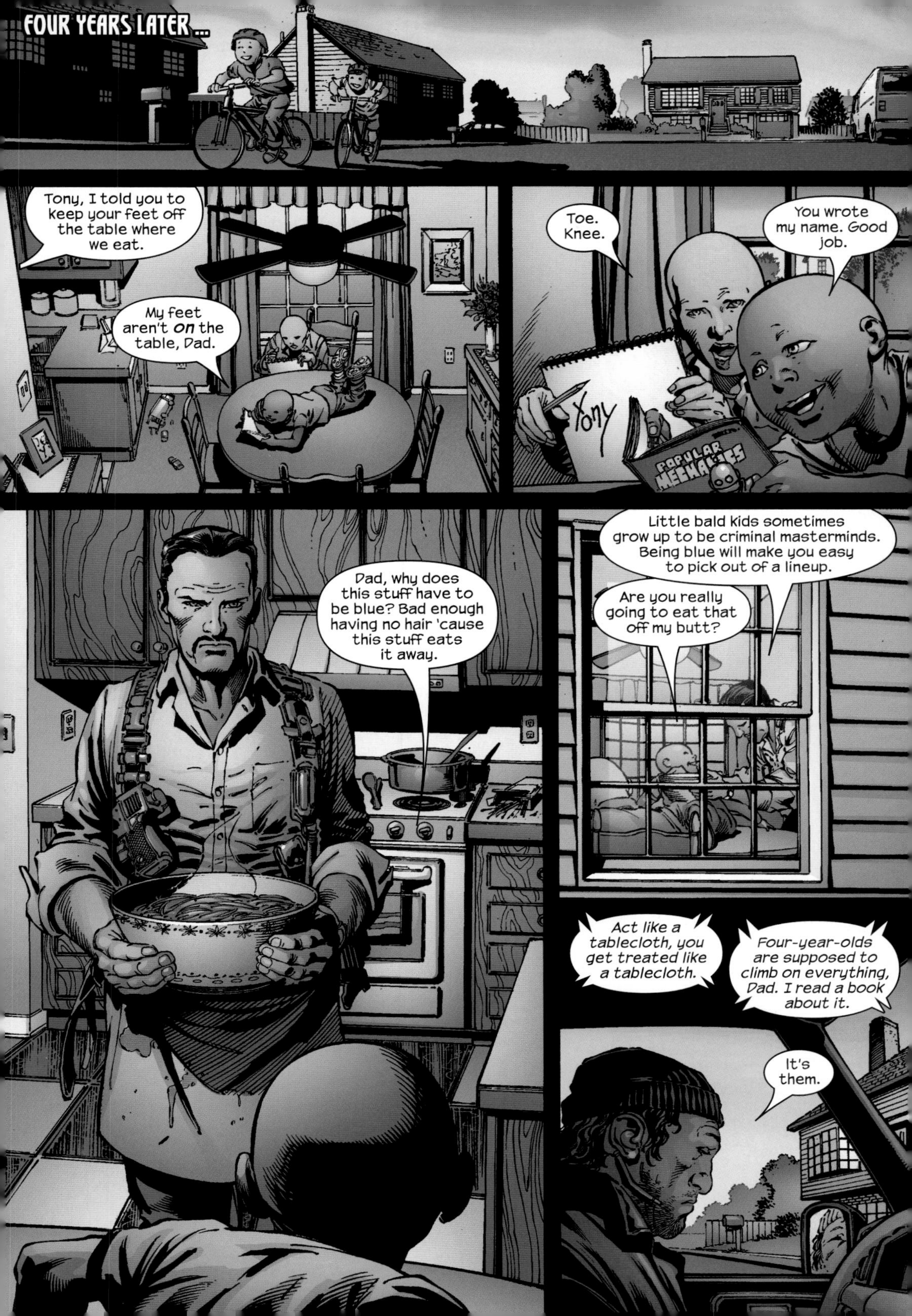
FOUR YEARS LATER ...
Tony, I told you to keep your feet off the table where we eat.
My feet aren't *on* the table, Dad.
Toe. Knee.
You wrote my name. Good job.
Tony
POPULAR MECHANICS
Dad, why does this stuff have to be blue? Bad enough having no hair 'cause this stuff eats it away.
Little bald kids sometimes grow up to be criminal masterminds. Being blue will make you easy to pick out of a lineup.
Are you really going to eat that off my butt?
Act like a tablecloth, you get treated like a tablecloth.
Four-year-olds are supposed to climb on everything, Dad. I read a book about it.
It's them.

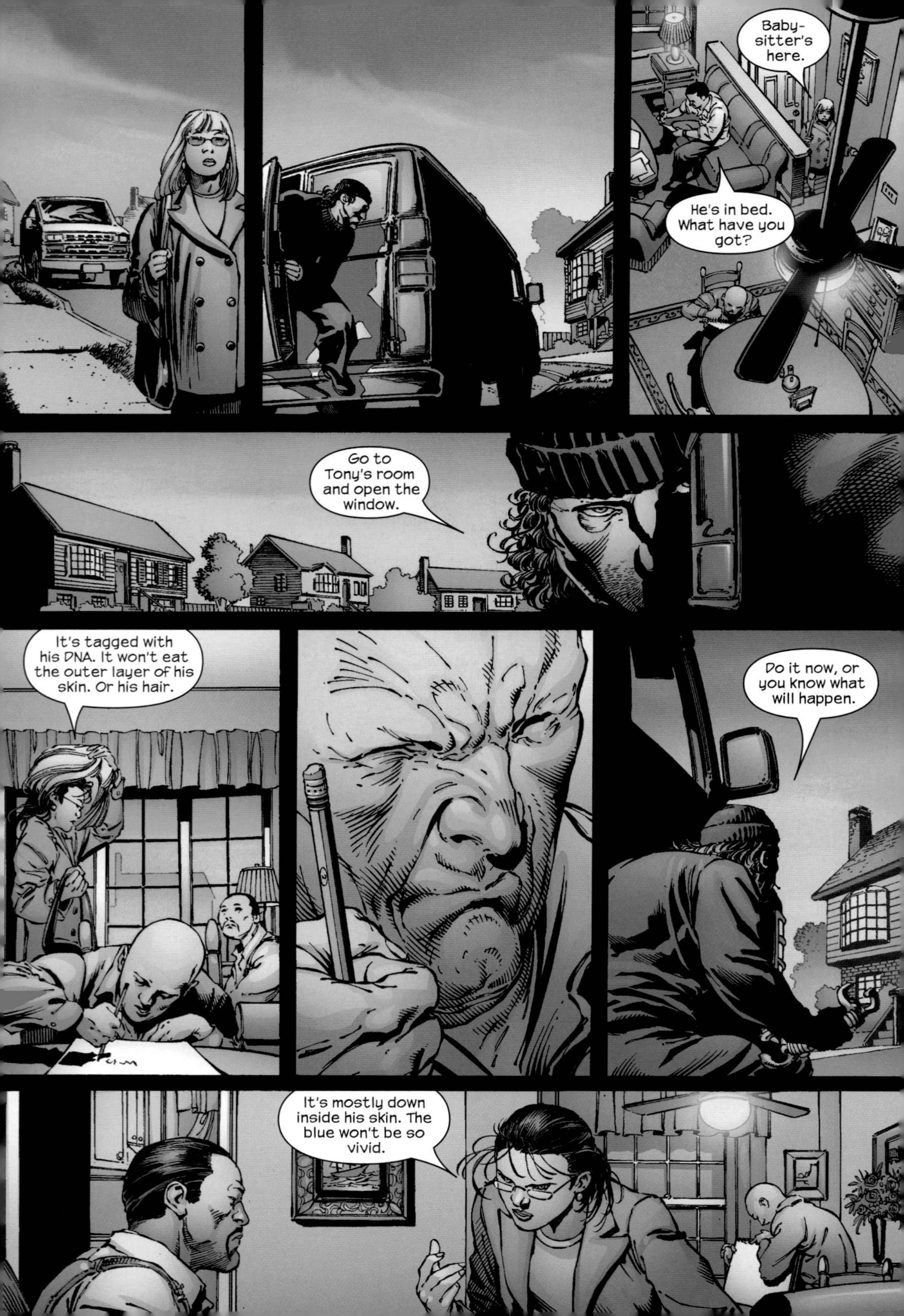

Baby-sitter's here.
He's in bed. What have you got?
Go to Tony's room and open the window.
It's tagged with his DNA. It won't eat the outer layer of his skin. Or his hair.
Do it now, or you know what will happen.
It's mostly down inside his skin. The blue won't be so vivid.

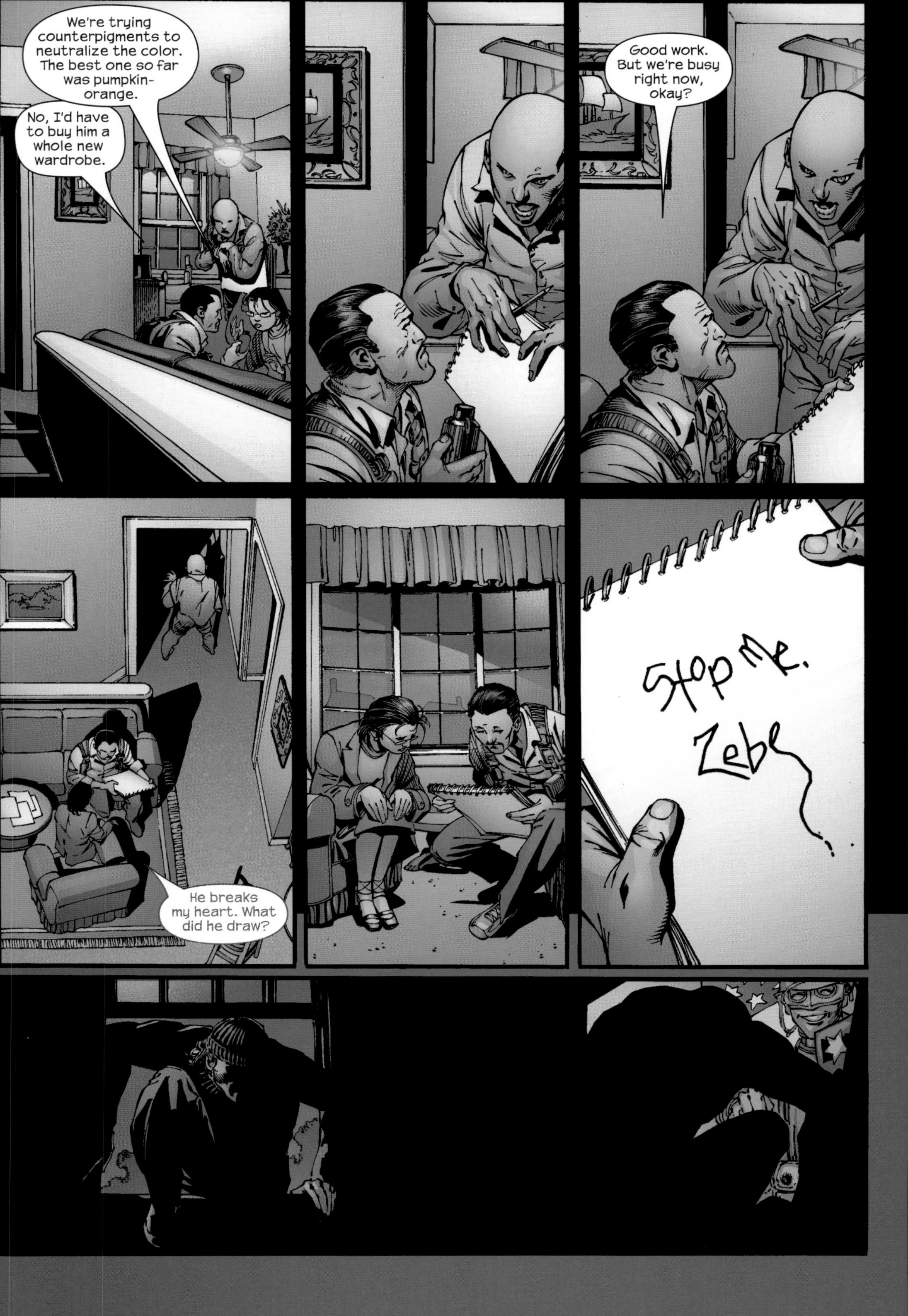

We're trying counterpigments to neutralize the color. The best one so far was pumpkin-orange.
No, I'd have to buy him a whole new wardrobe.
Good work. But we're busy right now, okay?
He breaks my heart. What did he draw?
Stop me.
Zebe

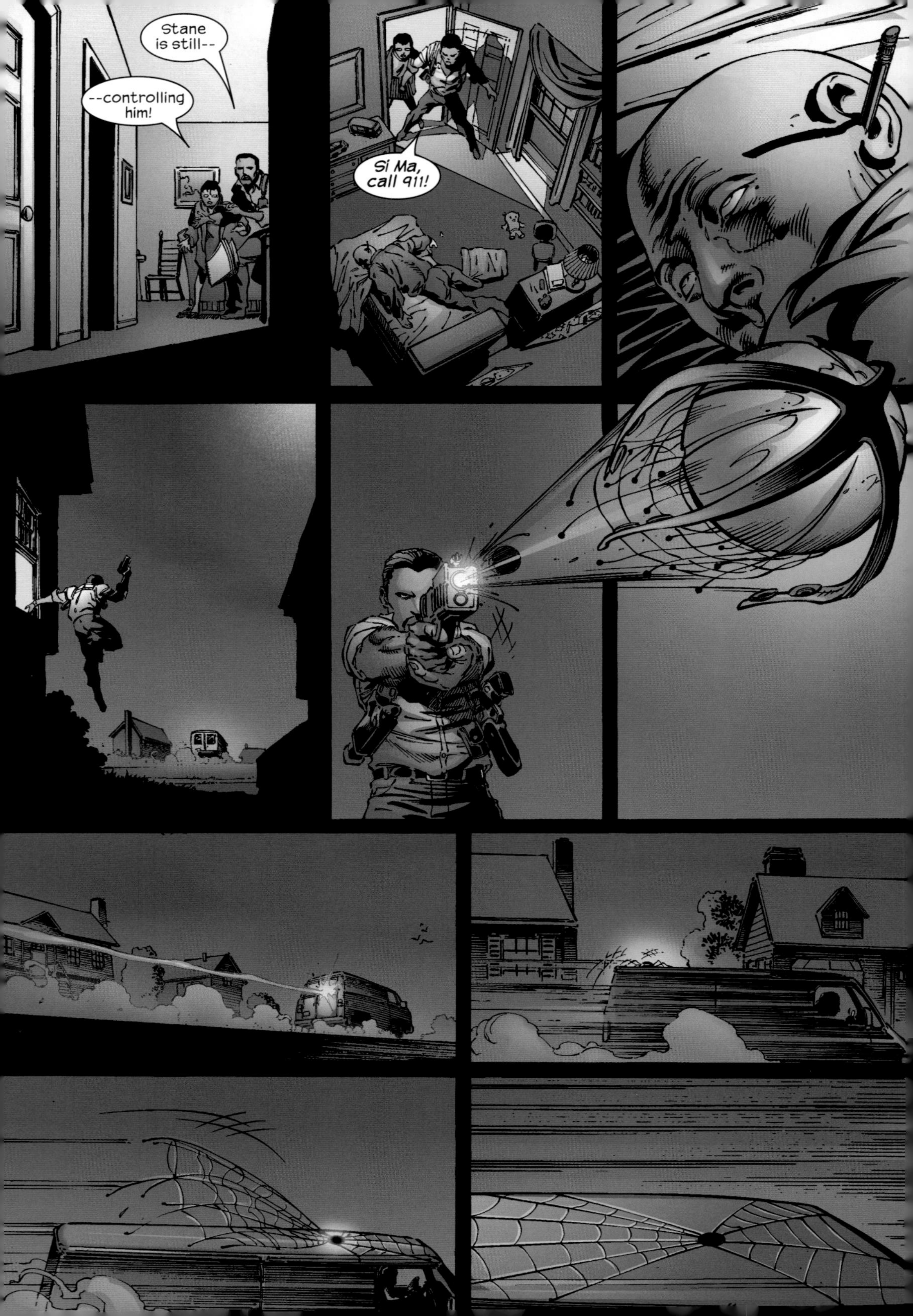

Stane is still--
--controlling him!
Si Ma, call 911!

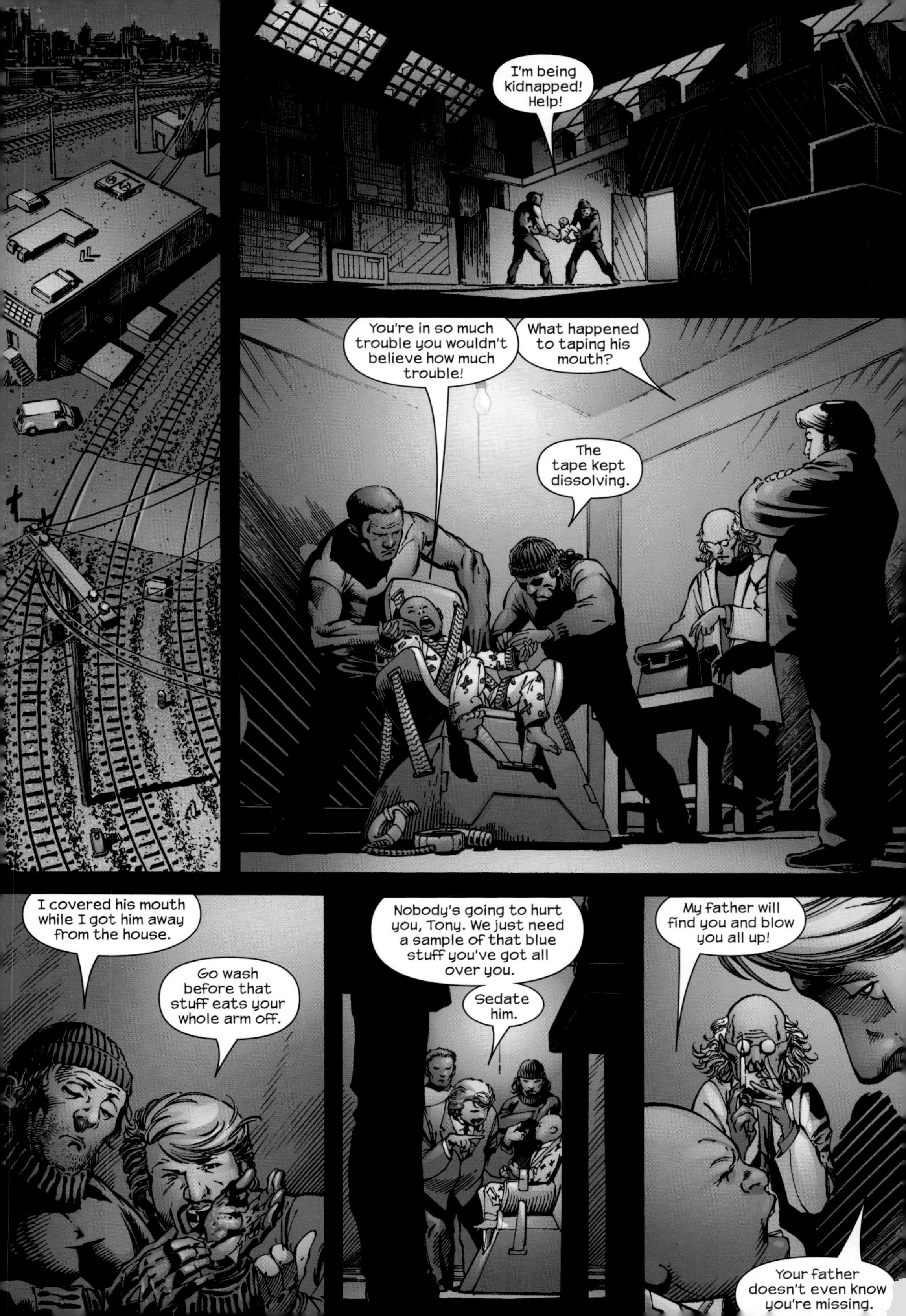
I'm being kidnapped! Help!
You're in so much trouble you wouldn't believe how much trouble!
What happened to taping his mouth?
The tape kept dissolving.
I covered his mouth while I got him away from the house.
Go wash before that stuff eats your whole arm off.
Nobody's going to hurt you, Tony. We just need a sample of that blue stuff you've got all over you.
Sedate him.
My father will find you and blow you all up!
Your father doesn't even know you're missing.

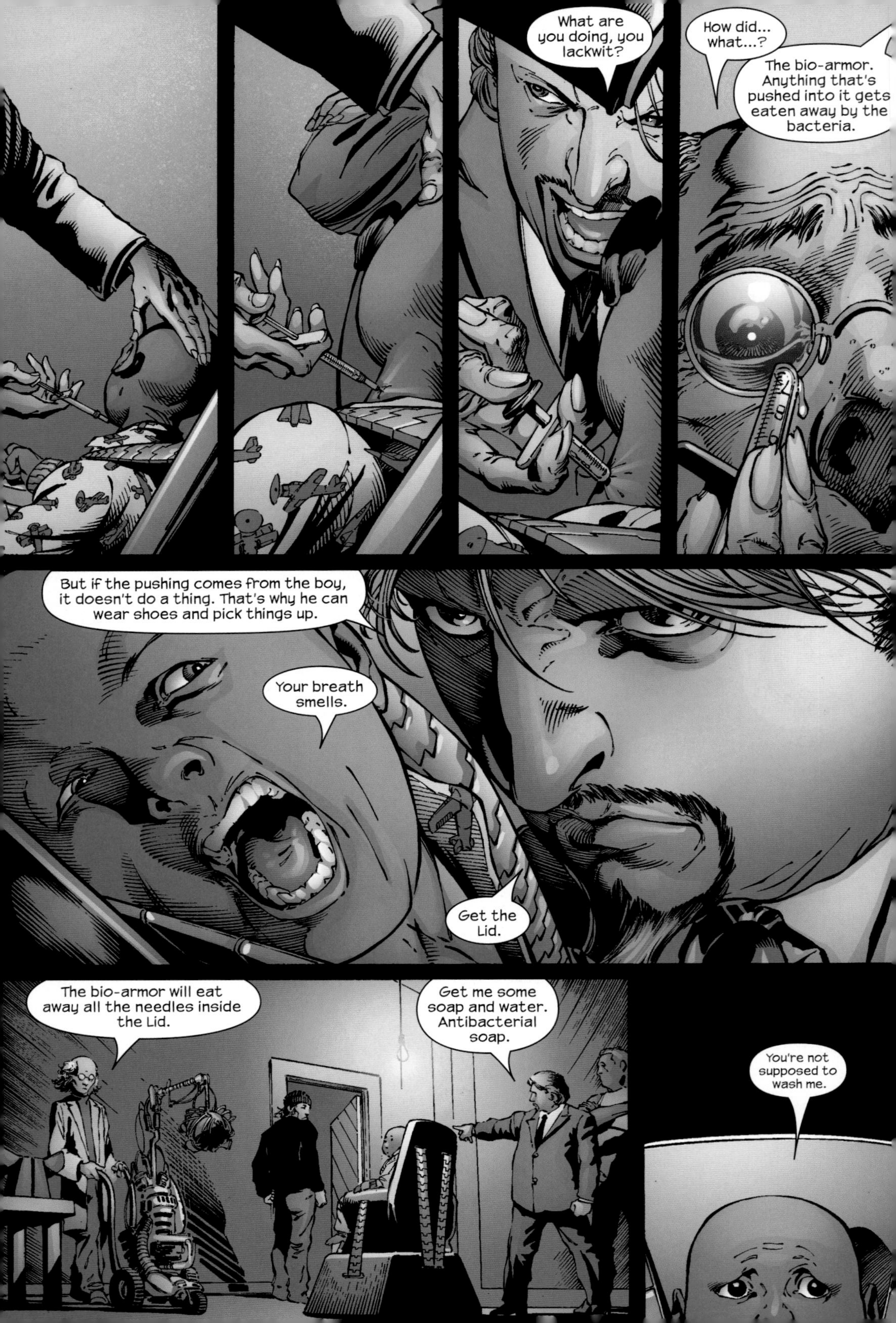
What are you doing, you lackwit?
How did... what...?
The bio-armor. Anything that's pushed into it gets eaten away by the bacteria.
But if the pushing comes from the boy, it doesn't do a thing. That's why he can wear shoes and pick things up.
Your breath smells.
Get the Lid.
The bio-armor will eat away all the needles inside the Lid.
Get me some soap and water. Antibacterial soap.
You're not supposed to wash me.

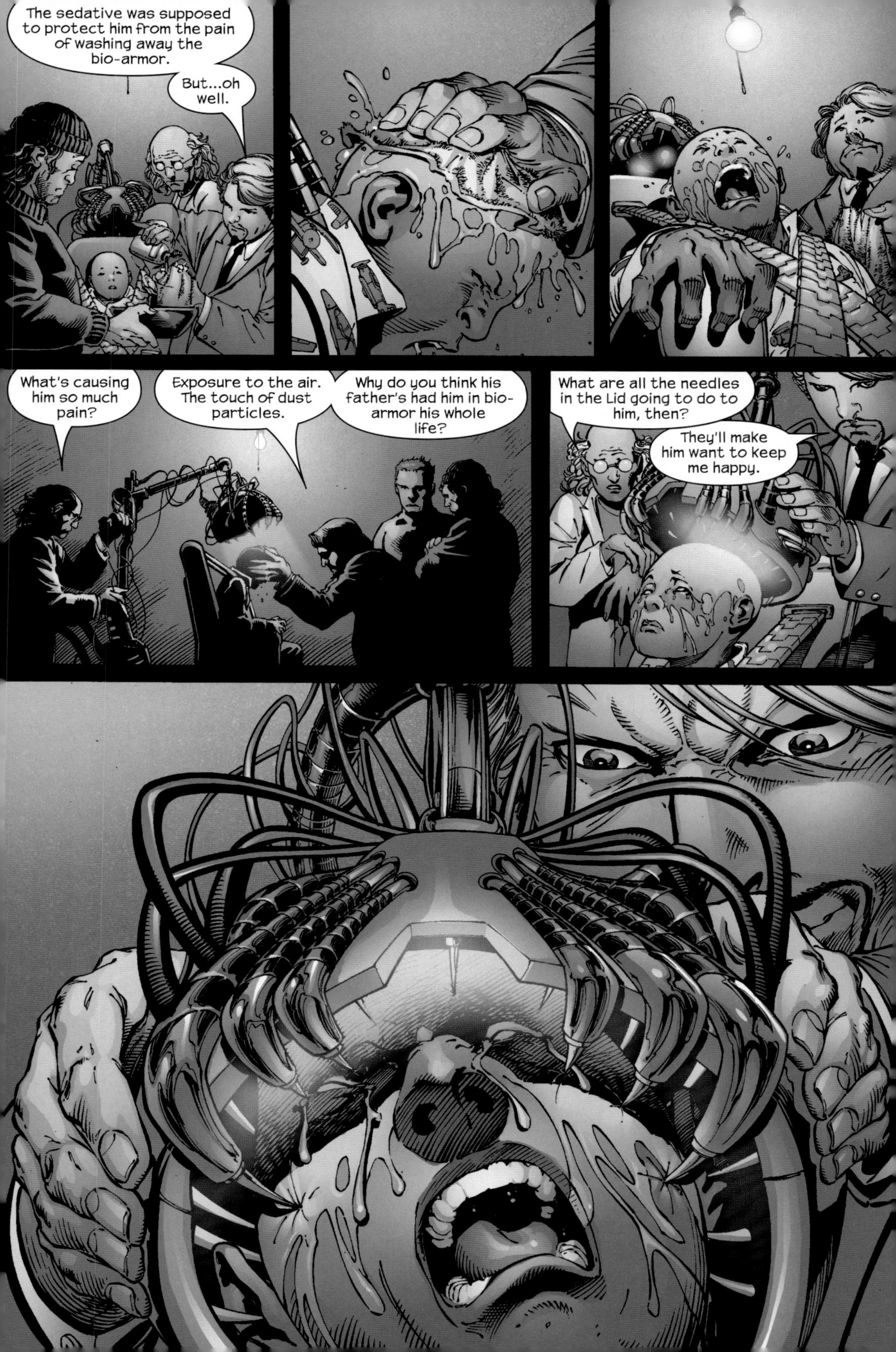
The sedative was supposed to protect him from the pain of washing away the bio-armor.
But...oh well.
What's causing him so much pain?
Exposure to the air. The touch of dust particles.
Why do you think his father's had him in bio-armor his whole life?
What are all the needles in the Lid going to do to him, then?
They'll make him want to keep me happy.

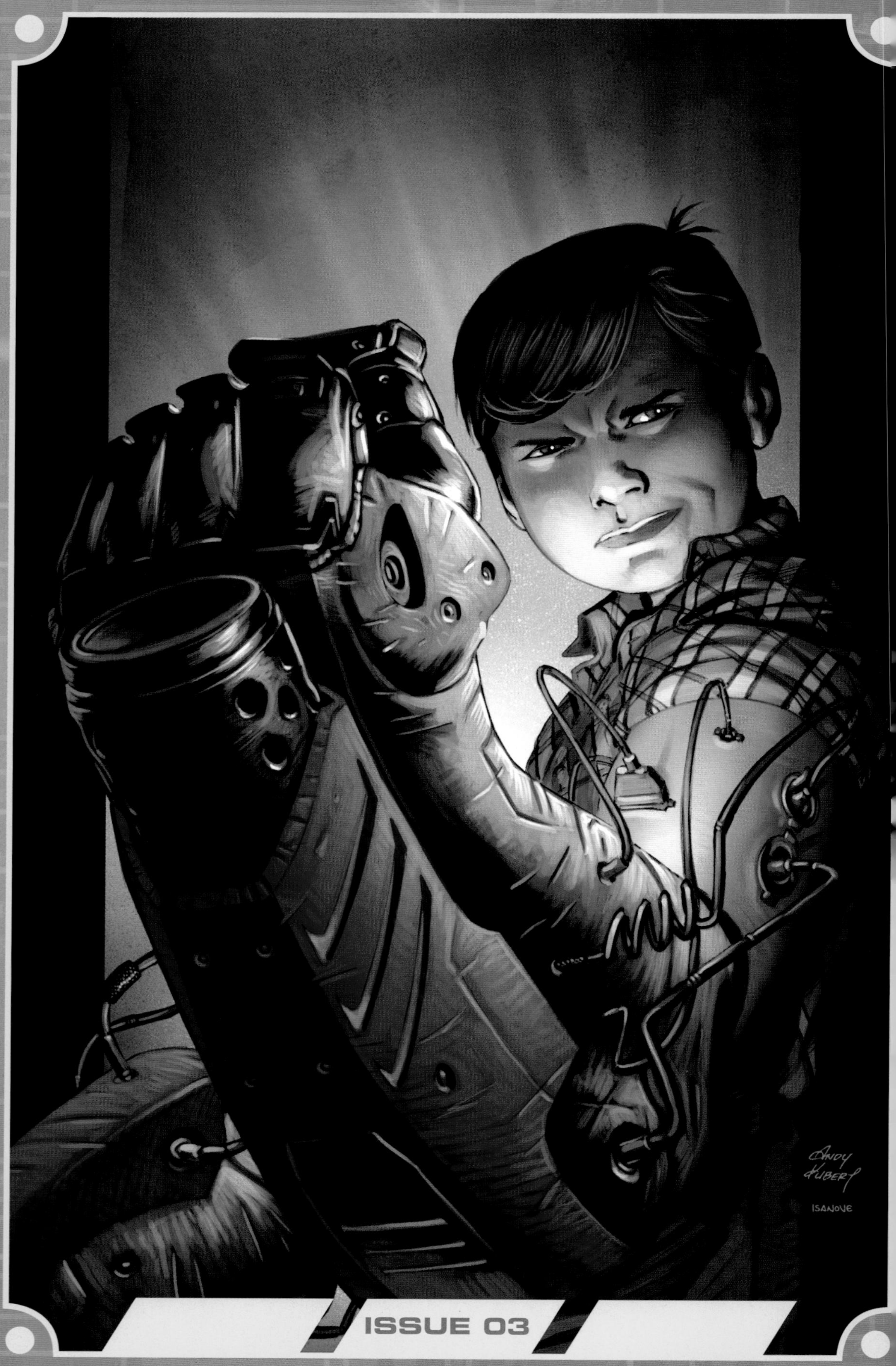
ANDY KUBERT
ISANOVE
ISSUE 03

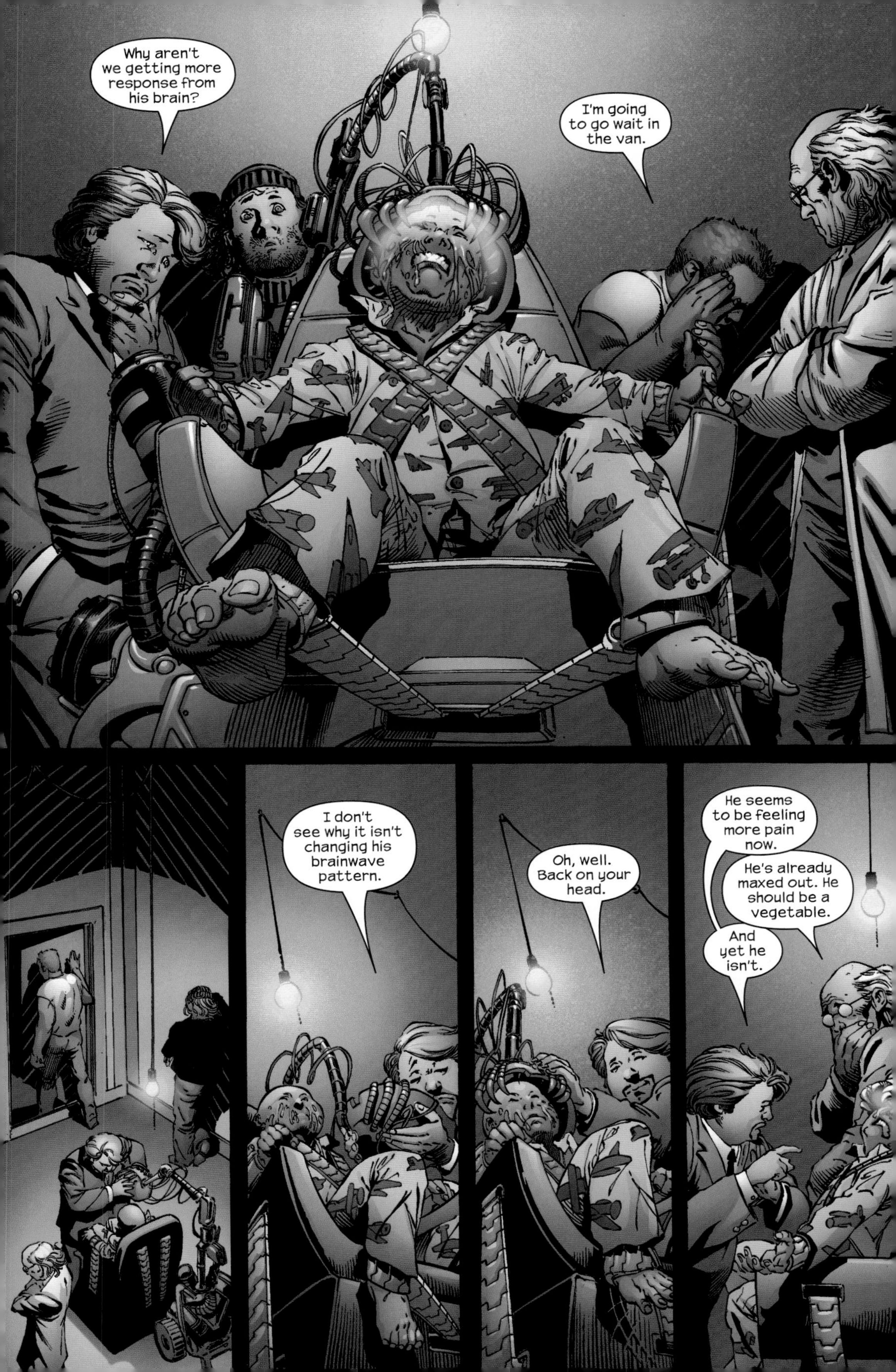
Why aren't we getting more response from his brain?
I'm going to go wait in the van.
I don't see why it isn't changing his brainwave pattern.
Oh, well. Back on your head.
He seems to be feeling more pain now.
He's already maxed out. He should be a vegetable.
And yet he isn't.

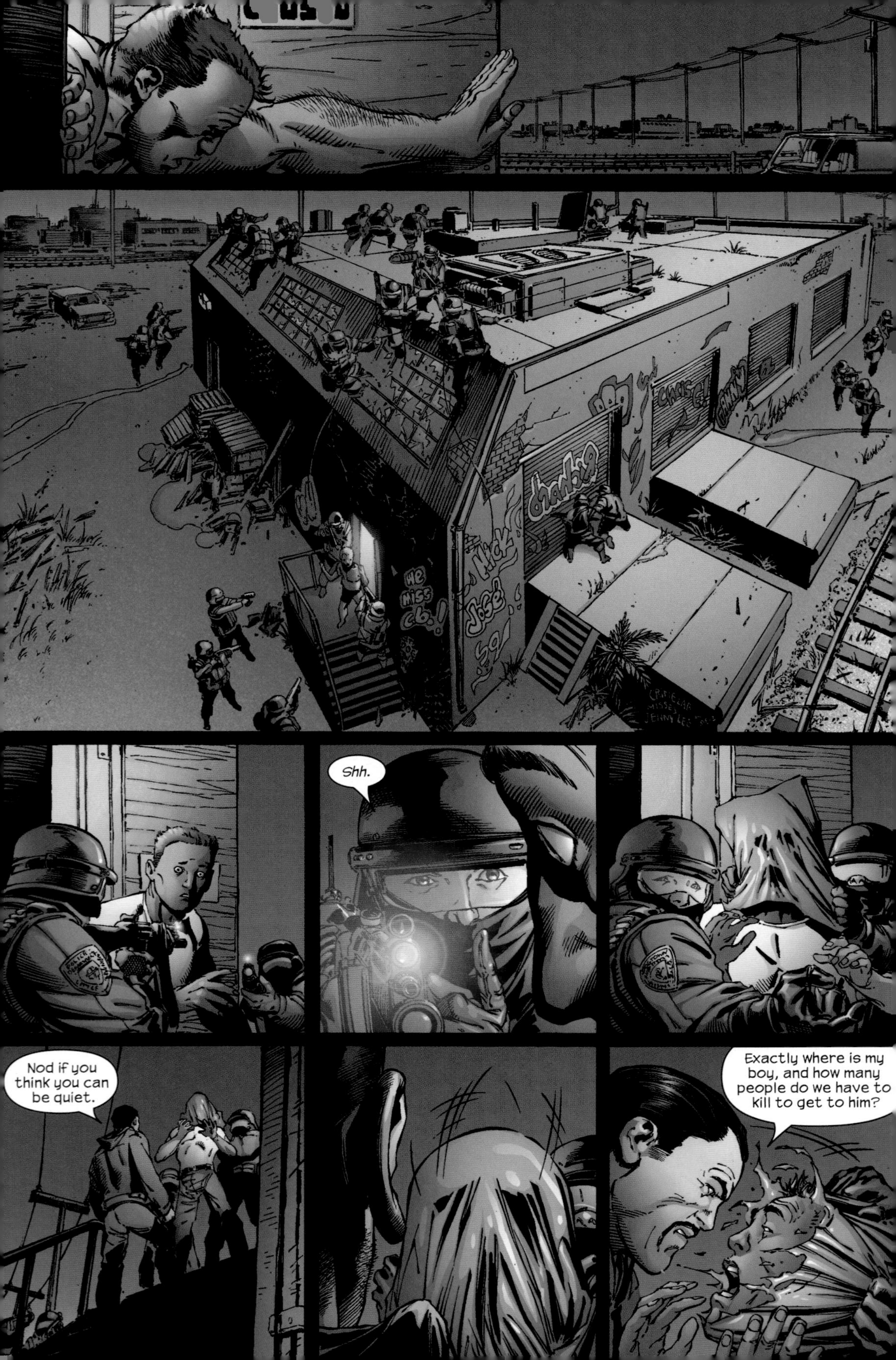
We miss C.B.!
Shh.
Nod if you think you can be quiet.
Exactly where is my boy, and how many people do we have to kill to get to him?

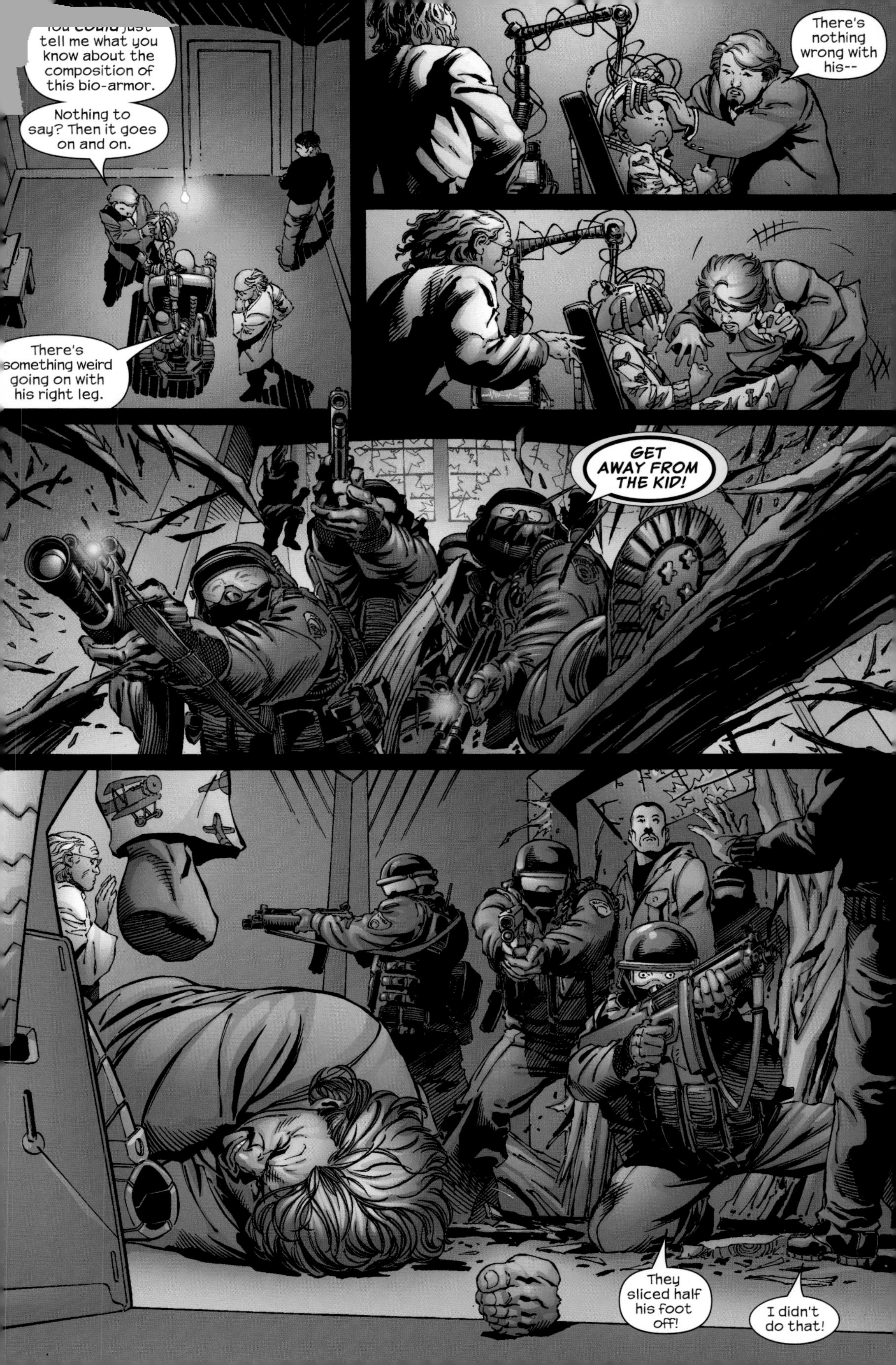
You could just tell me what you know about the composition of this bio-armor.
Nothing to say? Then it goes on and on.
There's something weird going on with his right leg.
There's nothing wrong with his--
GET AWAY FROM THE KID!
They sliced half his foot off!
I didn't do that!

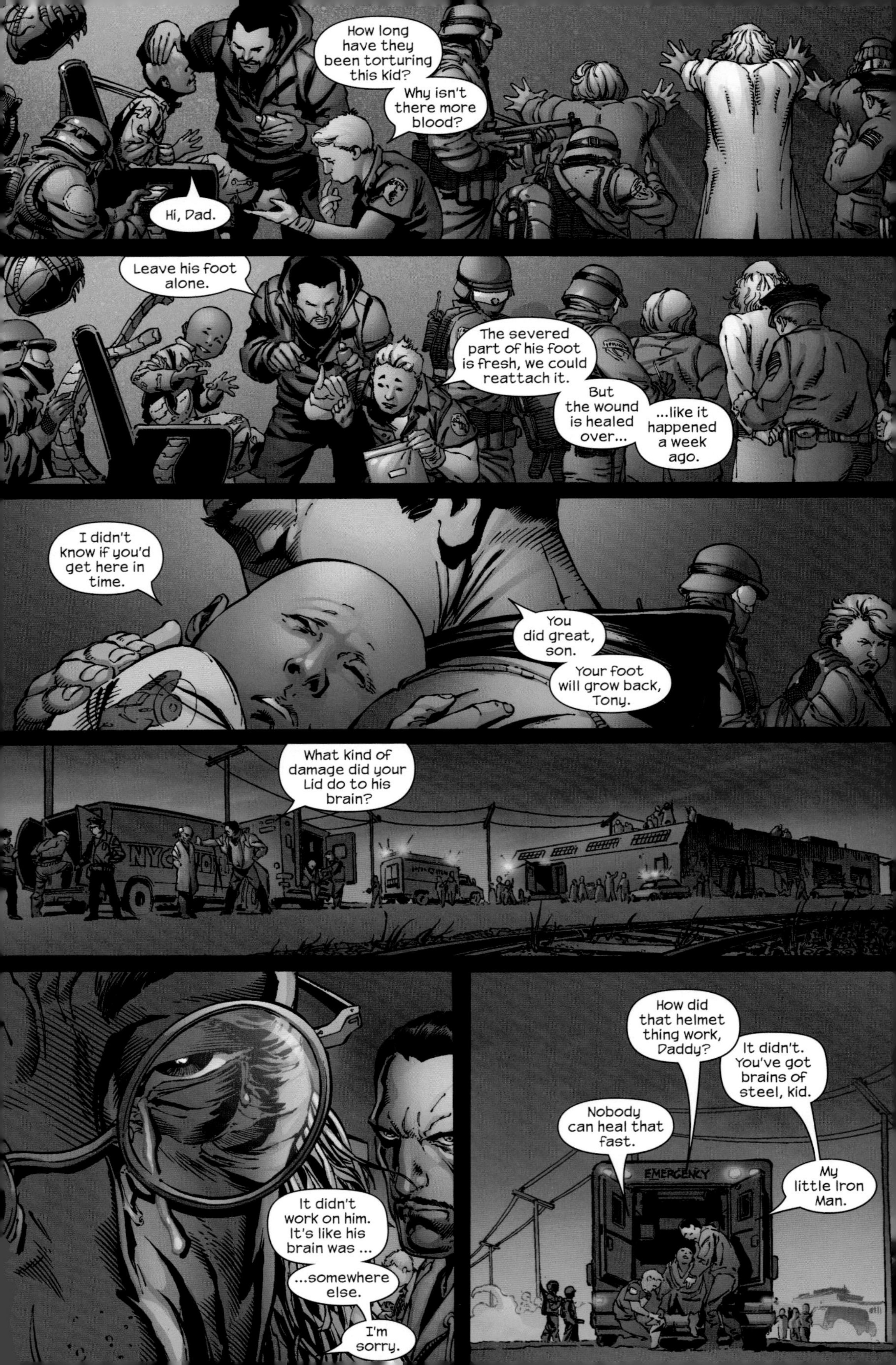
How long have they been torturing this kid?
Why isn't there more blood?
Hi, Dad.
Leave his foot alone.
The severed part of his foot is fresh, we could reattach it.
But the wound is healed over...
...like it happened a week ago.
I didn't know if you'd get here in time.
You did great, son.
Your foot will grow back, Tony.
What kind of damage did your Lid do to his brain?
NYC
It didn't work on him. It's like his brain was ...
...somewhere else.
I'm sorry.
How did that helmet thing work, Daddy?
It didn't. You've got brains of steel, kid.
Nobody can heal that fast.
EMERGENCY
My little Iron Man.

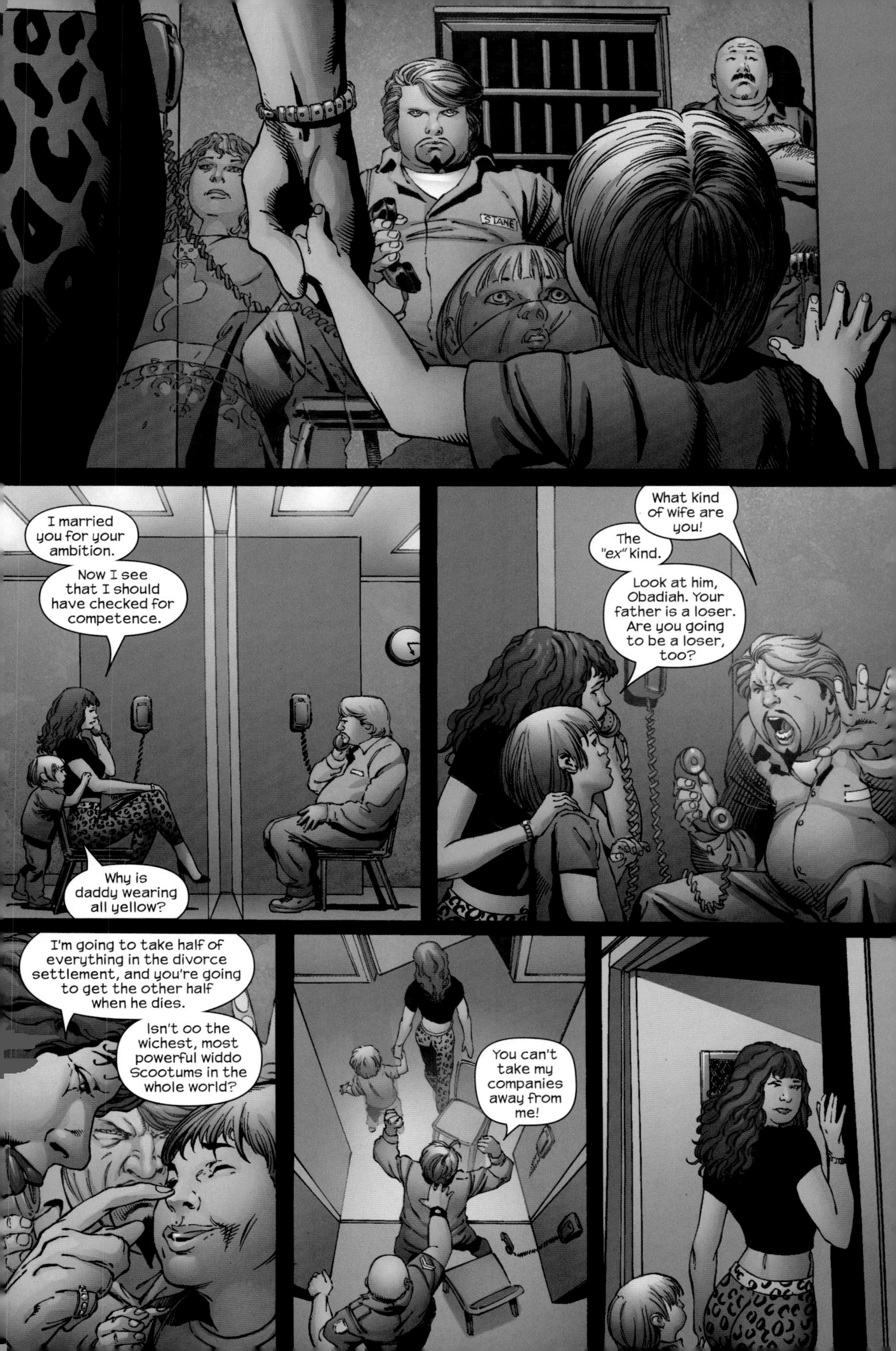
I married you for your ambition.
Now I see that I should have checked for competence.
Why is daddy wearing all yellow?
What kind of wife are you!
The "ex" kind.
Look at him, Obadiah. Your father is a loser. Are you going to be a loser, too?
I'm going to take half of everything in the divorce settlement, and you're going to get the other half when he dies.
Isn't oo the wichest, most powerful widdo Scootums in the whole world?
You can't take my companies away from me!
STANE

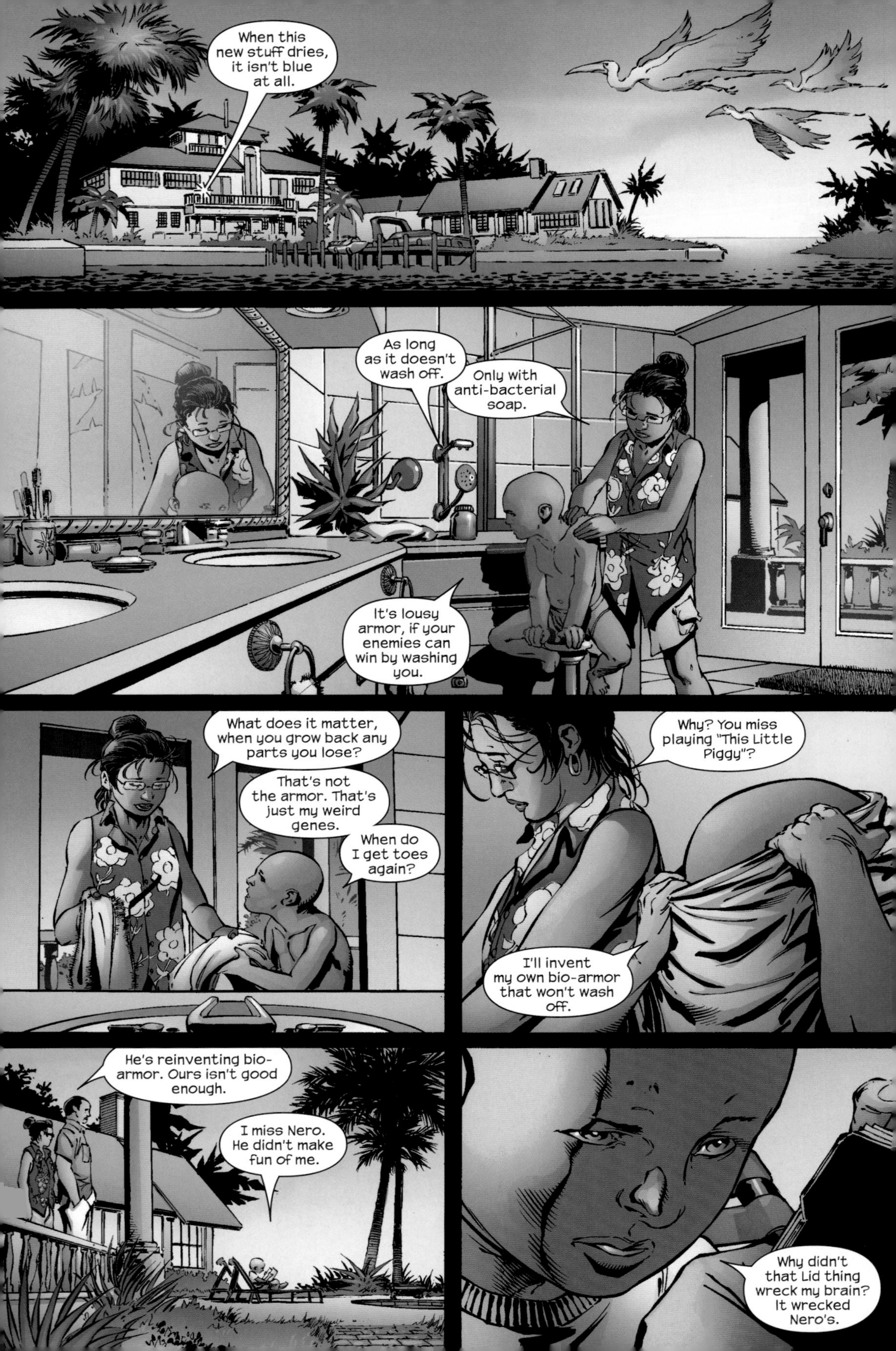
When this new stuff dries, it isn't blue at all.
As long as it doesn't wash off.
Only with anti-bacterial soap.
It's lousy armor, if your enemies can win by washing you.
What does it matter, when you grow back any parts you lose?
That's not the armor. That's just my weird genes.
When do I get toes again?
Why? You miss playing "This Little Piggy"?
I'll invent my own bio-armor that won't wash off.
He's reinventing bio-armor. Ours isn't good enough.
I miss Nero. He didn't make fun of me.
Why didn't that Lid thing wreck my brain? It wrecked Nero's.

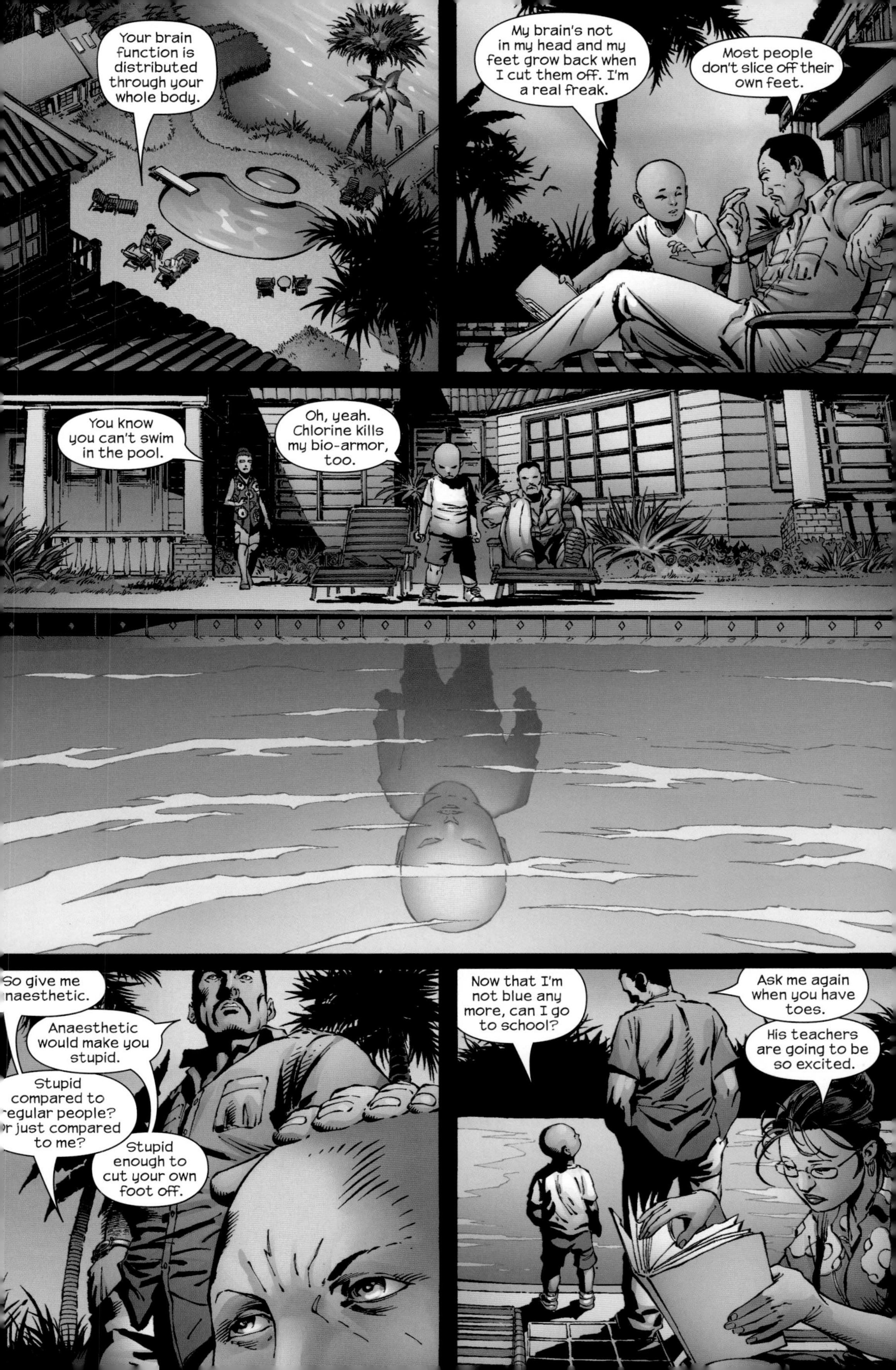
Your brain function is distributed through your whole body.
My brain's not in my head and my feet grow back when I cut them off. I'm a real freak.
Most people don't slice off their own feet.
You know you can't swim in the pool.
Oh, yeah. Chlorine kills my bio-armor, too.
So give me anaesthetic.
Anaesthetic would make you stupid.
Stupid compared to regular people? Or just compared to me?
Stupid enough to cut your own foot off.
Now that I'm not blue any more, can I go to school?
Ask me again when you have toes.
His teachers are going to be so excited.

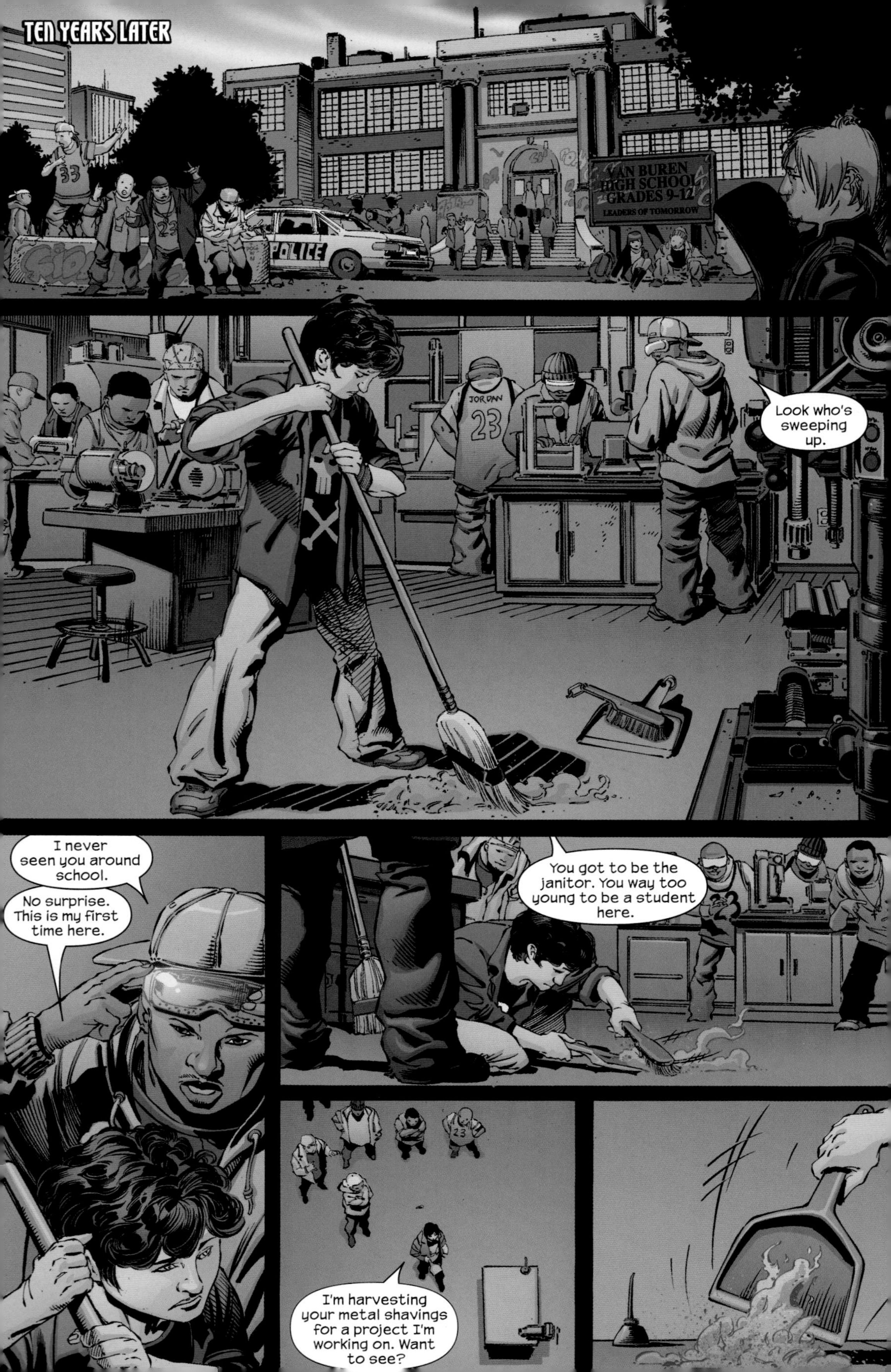
TEN YEARS LATER
VAN BUREN HIGH SCHOOL GRADES 9-12
LEADERS OF TOMORROW
POLICE
Look who's sweeping up.
I never seen you around school.
No surprise. This is my first time here.
You got to be the janitor. You way too young to be a student here.
I'm harvesting your metal shavings for a project I'm working on. Want to see?

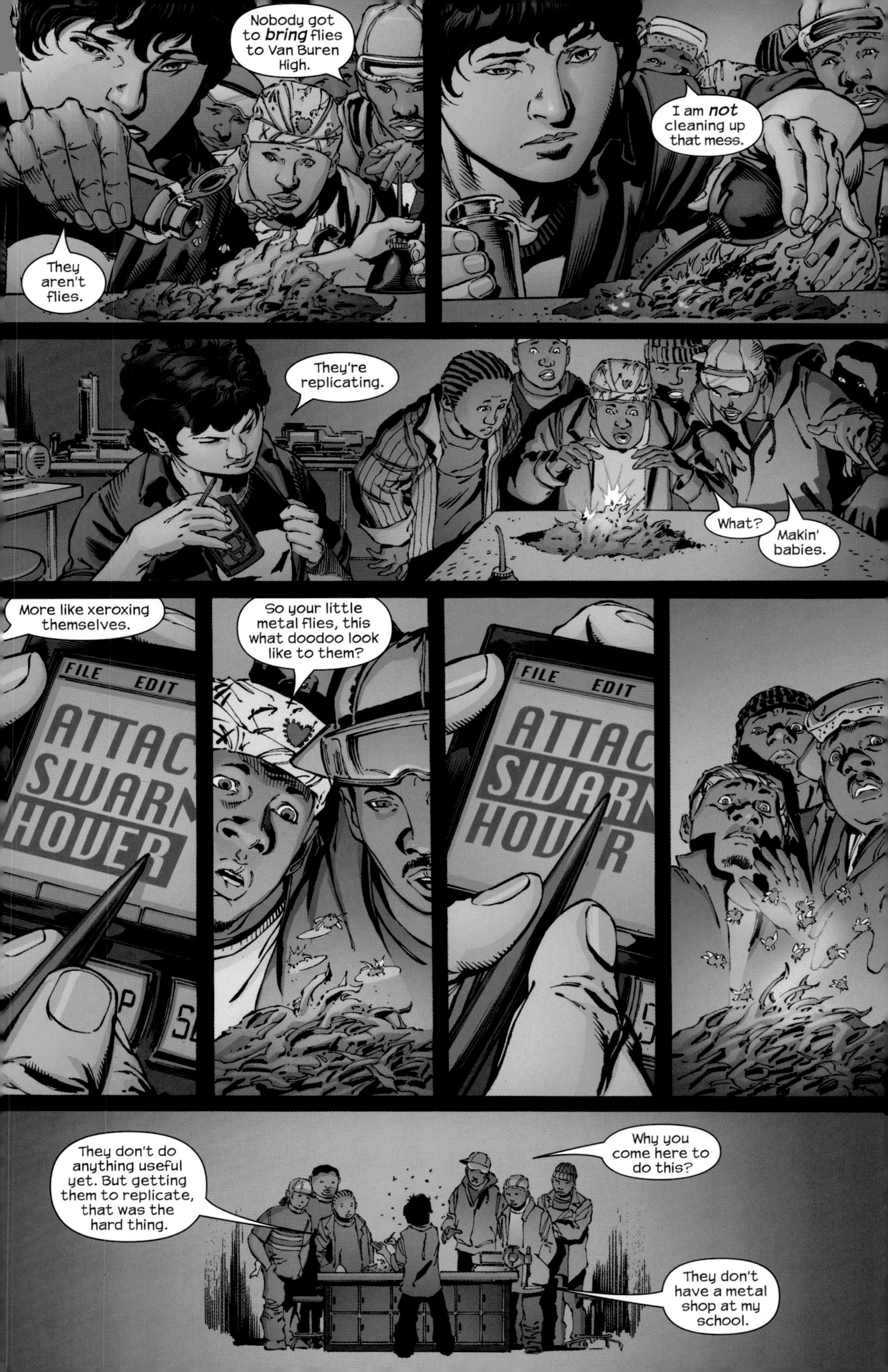

Nobody got to *bring* flies to Van Buren High.
They aren't flies.
I am *not* cleaning up that mess.
They're replicating.
What?
Makin' babies.
More like xeroxing themselves.
FILE EDIT
ATTAC SWARM HOVER
So your little metal flies, this what doodoo look like to them?
FILE EDIT
ATTAC SWARM HOVER
They don't do anything useful yet. But getting them to replicate, that was the hard thing.
Why you come here to do this?
They don't have a metal shop at my school.

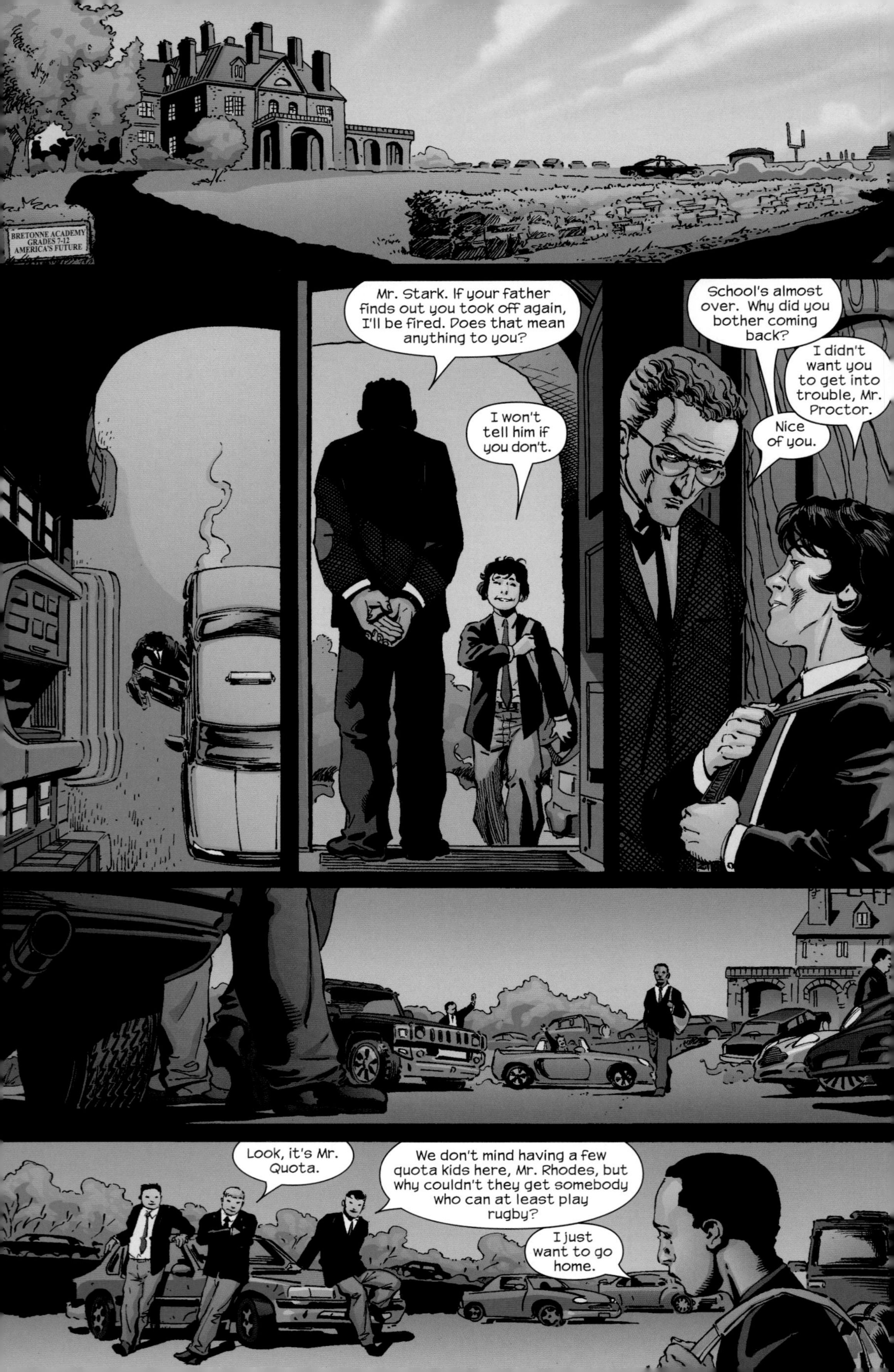
BRETONNE ACADEMY
GRADES 7-12
AMERICA'S FUTURE
Mr. Stark. If your father finds out you took off again, I'll be fired. Does that mean anything to you?
I won't tell him if you don't.
School's almost over. Why did you bother coming back?
I didn't want you to get into trouble, Mr. Proctor.
Nice of you.
Look, it's Mr. Quota.
We don't mind having a few quota kids here, Mr. Rhodes, but why couldn't they get somebody who can at least play rugby?
I just want to go home.

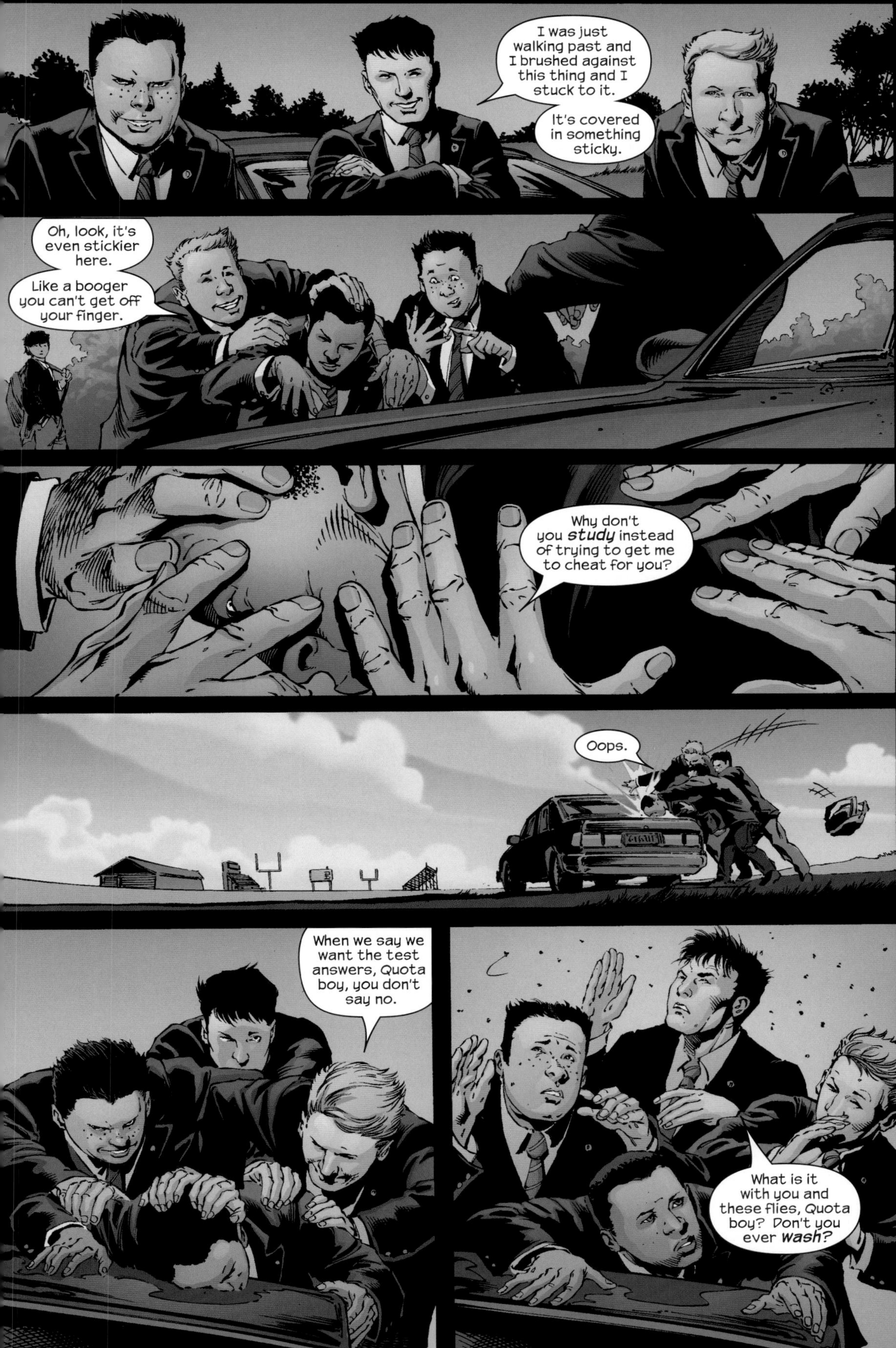
I was just walking past and I brushed against this thing and I stuck to it.
It's covered in something sticky.
Oh, look, it's even stickier here.
Like a booger you can't get off your finger.
Why don't you *study* instead of trying to get me to cheat for you?
Oops.
When we say we want the test answers, Quota boy, you don't say no.
What is it with you and these flies, Quota boy? Don't you ever *wash?*

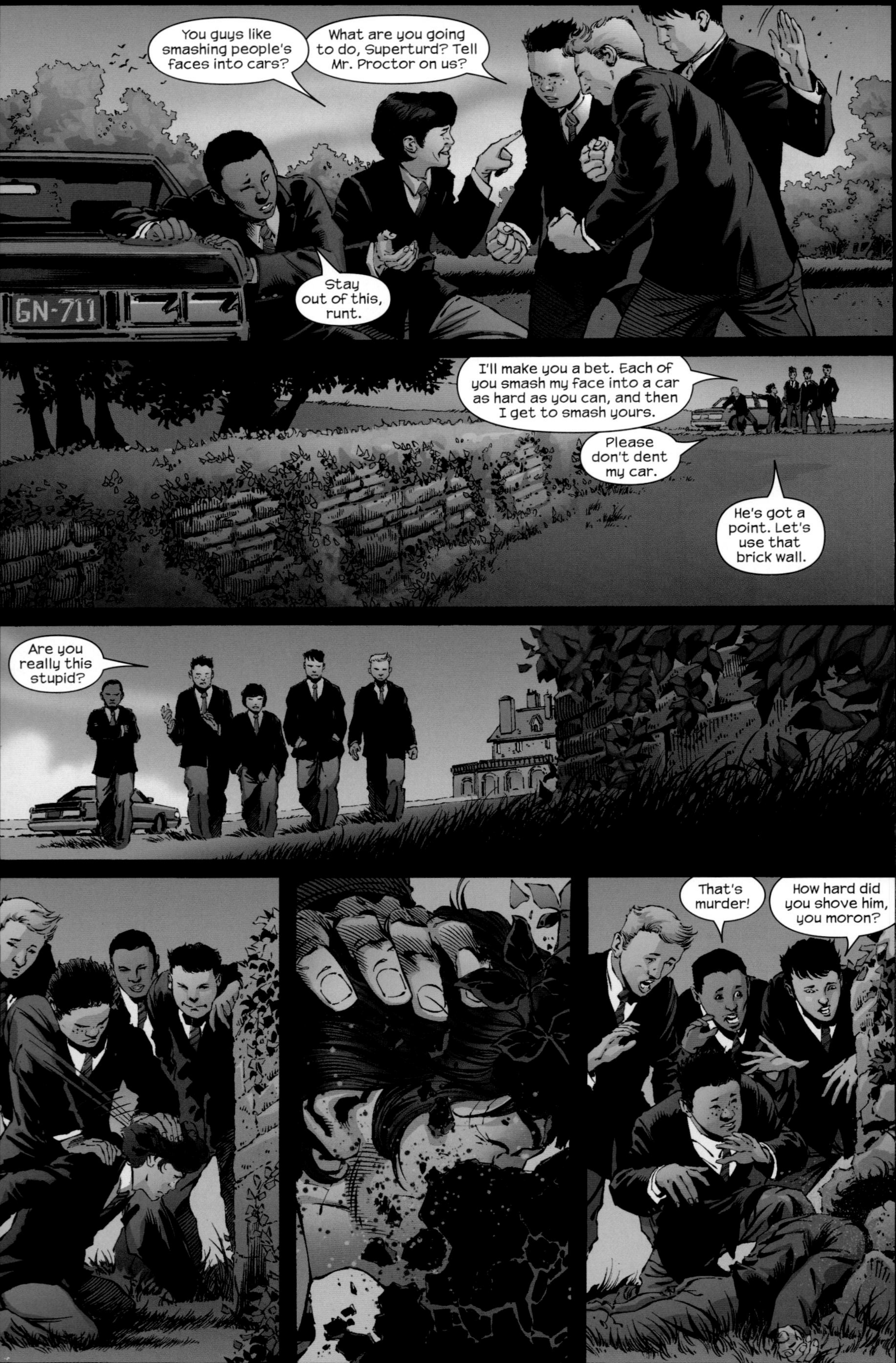
You guys like smashing people's faces into cars?
What are you going to do, Superturd? Tell Mr. Proctor on us?
Stay out of this, runt.
GN-711
I'll make you a bet. Each of you smash my face into a car as hard as you can, and then I get to smash yours.
Please don't dent my car.
He's got a point. Let's use that brick wall.
Are you really this stupid?
That's murder!
How hard did you shove him, you moron?

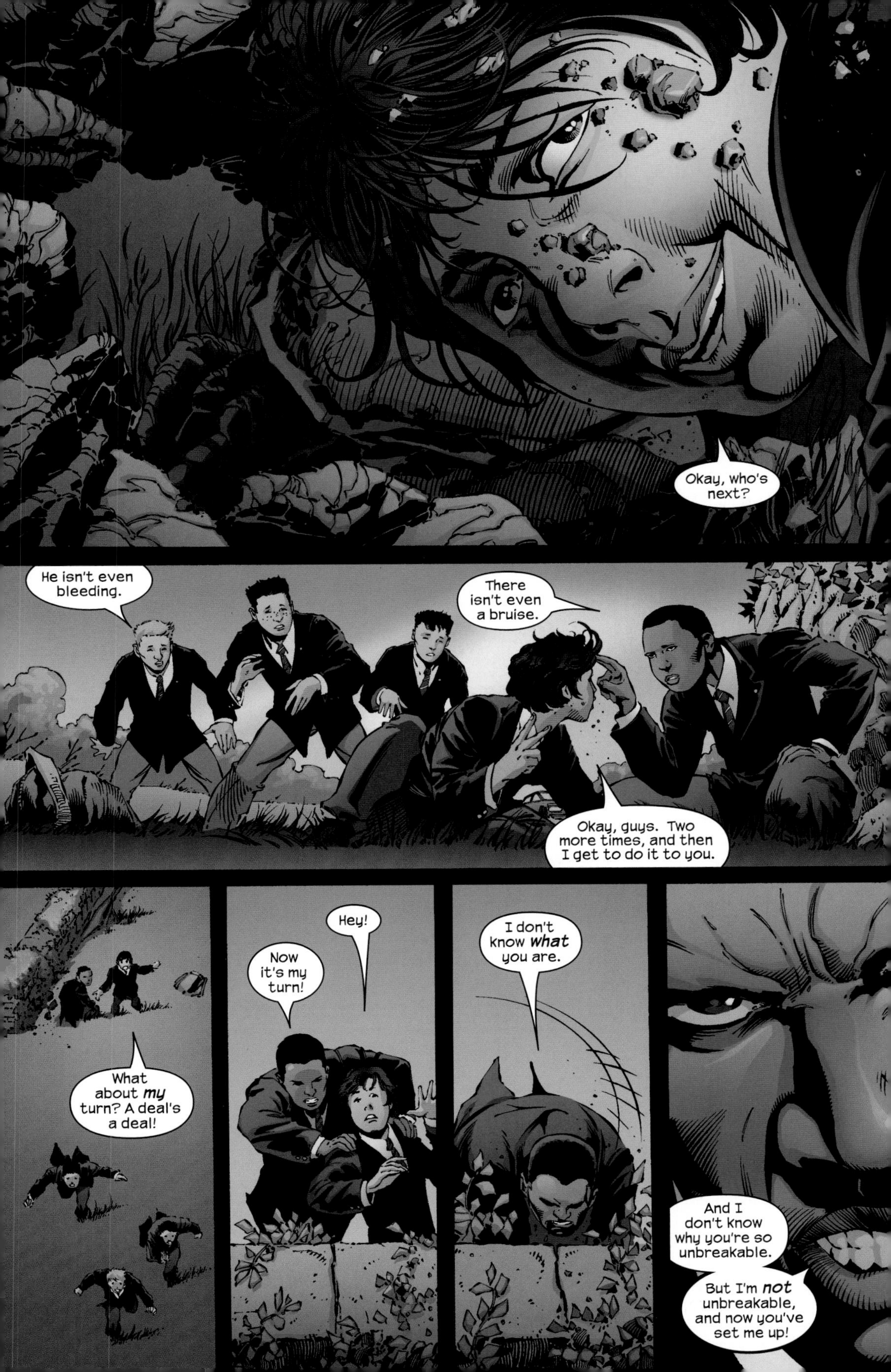
Okay, who's next?
He isn't even bleeding.
There isn't even a bruise.
Okay, guys. Two more times, and then I get to do it to you.
What about *my* turn? A deal's a deal!
Hey!
Now it's my turn!
I don't know *what* you are.
And I don't know why you're so unbreakable.
But I'm *not* unbreakable, and now you've set me up!

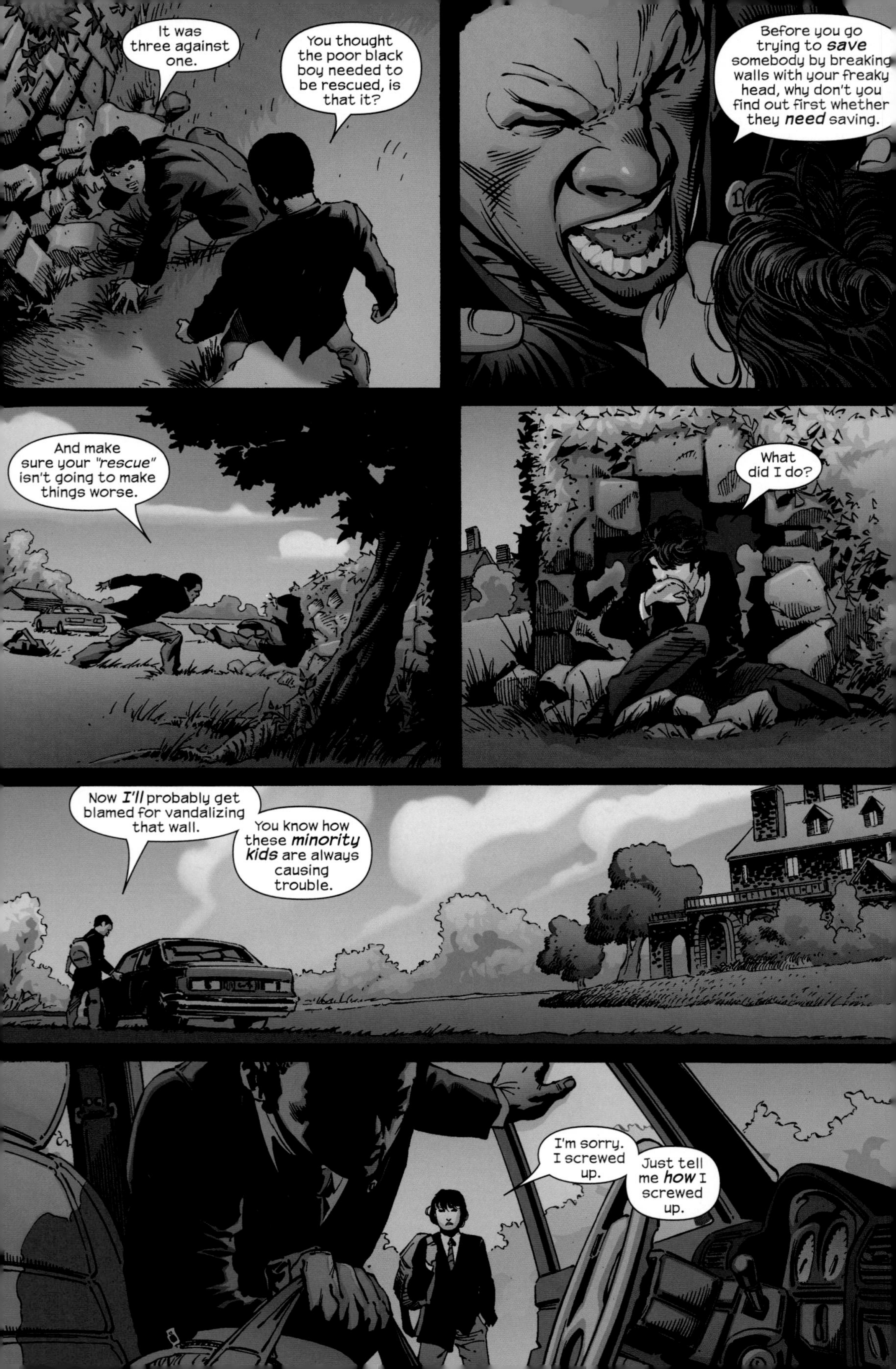
It was three against one.
You thought the poor black boy needed to be rescued, is that it?
Before you go trying to *save* somebody by breaking walls with your freaky head, why don't you find out first whether they *need* saving.
And make sure your *"rescue"* isn't going to make things worse.
What did I do?
Now *I'll* probably get blamed for vandalizing that wall.
You know how these *minority kids* are always causing trouble.
I'm sorry. I screwed up.
Just tell me *how* I screwed up.

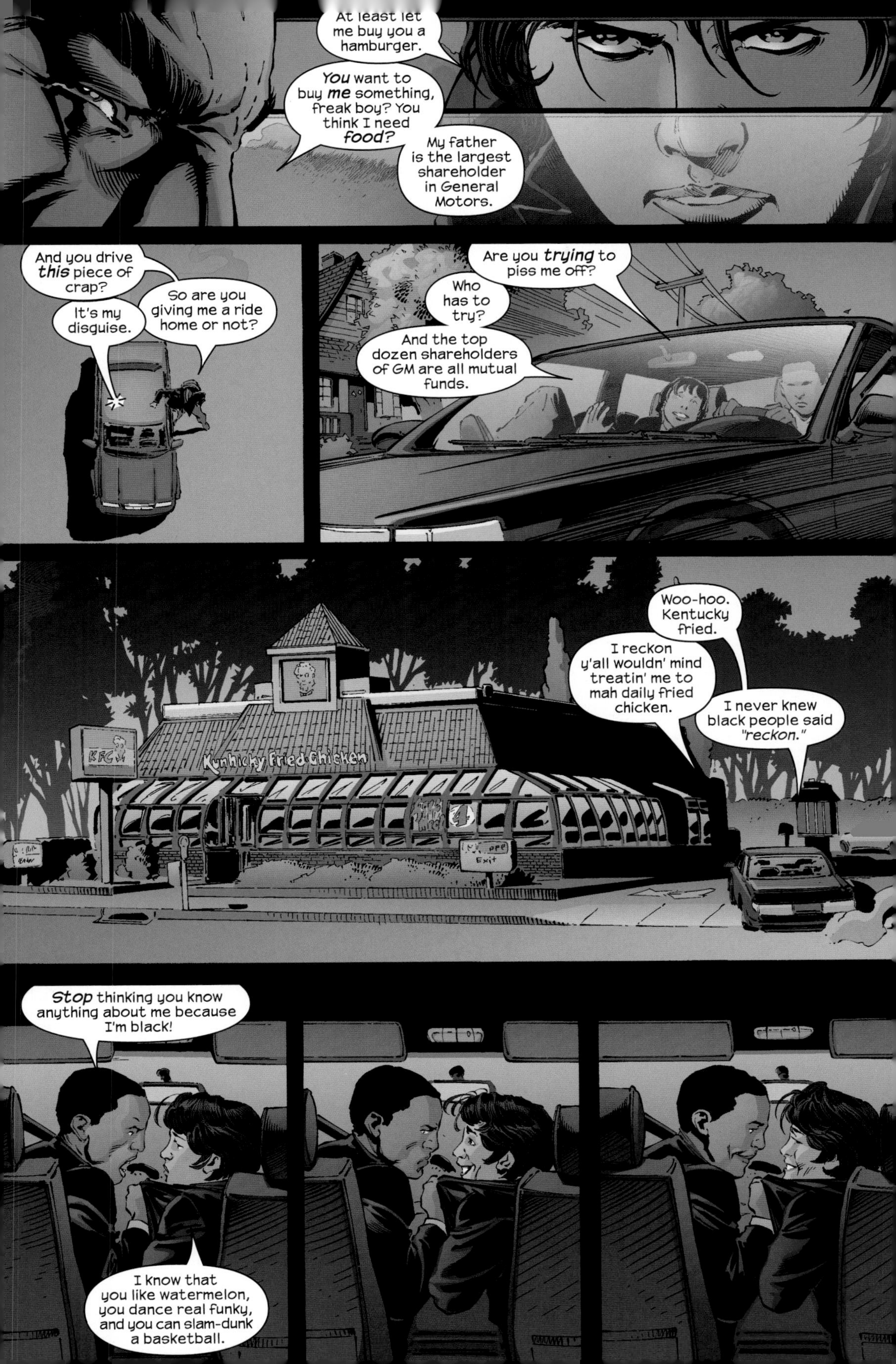
At least let me buy you a hamburger.
You want to buy me something, freak boy? You think I need food?
My father is the largest shareholder in General Motors.
And you drive this piece of crap?
It's my disguise.
So are you giving me a ride home or not?
Are you trying to piss me off?
Who has to try?
And the top dozen shareholders of GM are all mutual funds.
KFC
Kuntucky Fried Chicken
Exit
Woo-hoo. Kentucky fried.
I reckon y'all wouldn' mind treatin' me to mah daily fried chicken.
I never knew black people said "reckon."
Stop thinking you know anything about me because I'm black!
I know that you like watermelon, you dance real funky, and you can slam-dunk a basketball.

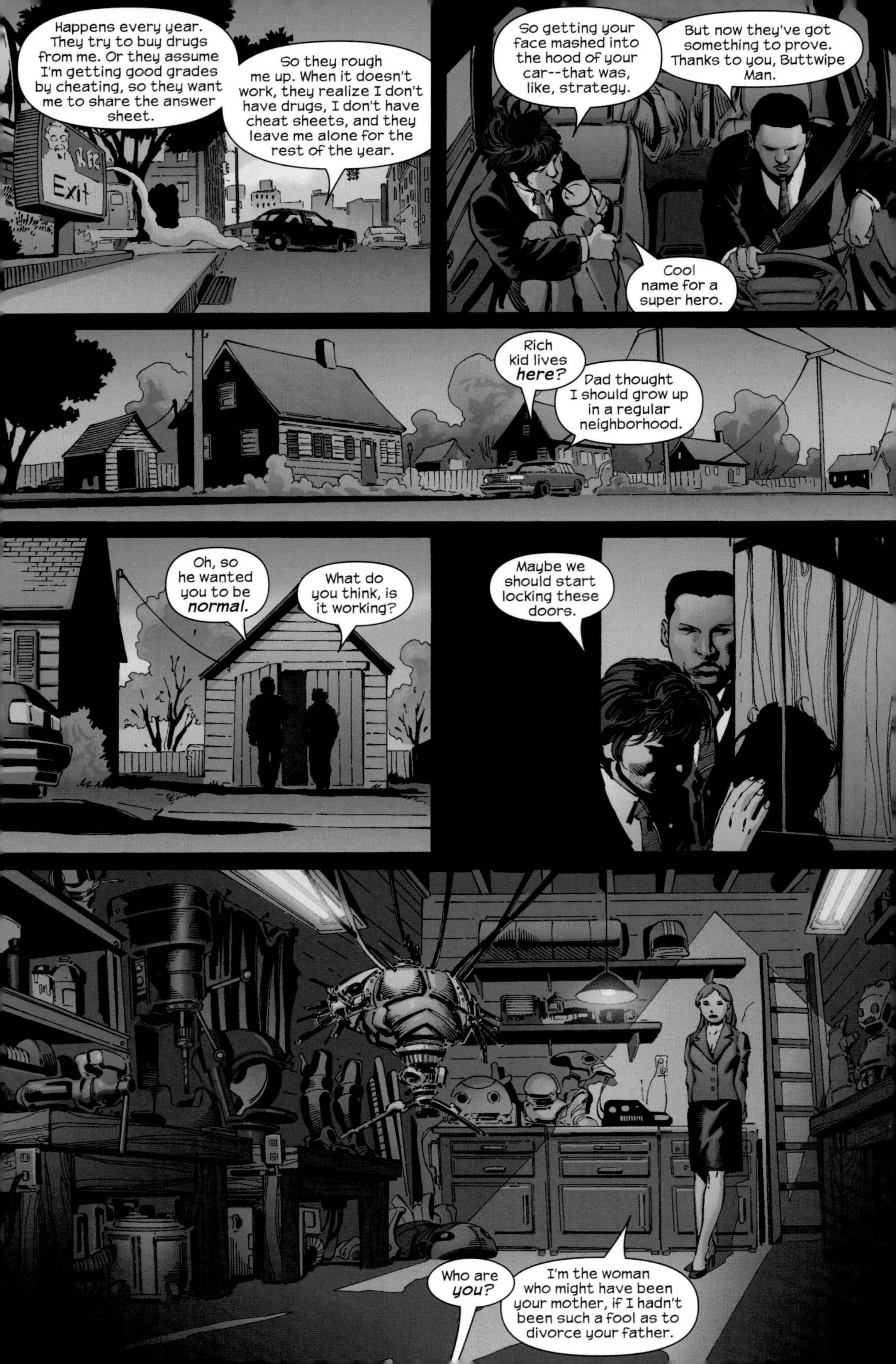
Happens every year. They try to buy drugs from me. Or they assume I'm getting good grades by cheating, so they want me to share the answer sheet.
So they rough me up. When it doesn't work, they realize I don't have drugs, I don't have cheat sheets, and they leave me alone for the rest of the year.
KFC
Exit
So getting your face mashed into the hood of your car--that was, like, strategy.
But now they've got something to prove. Thanks to you, Buttwipe Man.
Cool name for a super hero.
Rich kid lives *here?*
Dad thought I should grow up in a regular neighborhood.
Oh, so he wanted you to be *normal.*
What do you think, is it working?
Maybe we should start locking these doors.
Who are *you?*
I'm the woman who might have been your mother, if I hadn't been such a fool as to divorce your father.

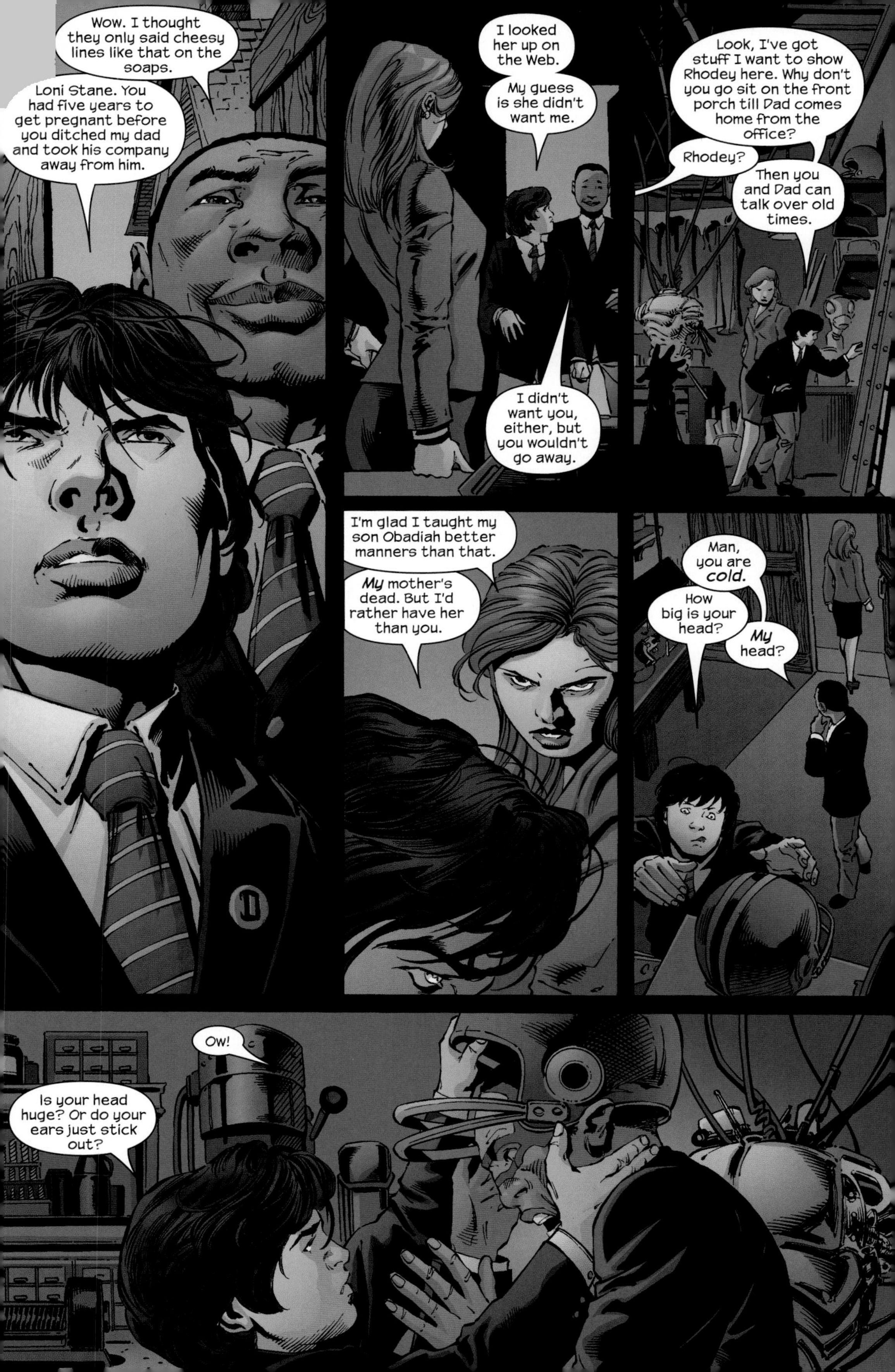
Wow. I thought they only said cheesy lines like that on the soaps.
Loni Stane. You had five years to get pregnant before you ditched my dad and took his company away from him.
I looked her up on the Web.
My guess is she didn't want me.
I didn't want you, either, but you wouldn't go away.
Look, I've got stuff I want to show Rhodey here. Why don't you go sit on the front porch till Dad comes home from the office?
Rhodey?
Then you and Dad can talk over old times.
I'm glad I taught my son Obadiah better manners than that.
My mother's dead. But I'd rather have her than you.
Man, you are *cold.*
How big is your head?
My head?
Ow!
Is your head huge? Or do your ears just stick out?

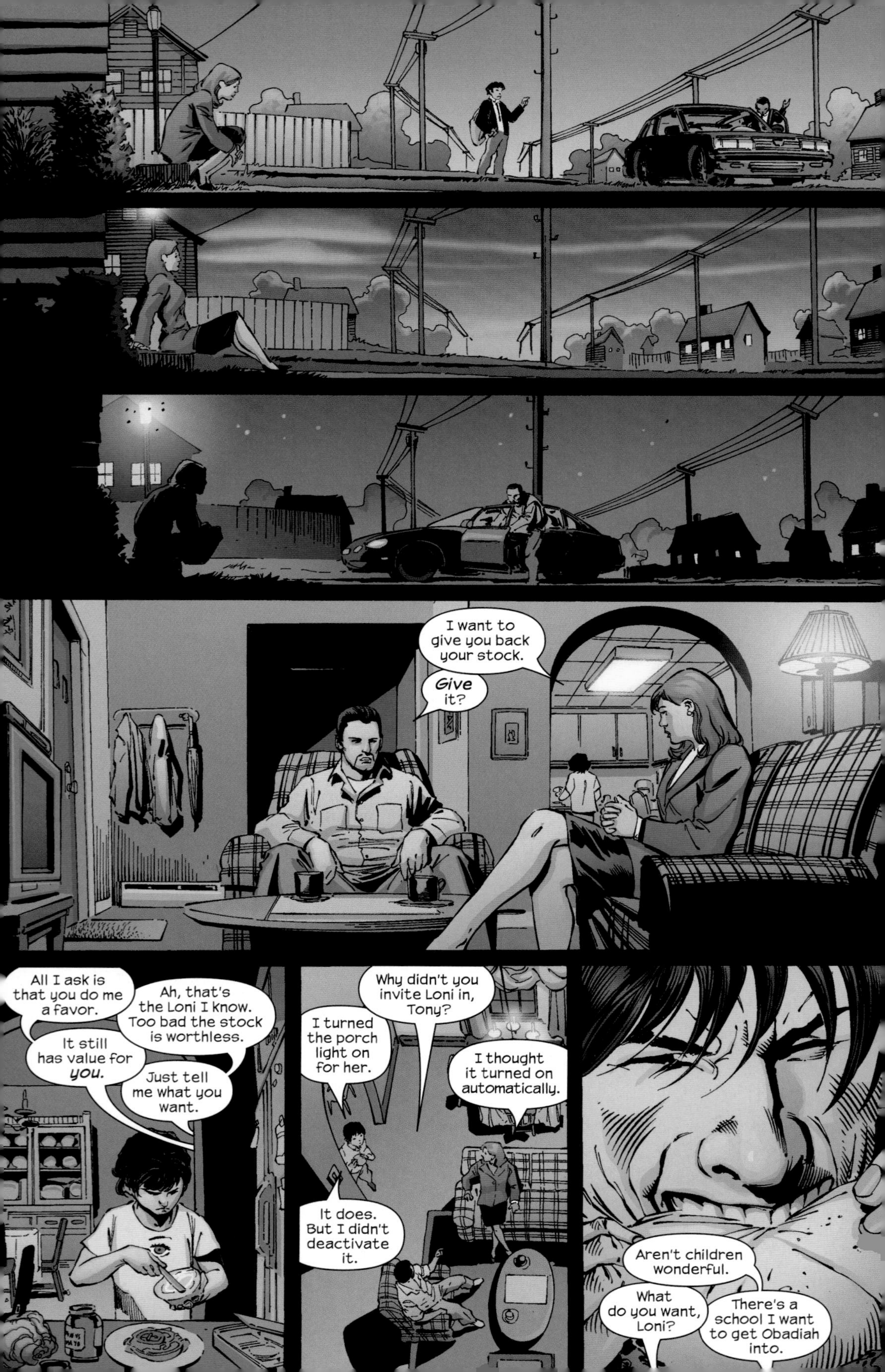

I want to give you back your stock.
Give it?
All I ask is that you do me a favor.
Ah, that's the Loni I know. Too bad the stock is worthless.
It still has value for you.
Just tell me what you want.
Why didn't you invite Loni in, Tony?
I turned the porch light on for her.
I thought it turned on automatically.
It does. But I didn't deactivate it.
Aren't children wonderful.
What do you want, Loni?
There's a school I want to get Obadiah into.

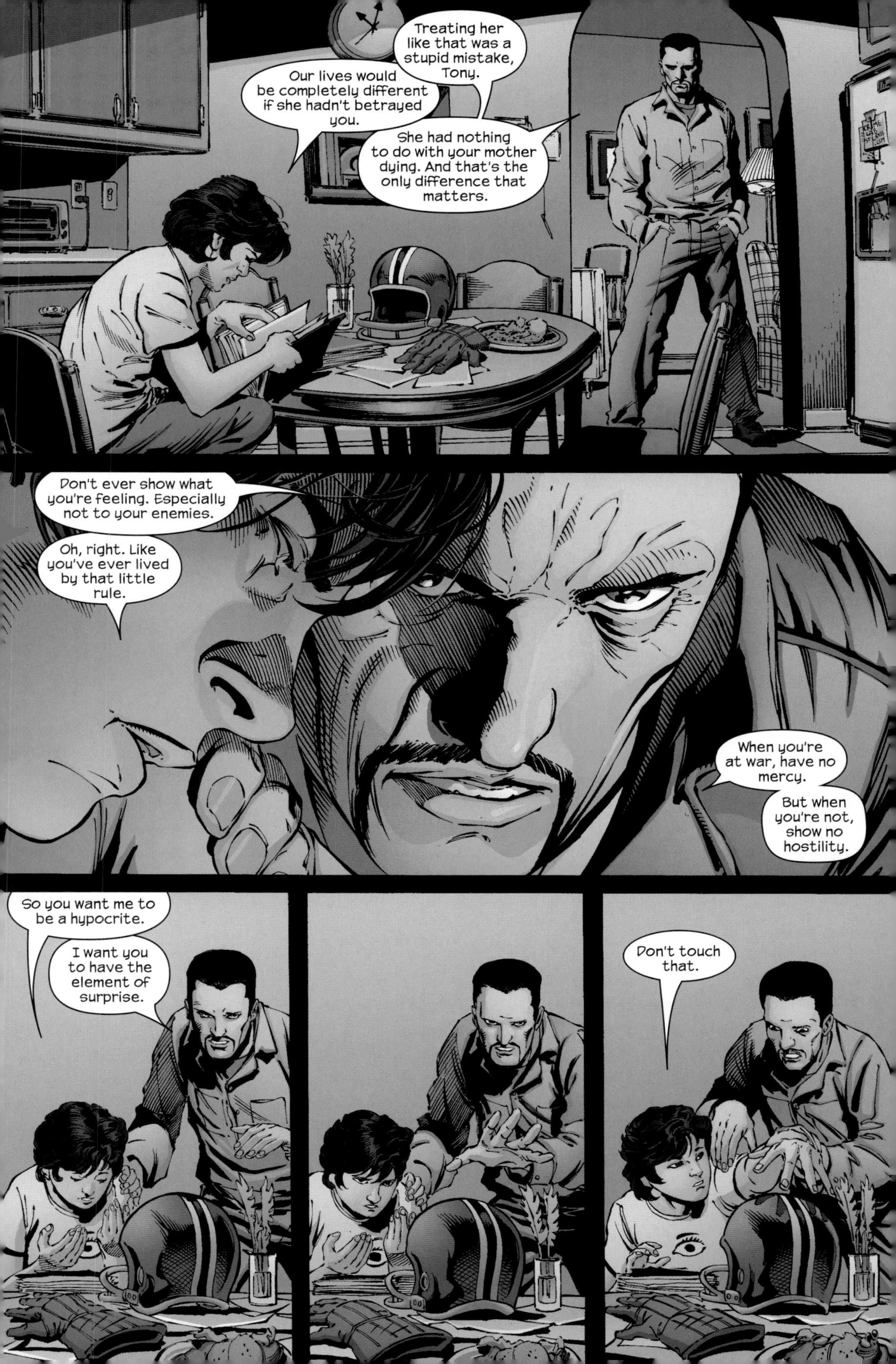
Treating her like that was a stupid mistake, Tony.
Our lives would be completely different if she hadn't betrayed you.
She had nothing to do with your mother dying. And that's the only difference that matters.
Don't ever show what you're feeling. Especially not to your enemies.
Oh, right. Like you've ever lived by that little rule.
When you're at war, have no mercy.
But when you're not, show no hostility.
So you want me to be a hypocrite.
I want you to have the element of surprise.
Don't touch that.

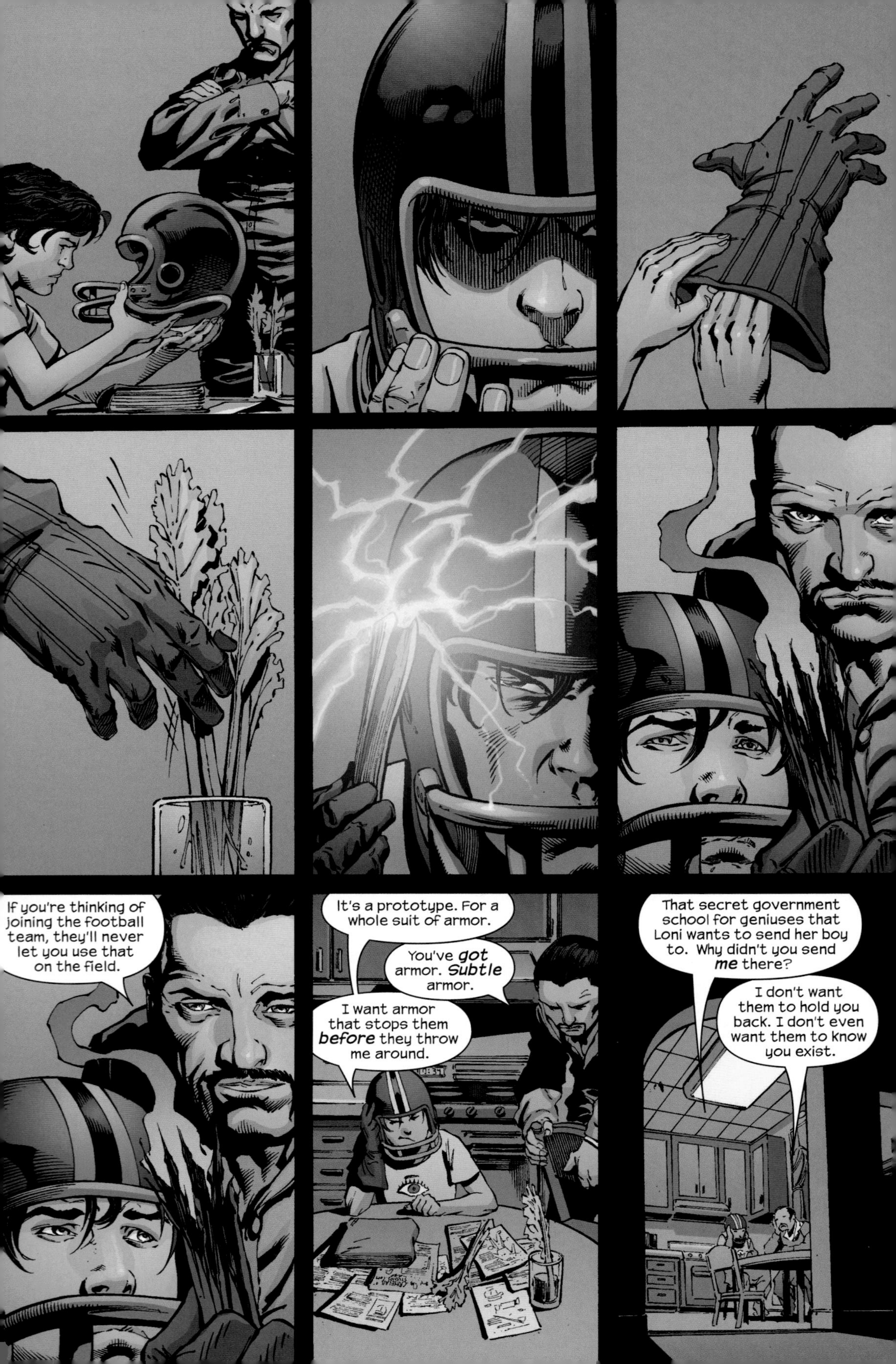
If you're thinking of joining the football team, they'll never let you use that on the field.
It's a prototype. For a whole suit of armor.
You've got armor. Subtle armor.
I want armor that stops them before they throw me around.
That secret government school for geniuses that Loni wants to send her boy to. Why didn't you send me there?
I don't want them to hold you back. I don't even want them to know you exist.

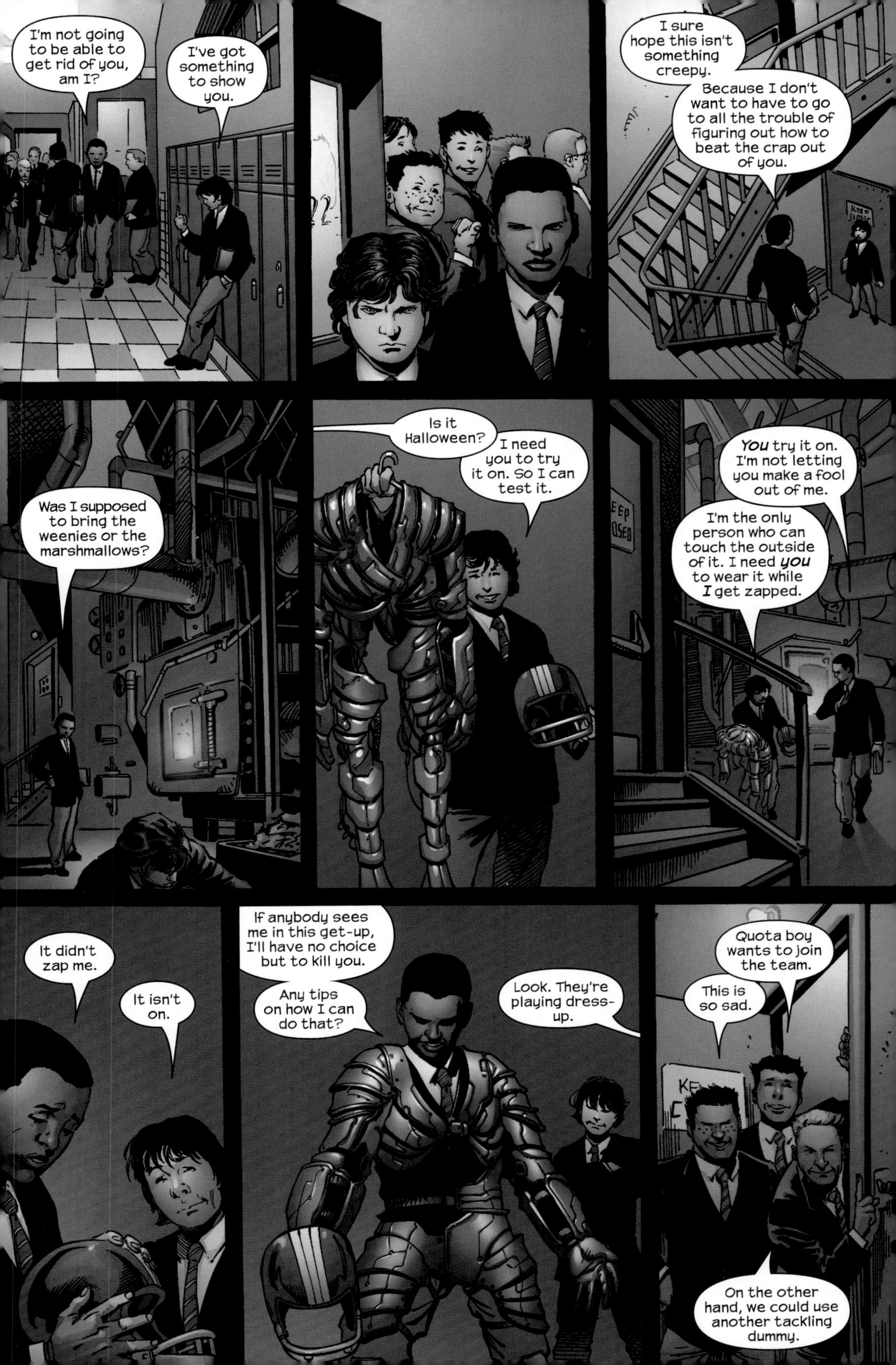

I'm not going to be able to get rid of you, am I?
I've got something to show you.
I sure hope this isn't something creepy.
Because I don't want to have to go to all the trouble of figuring out how to beat the crap out of you.
KEEP CLOSED
Was I supposed to bring the weenies or the marshmallows?
Is it Halloween?
I need you to try it on. So I can test it.
KEEP CLOSED
YOU try it on. I'm not letting you make a fool out of me.
I'm the only person who can touch the outside of it. I need *YOU* to wear it while *I* get zapped.
It didn't zap me.
It isn't on.
If anybody sees me in this get-up, I'll have no choice but to kill you.
Any tips on how I can do that?
Look. They're playing dress-up.
Quota boy wants to join the team.
This is so sad.
On the other hand, we could use another tackling dummy.

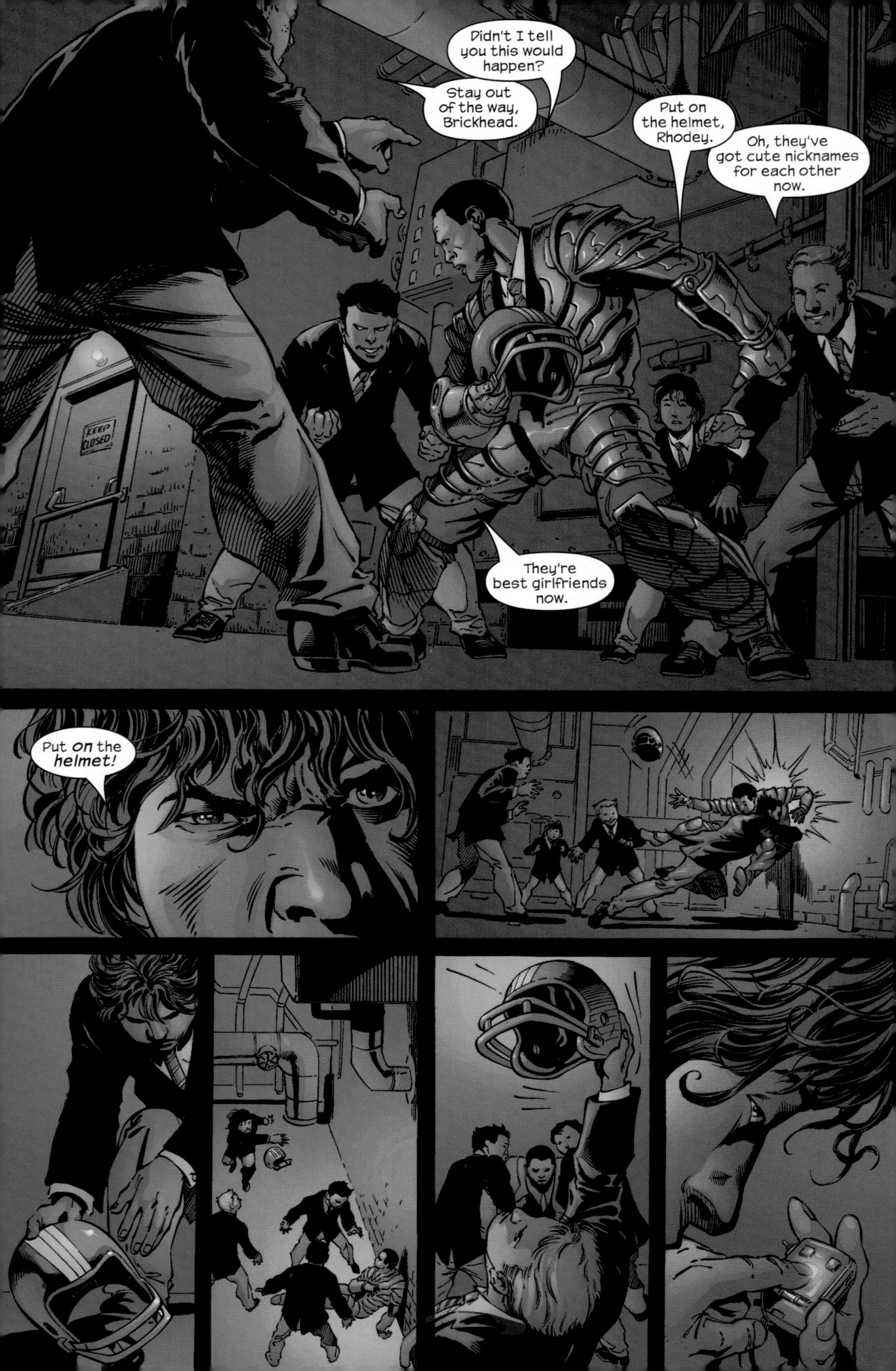
Stay out of the way, Brickhead.
Didn't I tell you this would happen?
Put on the helmet, Rhodey.
Oh, they've got cute nicknames for each other now.
They're best girlfriends now.
KEEP CLOSED
Put **on** the ***helmet!***

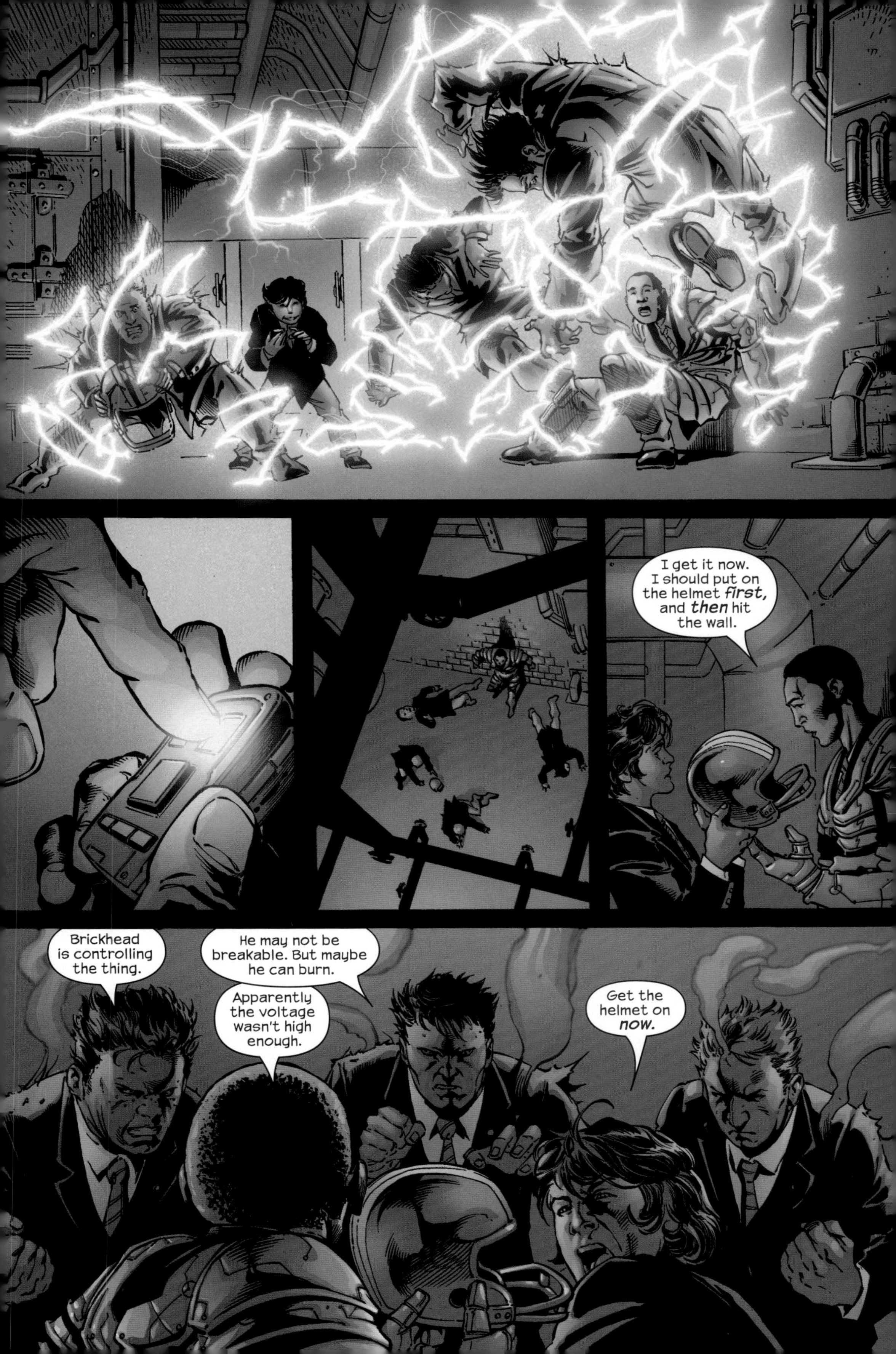

I get it now. I should put on the helmet *first,* and *then* hit the wall.
Brickhead is controlling the thing.
He may not be breakable. But maybe he can burn.
Apparently the voltage wasn't high enough.
Get the helmet on *now.*

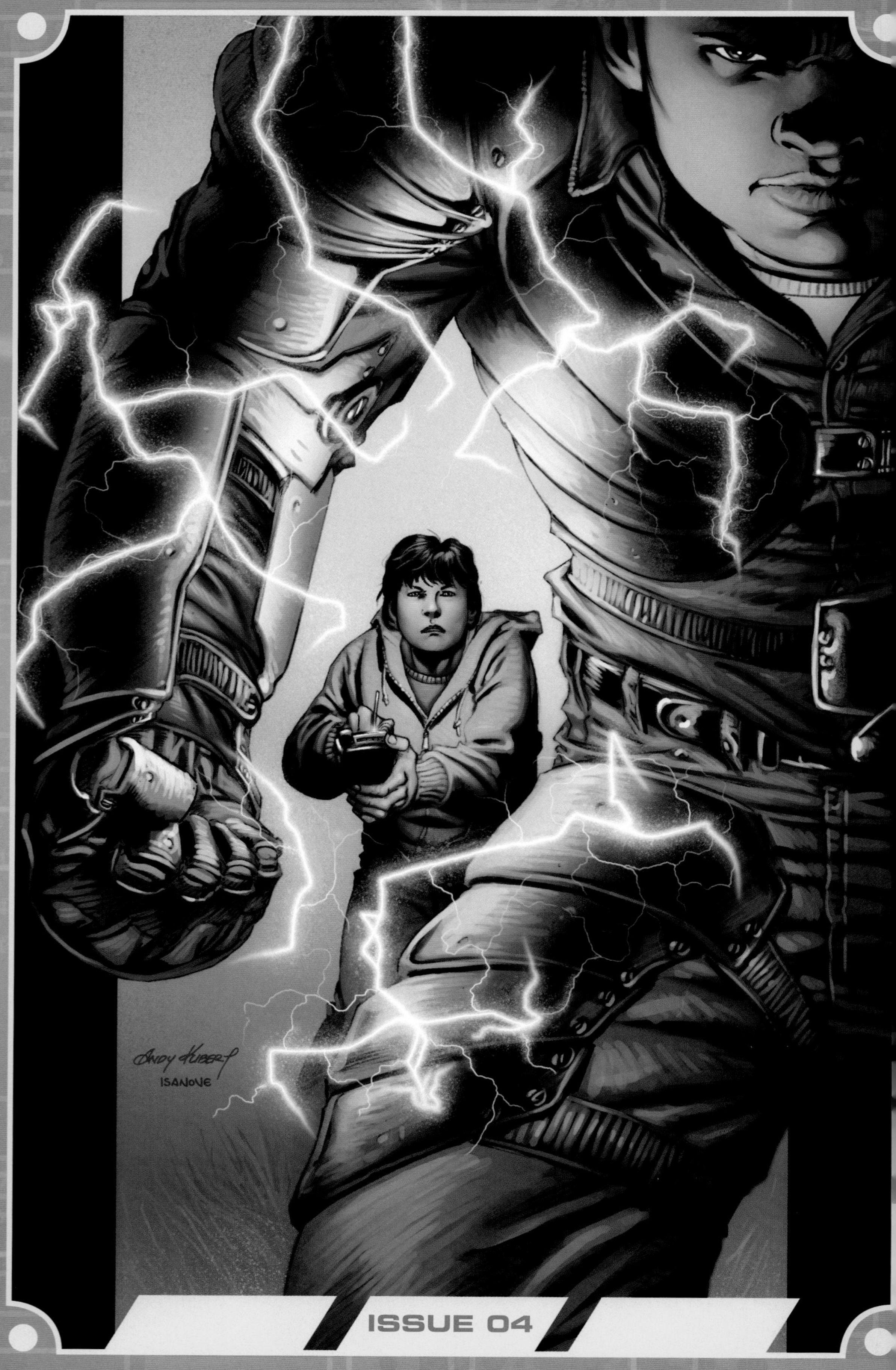
ANDY KUBERT
ISANOVE
ISSUE 04

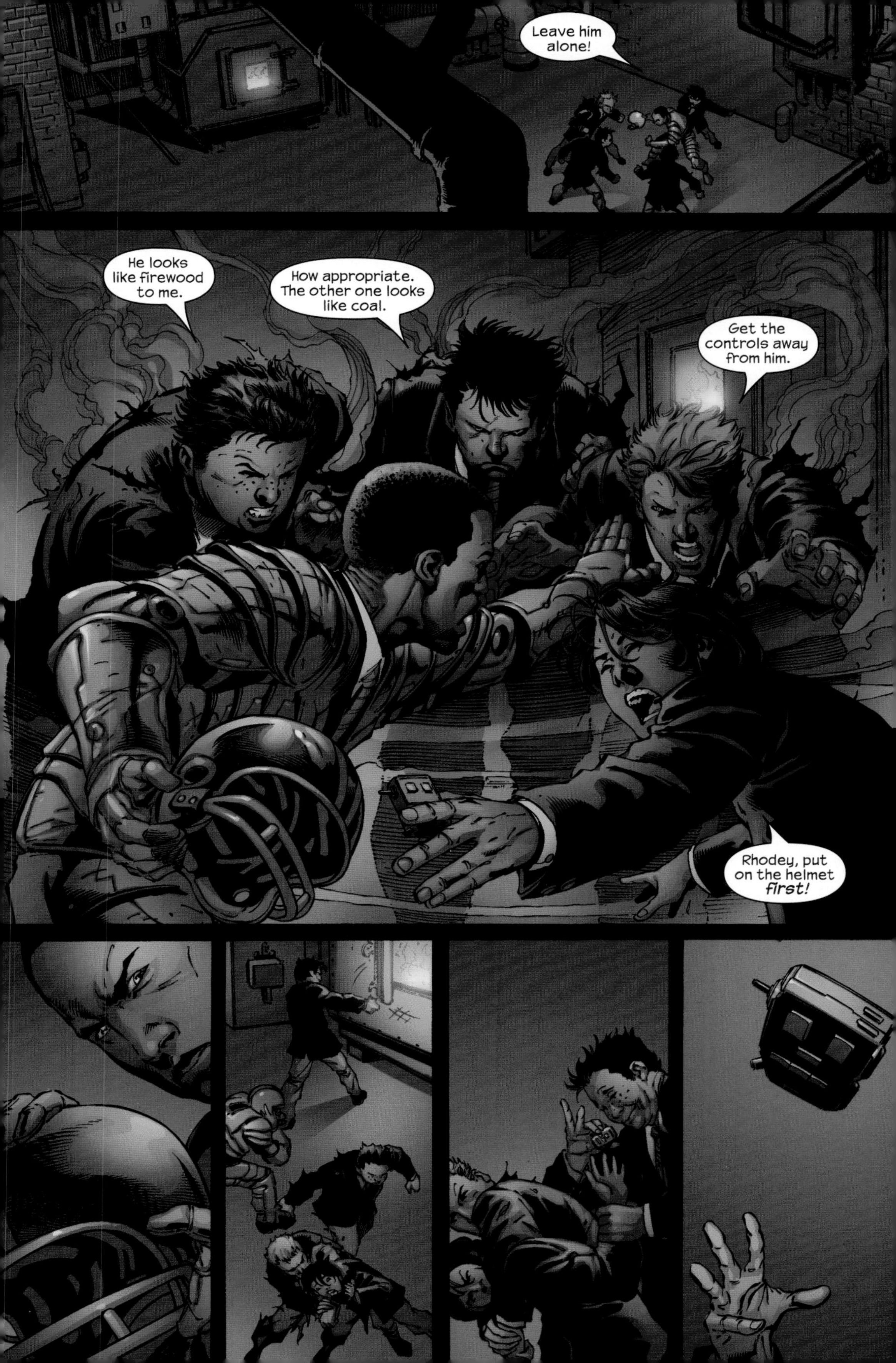
Leave him alone!
He looks like firewood to me.
How appropriate. The other one looks like coal.
Get the controls away from him.
Rhodey, put on the helmet *first!*

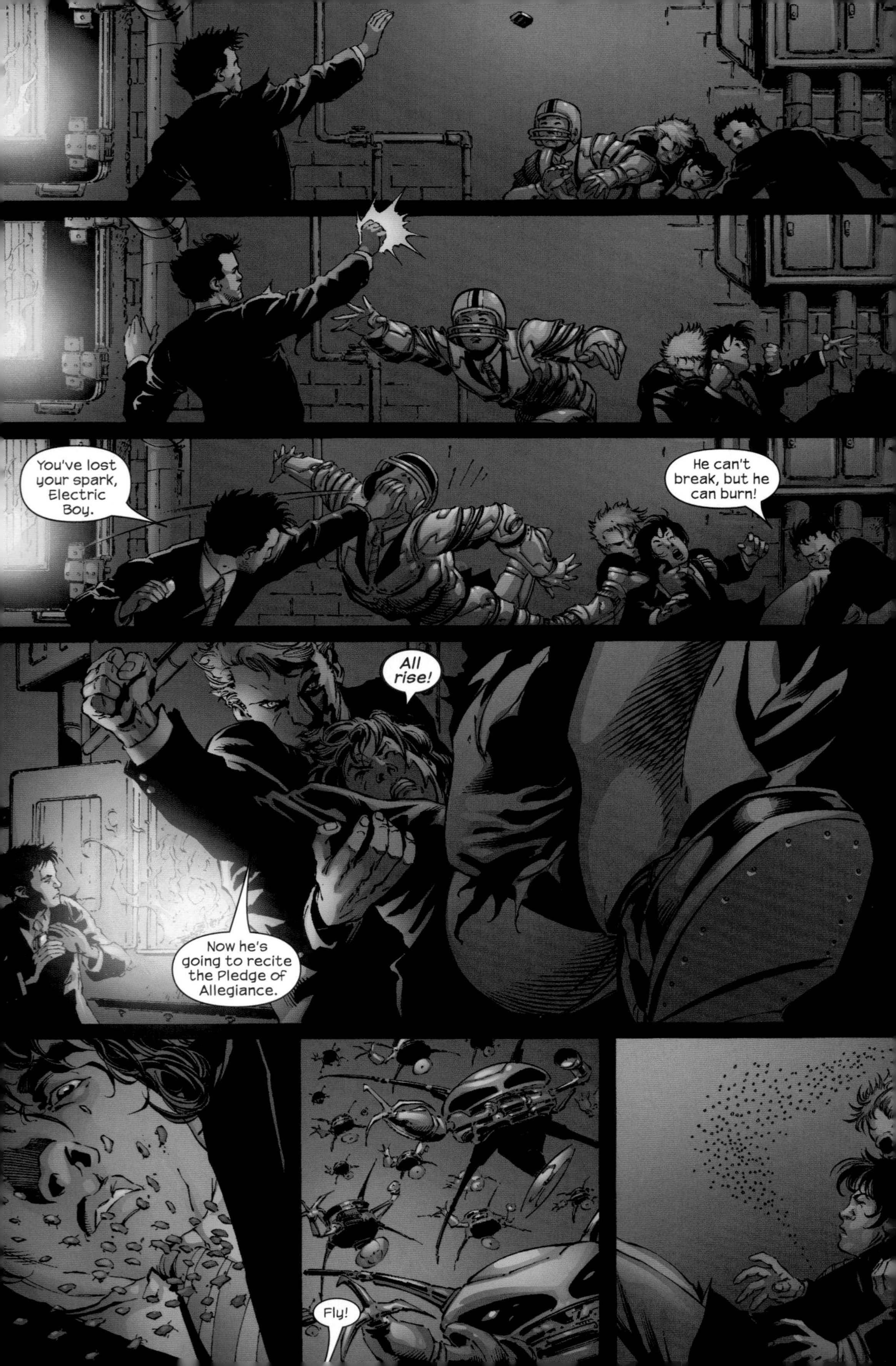
You've lost your spark, Electric Boy.
He can't break, but he can burn!
All rise!
Now he's going to recite the Pledge of Allegiance.
Fly!

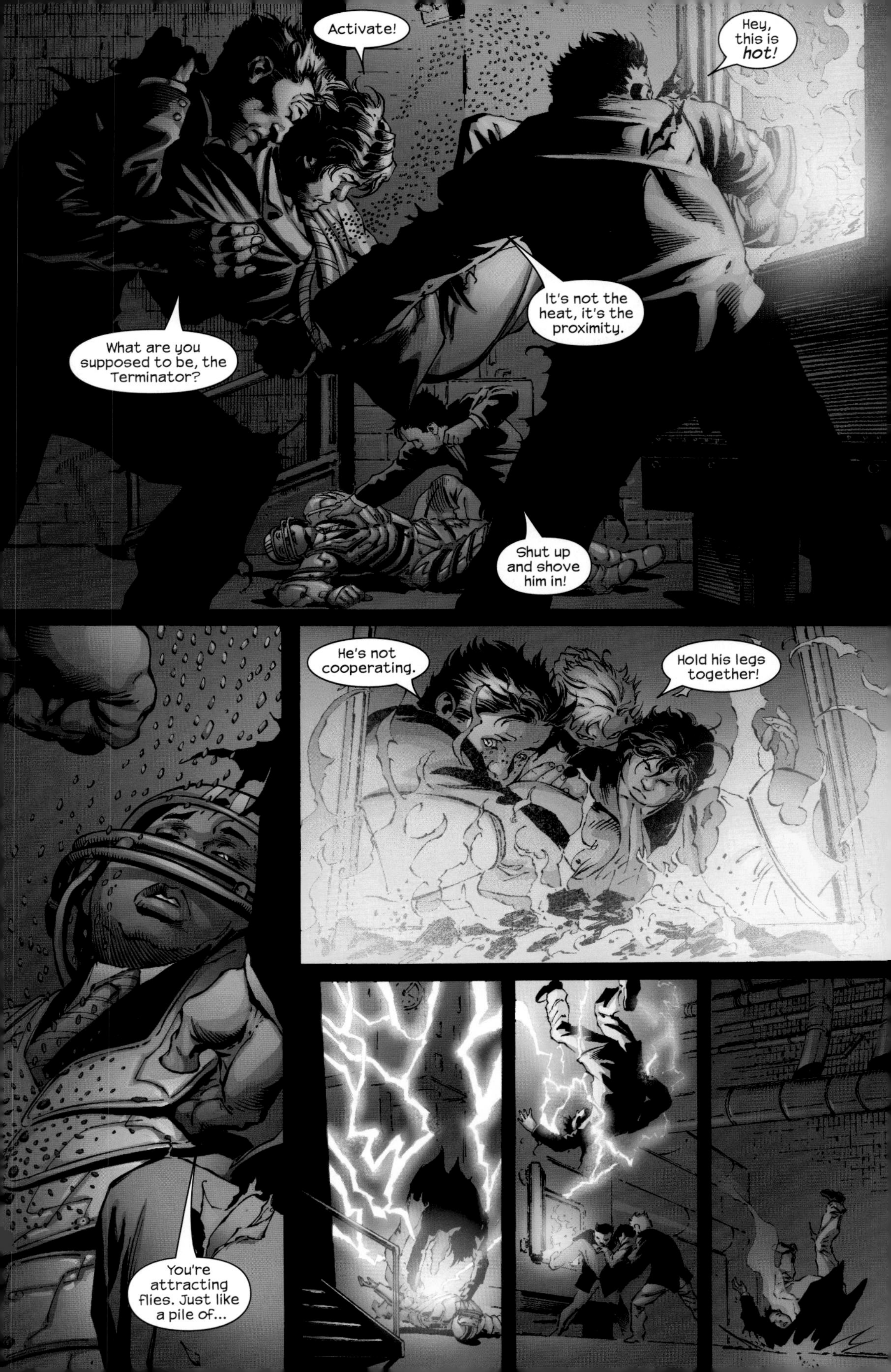
Activate!
Hey, this is *hot!*
What are you supposed to be, the Terminator?
It's not the heat, it's the proximity.
Shut up and shove him in!
He's not cooperating.
Hold his legs together!
You're attracting flies. Just like a pile of...

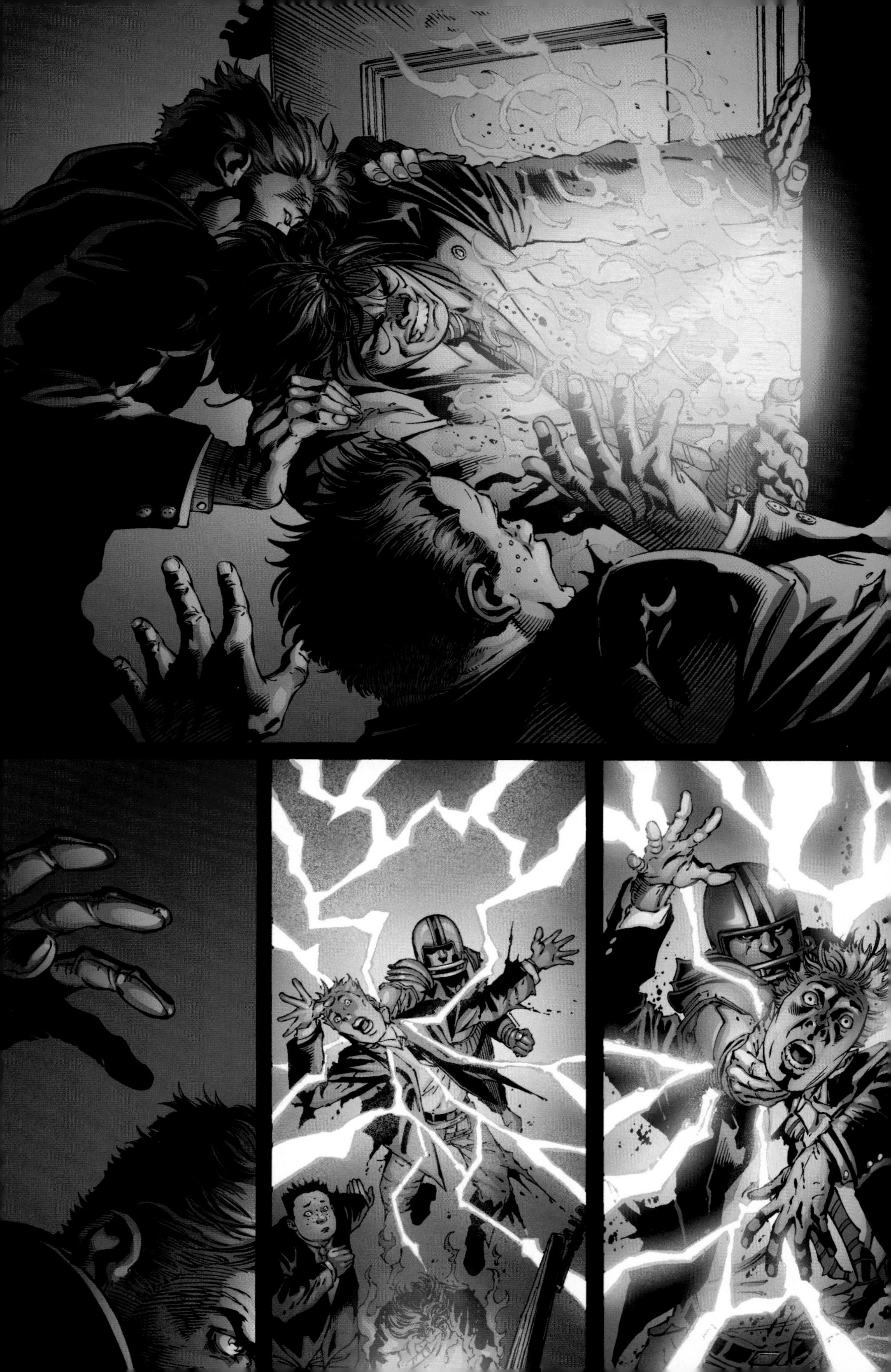

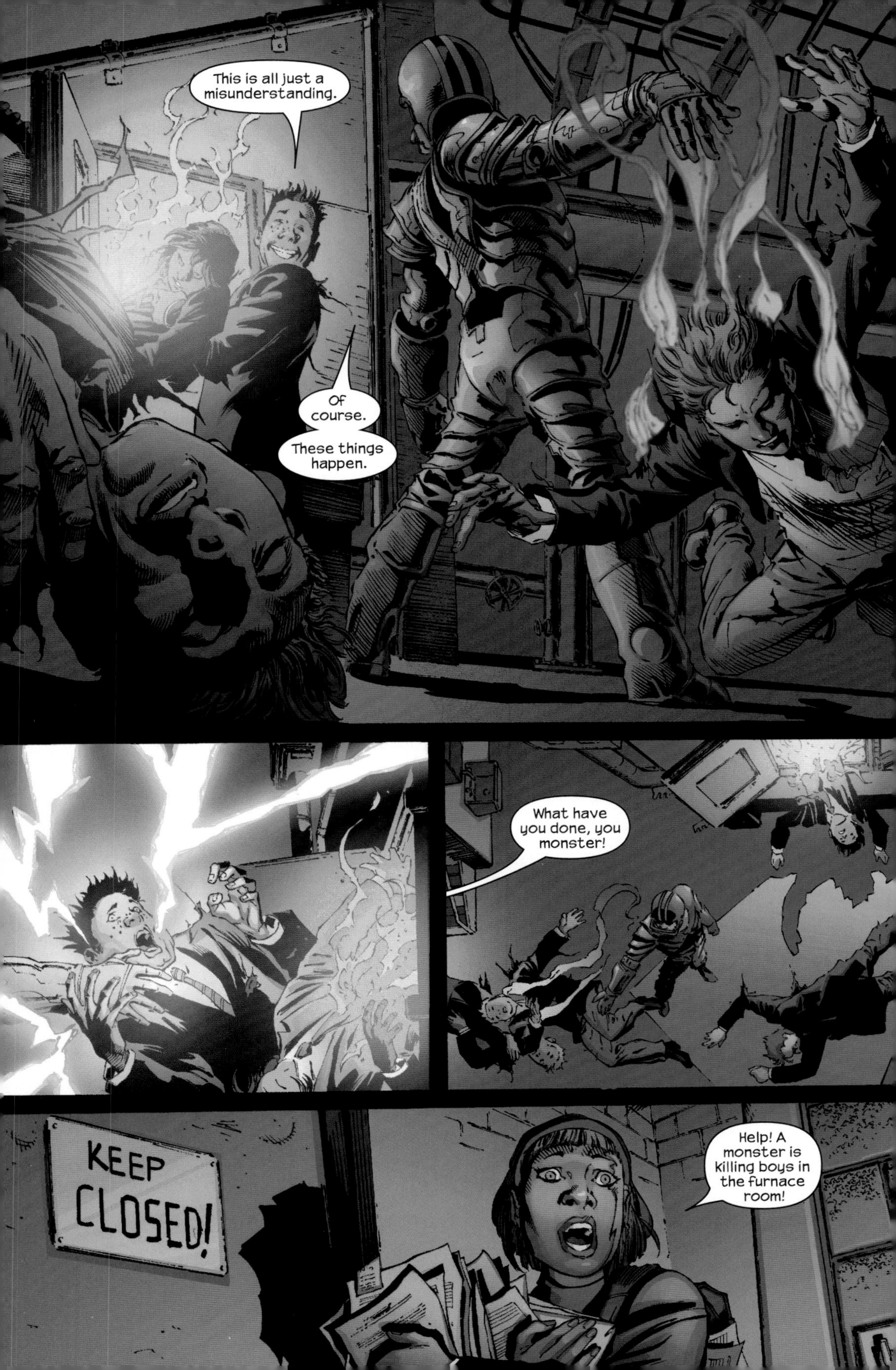
This is all just a misunderstanding.
Of course.
These things happen.
What have you done, you monster!
KEEP CLOSED!
Help! A monster is killing boys in the furnace room!

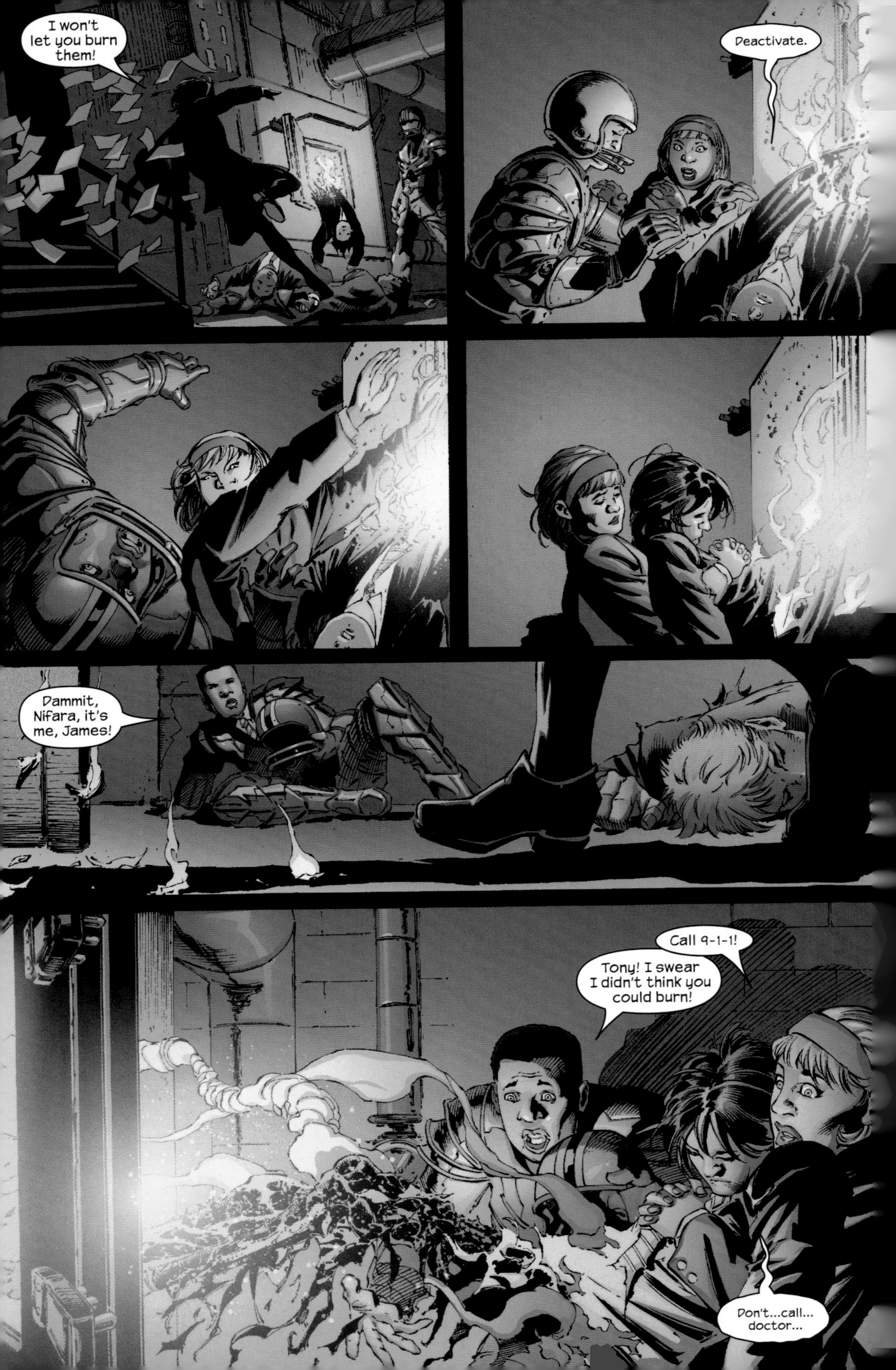
I won't let you burn them!
Deactivate.
Dammit, Nifara, it's me, James!
Call 9-1-1!
Tony! I swear I didn't think you could burn!
Don't...call... doctor...

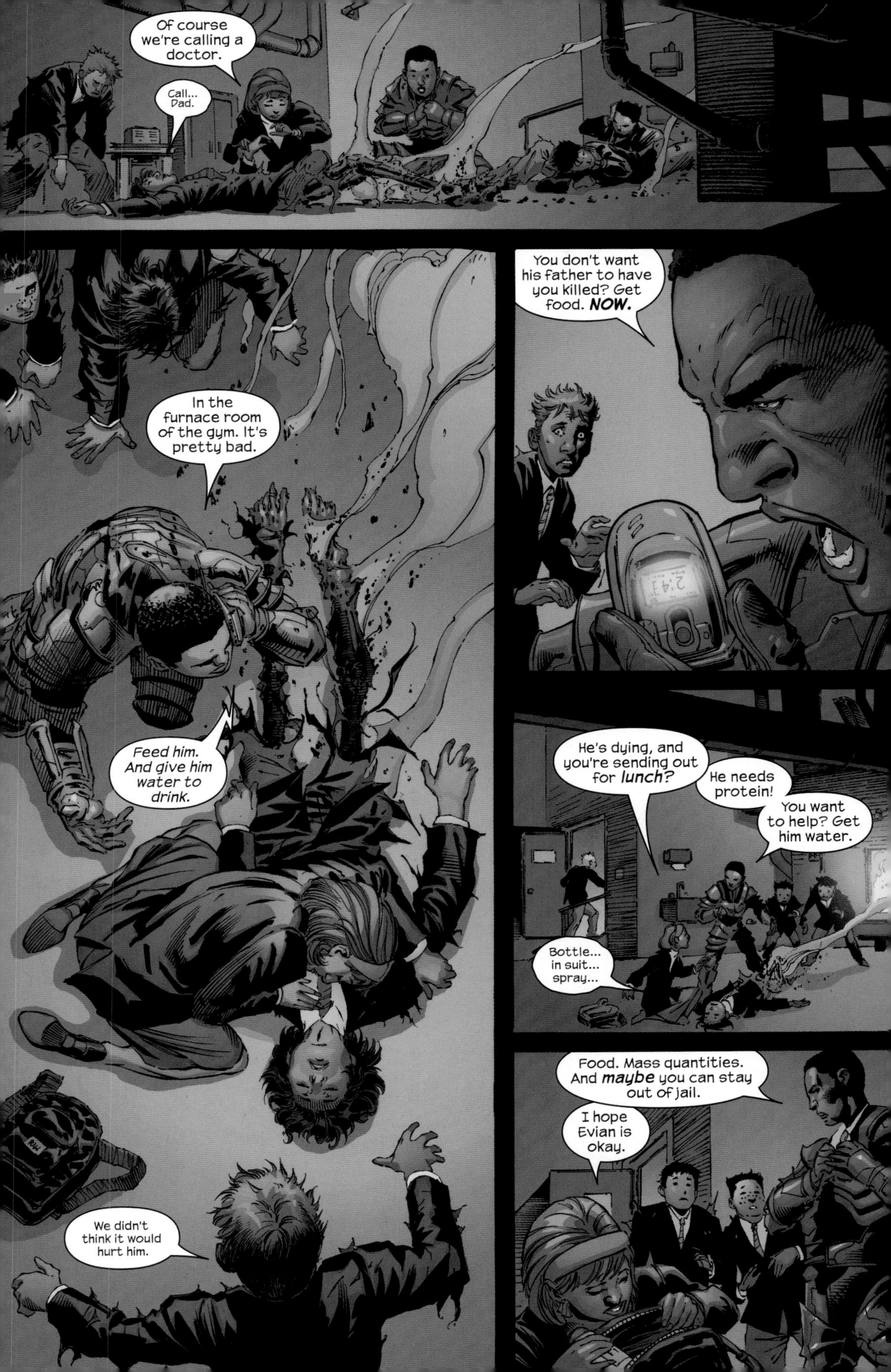

Of course we're calling a doctor.
Call... Dad.
In the furnace room of the gym. It's pretty bad.
Feed him. And give him water to drink.
We didn't think it would hurt him.
You don't want his father to have you killed? Get food. NOW.
He's dying, and you're sending out for lunch?
He needs protein!
You want to help? Get him water.
Bottle... in suit... spray...
Food. Mass quantities. And maybe you can stay out of jail.
I hope Evian is okay.

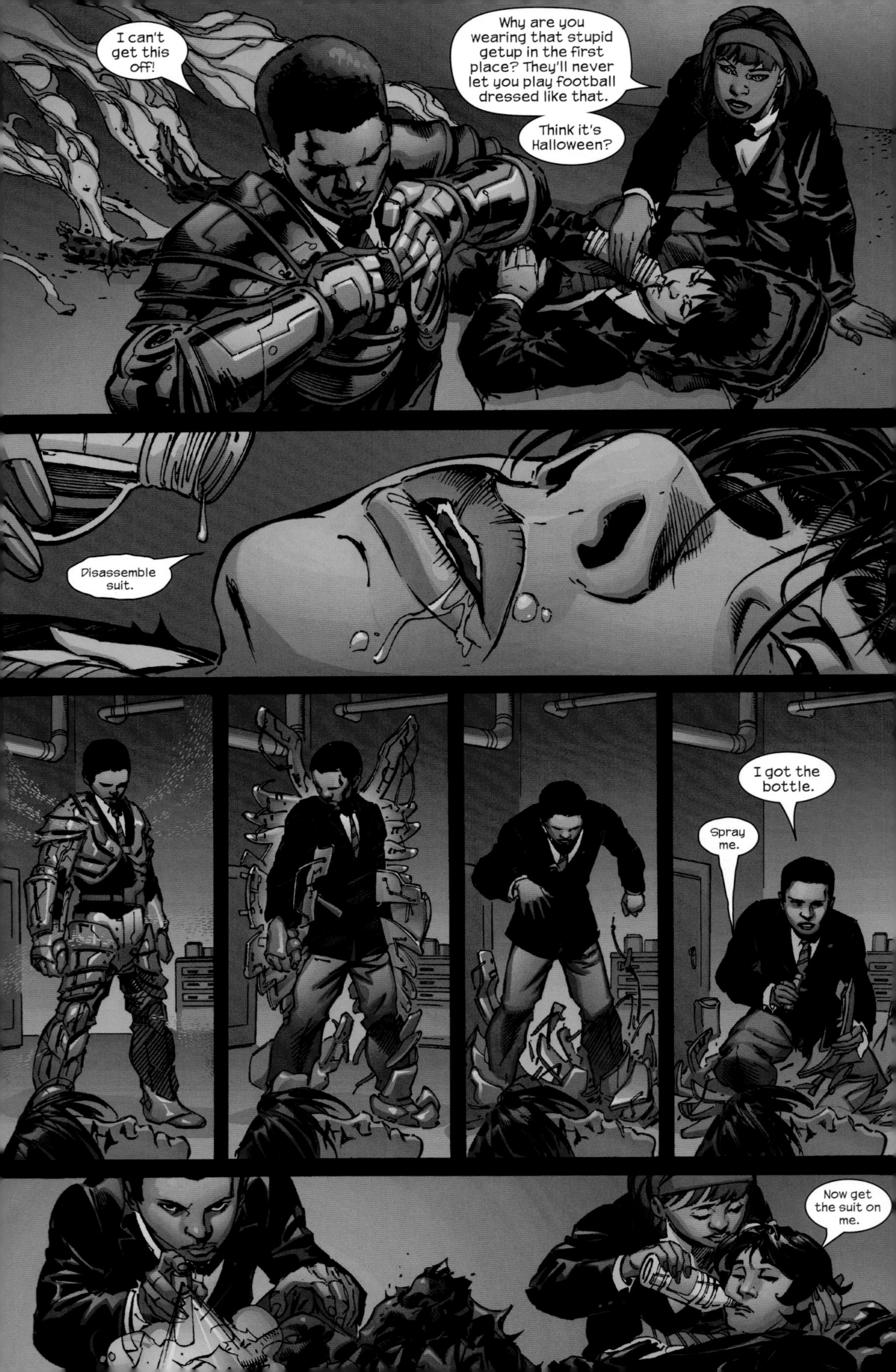
I can't get this off!
Why are you wearing that stupid getup in the first place? They'll never let you play football dressed like that.
Think it's Halloween?
Disassemble suit.
I got the bottle.
Spray me.
Now get the suit on me.

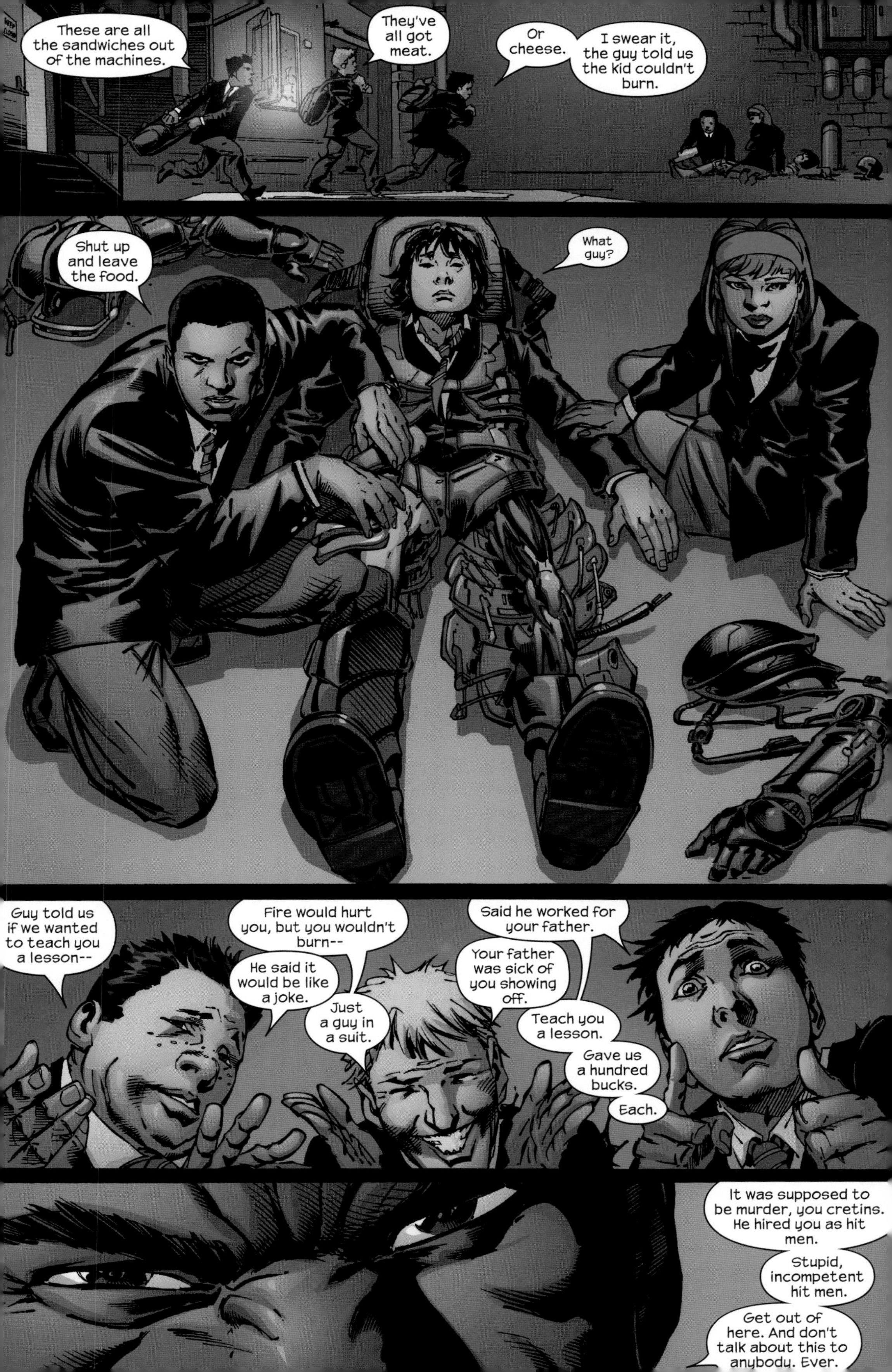

These are all the sandwiches out of the machines.
They've all got meat.
Or cheese.
I swear it, the guy told us the kid couldn't burn.
Shut up and leave the food.
What guy?
Guy told us if we wanted to teach you a lesson--
Fire would hurt you, but you wouldn't burn--
He said it would be like a joke.
Just a guy in a suit.
Said he worked for your father.
Your father was sick of you showing off.
Teach you a lesson.
Gave us a hundred bucks.
Each.
It was supposed to be murder, you cretins. He hired you as hit men.
Stupid, incompetent hit men.
Get out of here. And don't talk about this to anybody. Ever.

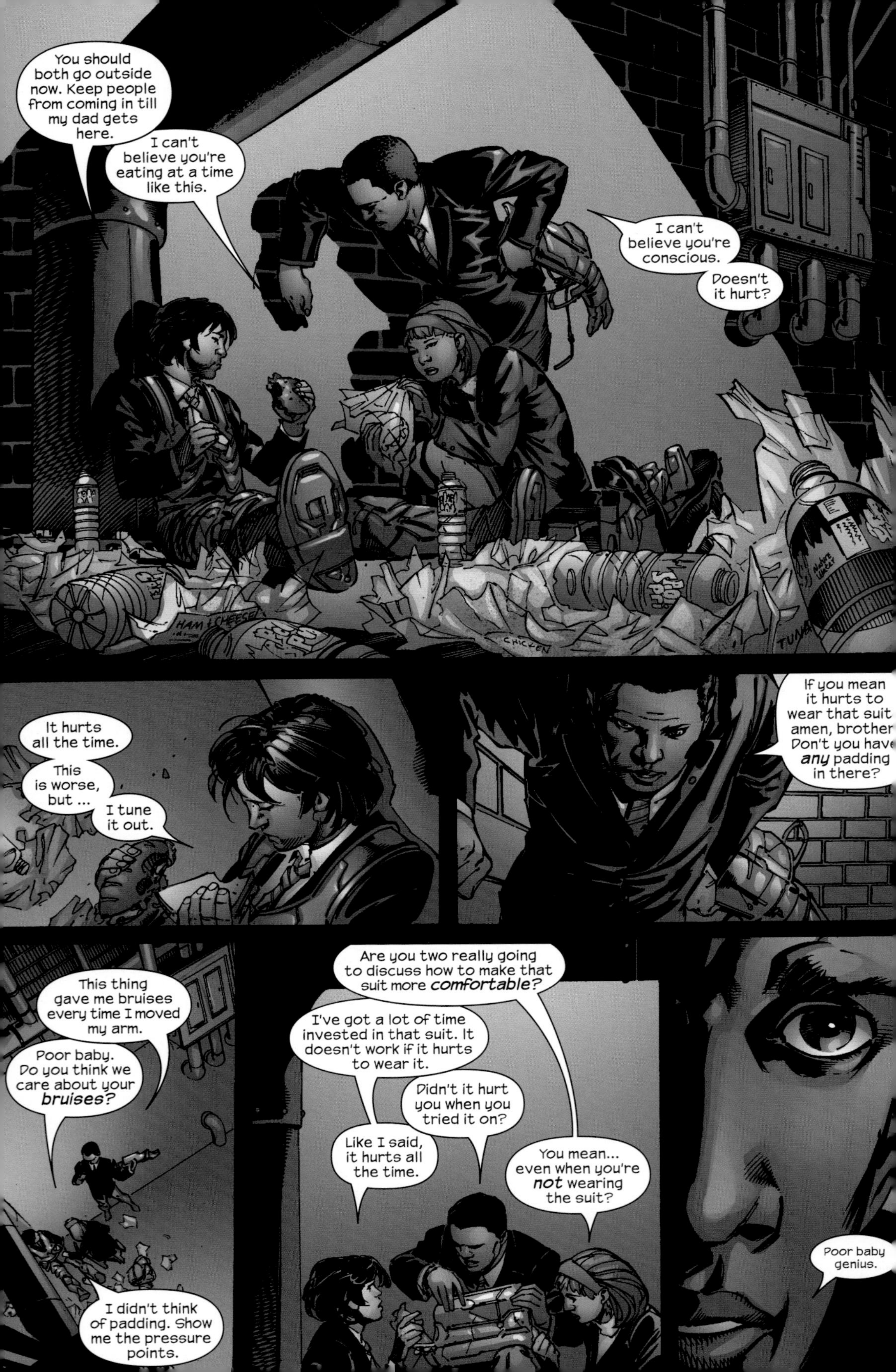

You should both go outside now. Keep people from coming in till my dad gets here.
I can't believe you're eating at a time like this.
I can't believe you're conscious.
Doesn't it hurt?
HAM + CHEESE
CHICKEN
TUNA
It hurts all the time.
This is worse, but ...
I tune it out.
If you mean it hurts to wear that suit amen, brother Don't you have *any* padding in there?
This thing gave me bruises every time I moved my arm.
Poor baby. Do you think we care about your *bruises?*
I didn't think of padding. Show me the pressure points.
Are you two really going to discuss how to make that suit more *comfortable?*
I've got a lot of time invested in that suit. It doesn't work if it hurts to wear it.
Didn't it hurt you when you tried it on?
Like I said, it hurts all the time.
You mean... even when you're *not* wearing the suit?
Poor baby genius.

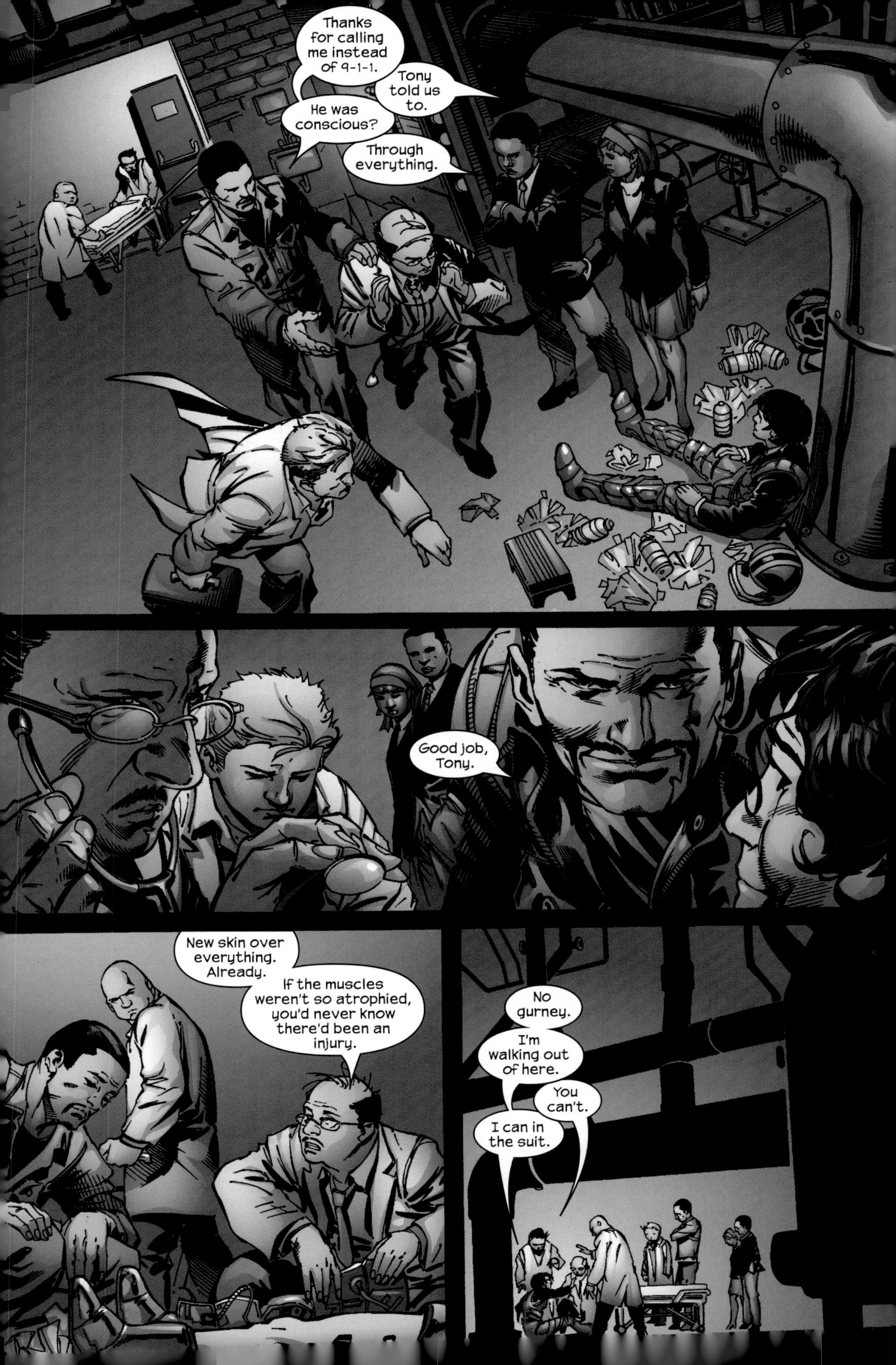
Thanks for calling me instead of 9-1-1.
Tony told us to.
He was conscious?
Through everything.
Good job, Tony.
New skin over everything. Already.
If the muscles weren't so atrophied, you'd never know there'd been an injury.
No gurney.
I'm walking out of here.
You can't.
I can in the suit.

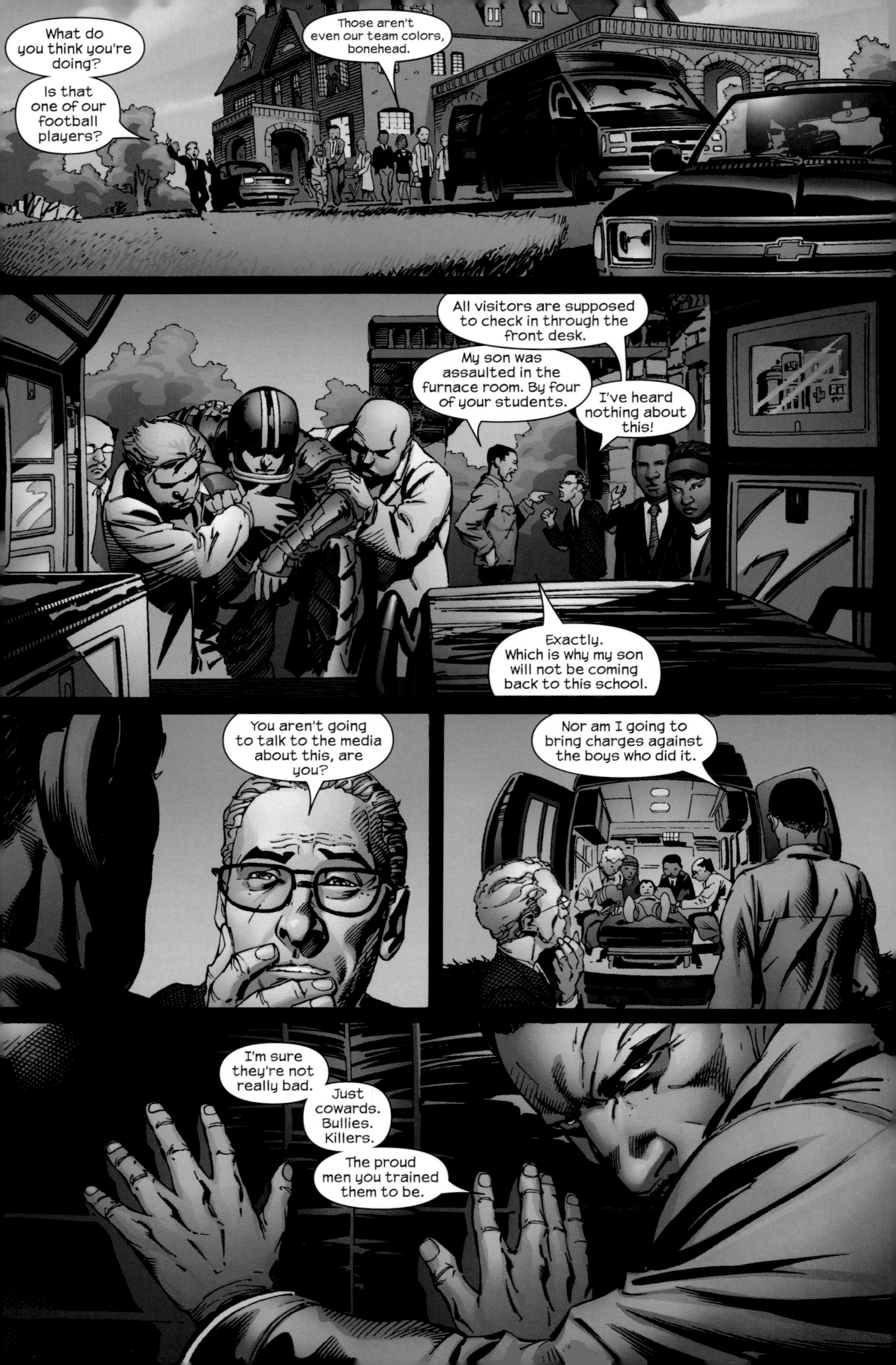
What do you think you're doing?
Is that one of our football players?
Those aren't even our team colors, bonehead.
All visitors are supposed to check in through the front desk.
My son was assaulted in the furnace room. By four of your students.
I've heard nothing about this!
Exactly. Which is why my son will not be coming back to this school.
You aren't going to talk to the media about this, are you?
Nor am I going to bring charges against the boys who did it.
I'm sure they're not really bad.
Just cowards. Bullies. Killers.
The proud men you trained them to be.

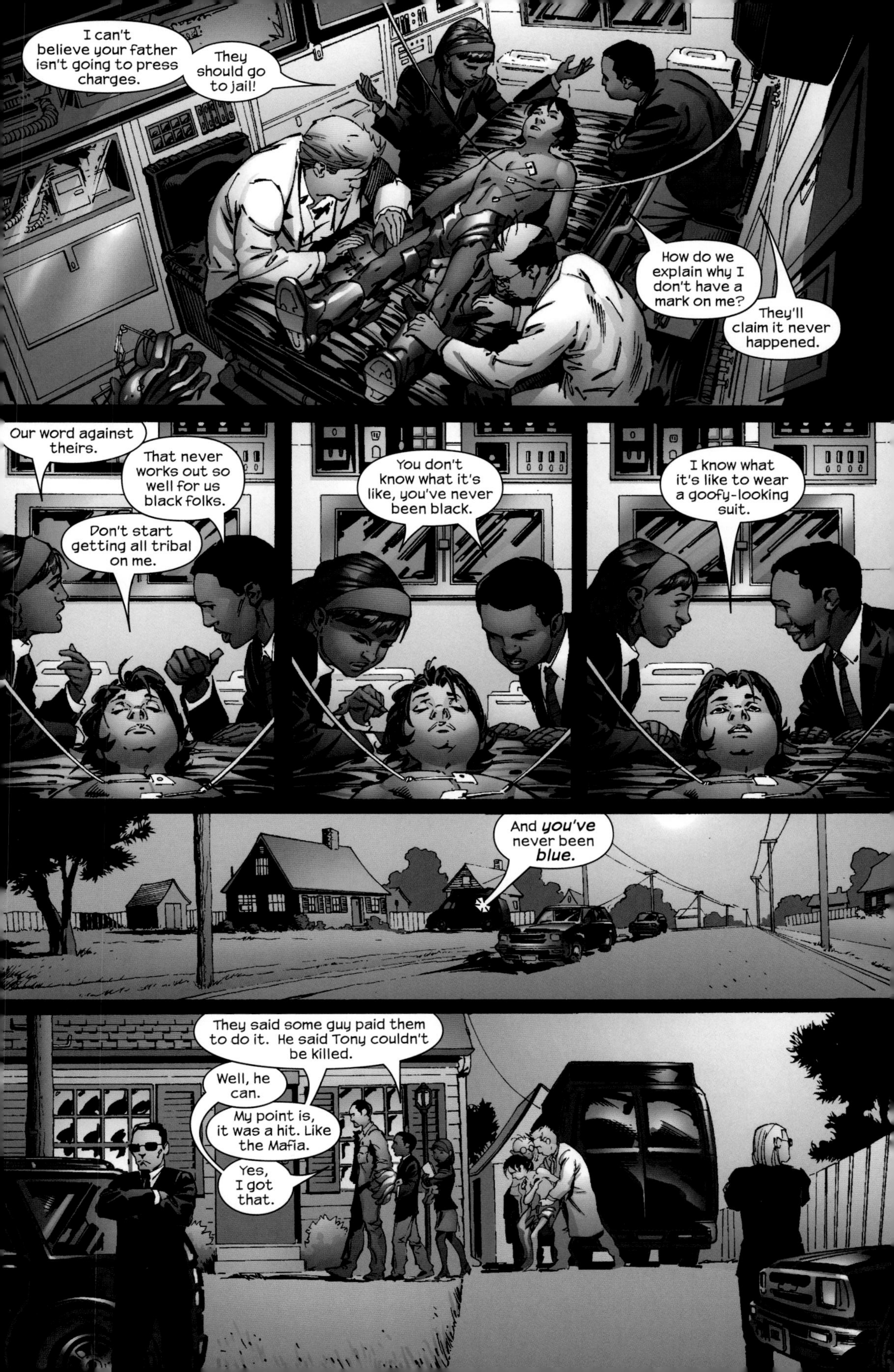
I can't believe your father isn't going to press charges.
They should go to jail!
How do we explain why I don't have a mark on me?
They'll claim it never happened.
Our word against theirs.
That never works out so well for us black folks.
Don't start getting all tribal on me.
You don't know what it's like, you've never been black.
I know what it's like to wear a goofy-looking suit.
And *you've* never been *blue.*
They said some guy paid them to do it. He said Tony couldn't be killed.
Well, he can.
My point is, it was a hit. Like the Mafia.
Yes, I got that.

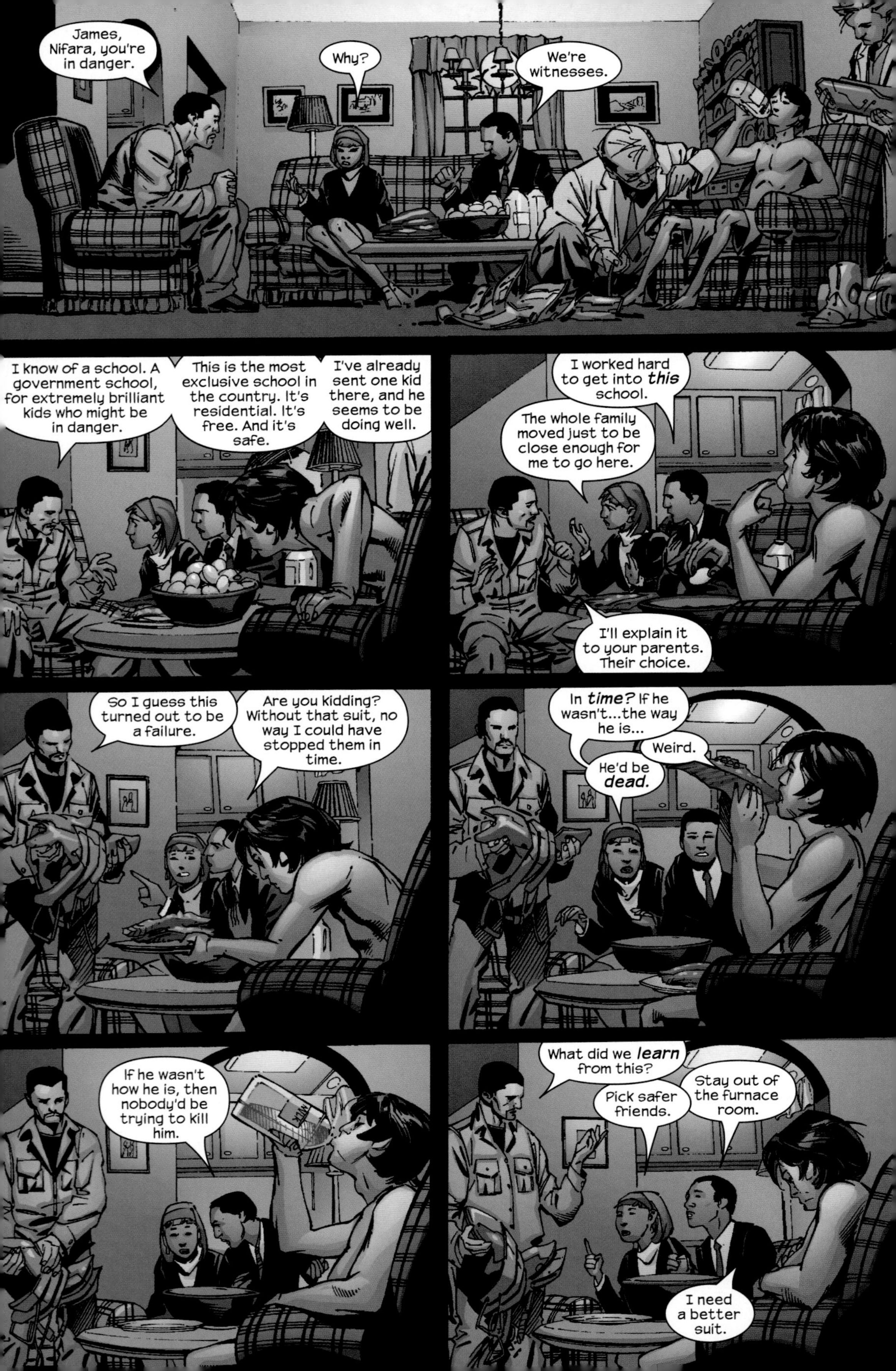
James, Nifara, you're in danger.
Why?
We're witnesses.
I know of a school. A government school, for extremely brilliant kids who might be in danger.
This is the most exclusive school in the country. It's residential. It's free. And it's safe.
I've already sent one kid there, and he seems to be doing well.
I worked hard to get into *this* school.
The whole family moved just to be close enough for me to go here.
I'll explain it to your parents. Their choice.
So I guess this turned out to be a failure.
Are you kidding? Without that suit, no way I could have stopped them in time.
In *time?* If he wasn't...the way he is...
Weird.
He'd be *dead.*
If he wasn't how he is, then nobody'd be trying to kill him.
MILK
What did we *learn* from this?
Pick safer friends.
Stay out of the furnace room.
I need a better suit.

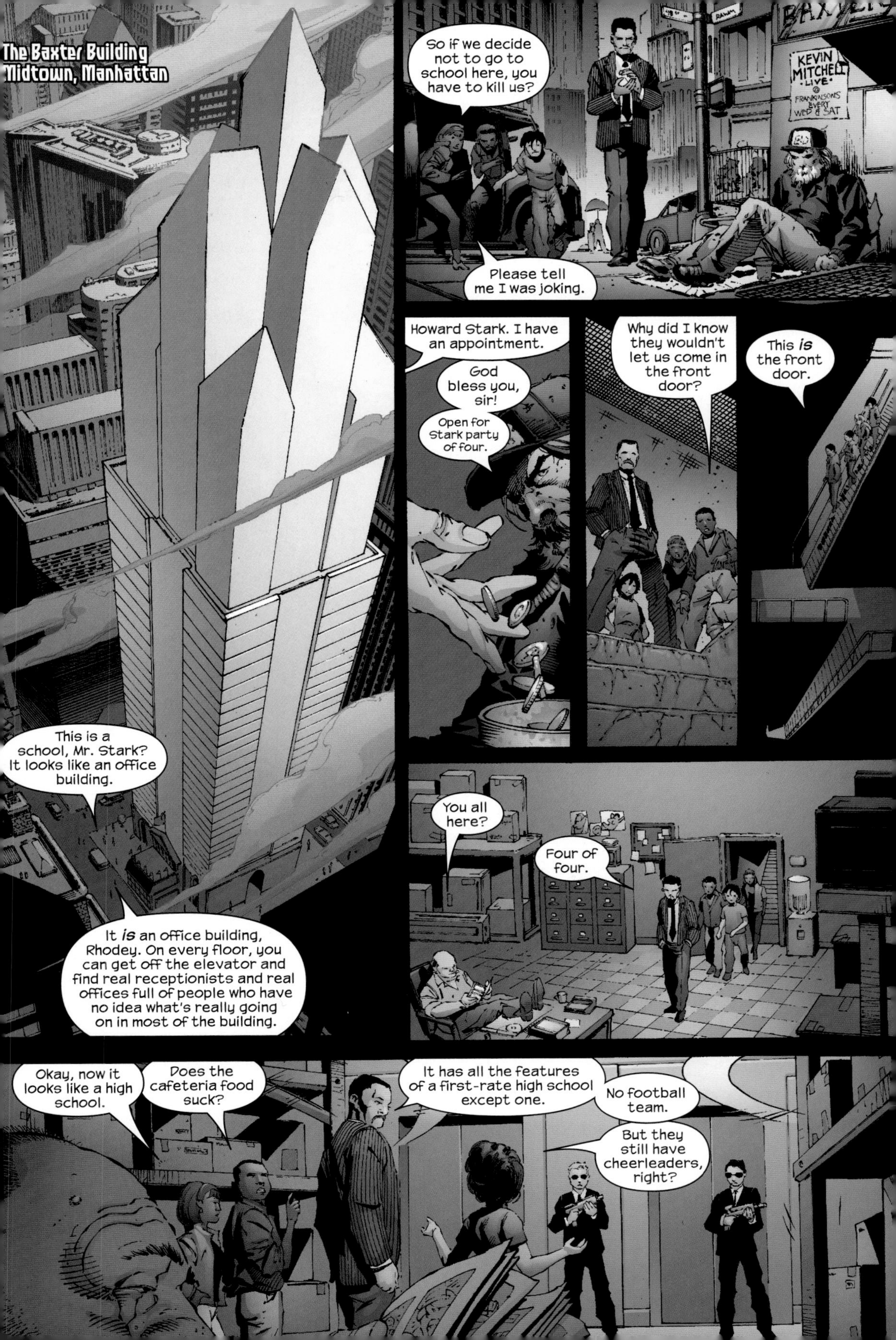
The Baxter Building
Midtown, Manhattan
This is a school, Mr. Stark? It looks like an office building.
It *is* an office building, Rhodey. On every floor, you can get off the elevator and find real receptionists and real offices full of people who have no idea what's really going on in most of the building.
So if we decide not to go to school here, you have to kill us?
Please tell me I was joking.
KEVIN MITCHELL LIVE @ FRANKINSONS EVERY WED & SAT
Howard Stark. I have an appointment.
God bless you, sir!
Open for Stark party of four.
Why did I know they wouldn't let us come in the front door?
This *is* the front door.
You all here?
Four of four.
Okay, now it looks like a high school.
Does the cafeteria food suck?
It has all the features of a first-rate high school except one.
No football team.
But they still have cheerleaders, right?

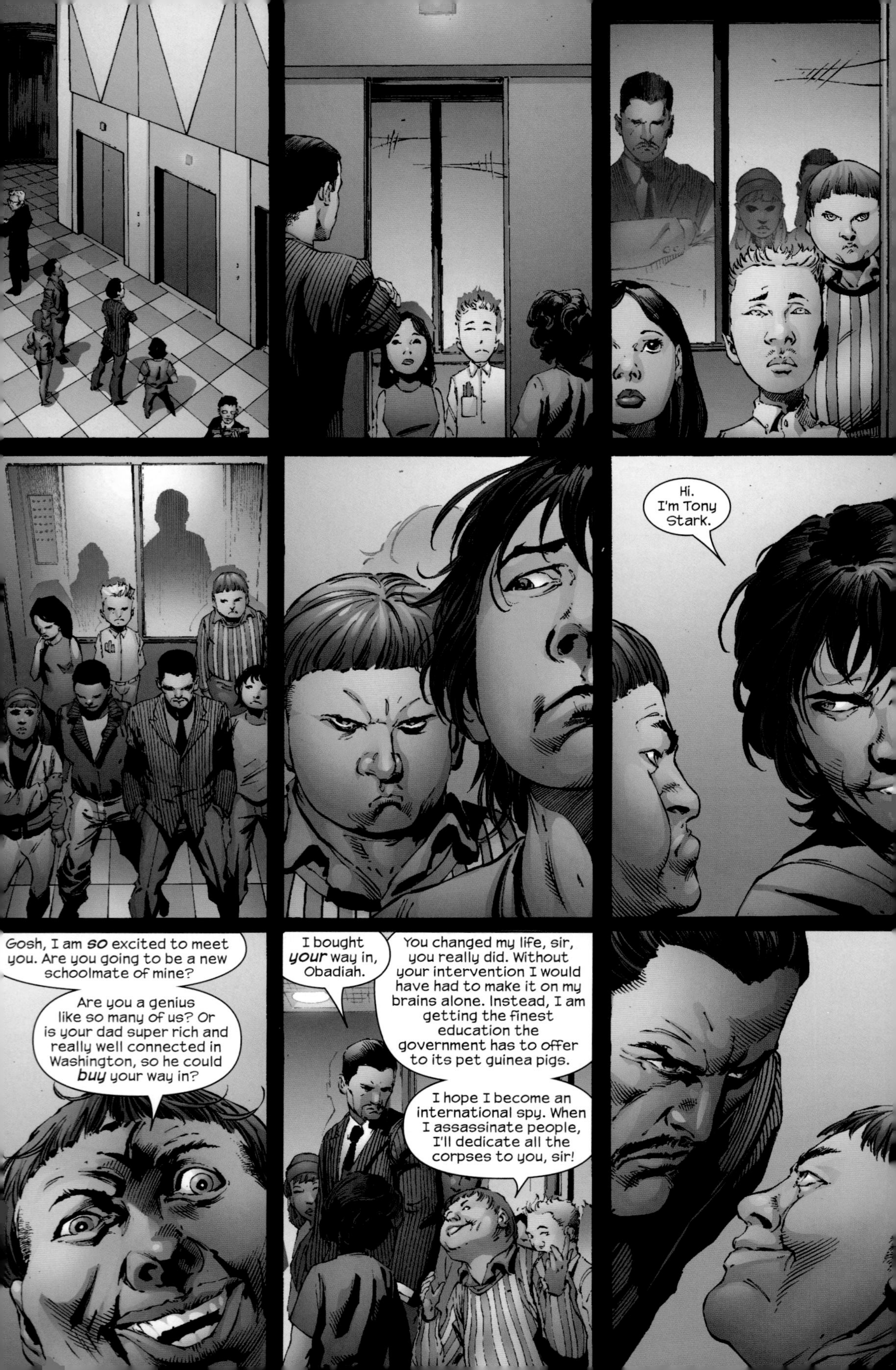
Hi. I'm Tony Stark.
Gosh, I am SO excited to meet you. Are you going to be a new schoolmate of mine?
Are you a genius like so many of us? Or is your dad super rich and really well connected in Washington, so he could buy your way in?
I bought your way in, Obadiah.
You changed my life, sir, you really did. Without your intervention I would have had to make it on my brains alone. Instead, I am getting the finest education the government has to offer to its pet guinea pigs.
I hope I become an international spy. When I assassinate people, I'll dedicate all the corpses to you, sir!

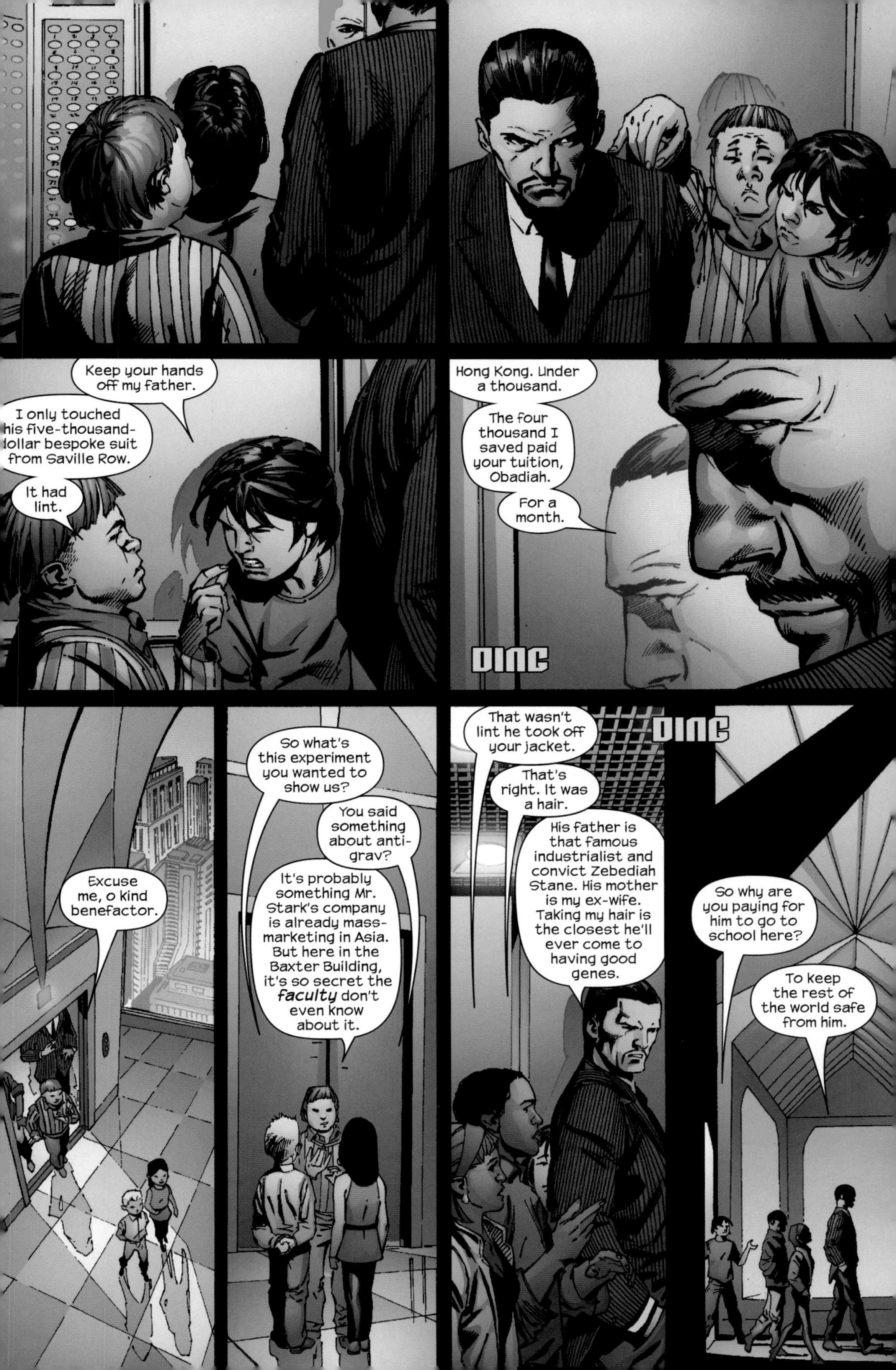

Keep your hands off my father.
I only touched his five-thousand-dollar bespoke suit from Saville Row.
It had lint.
Hong Kong. Under a thousand.
The four thousand I saved paid your tuition, Obadiah.
For a month.
DING
Excuse me, o kind benefactor.
So what's this experiment you wanted to show us?
You said something about anti-grav?
It's probably something Mr. Stark's company is already mass-marketing in Asia. But here in the Baxter Building, it's so secret the *faculty* don't even know about it.
That wasn't lint he took off your jacket.
DING
That's right. It was a hair.
His father is that famous industrialist and convict Zebediah Stane. His mother is my ex-wife. Taking my hair is the closest he'll ever come to having good genes.
So why are you paying for him to go to school here?
To keep the rest of the world safe from him.

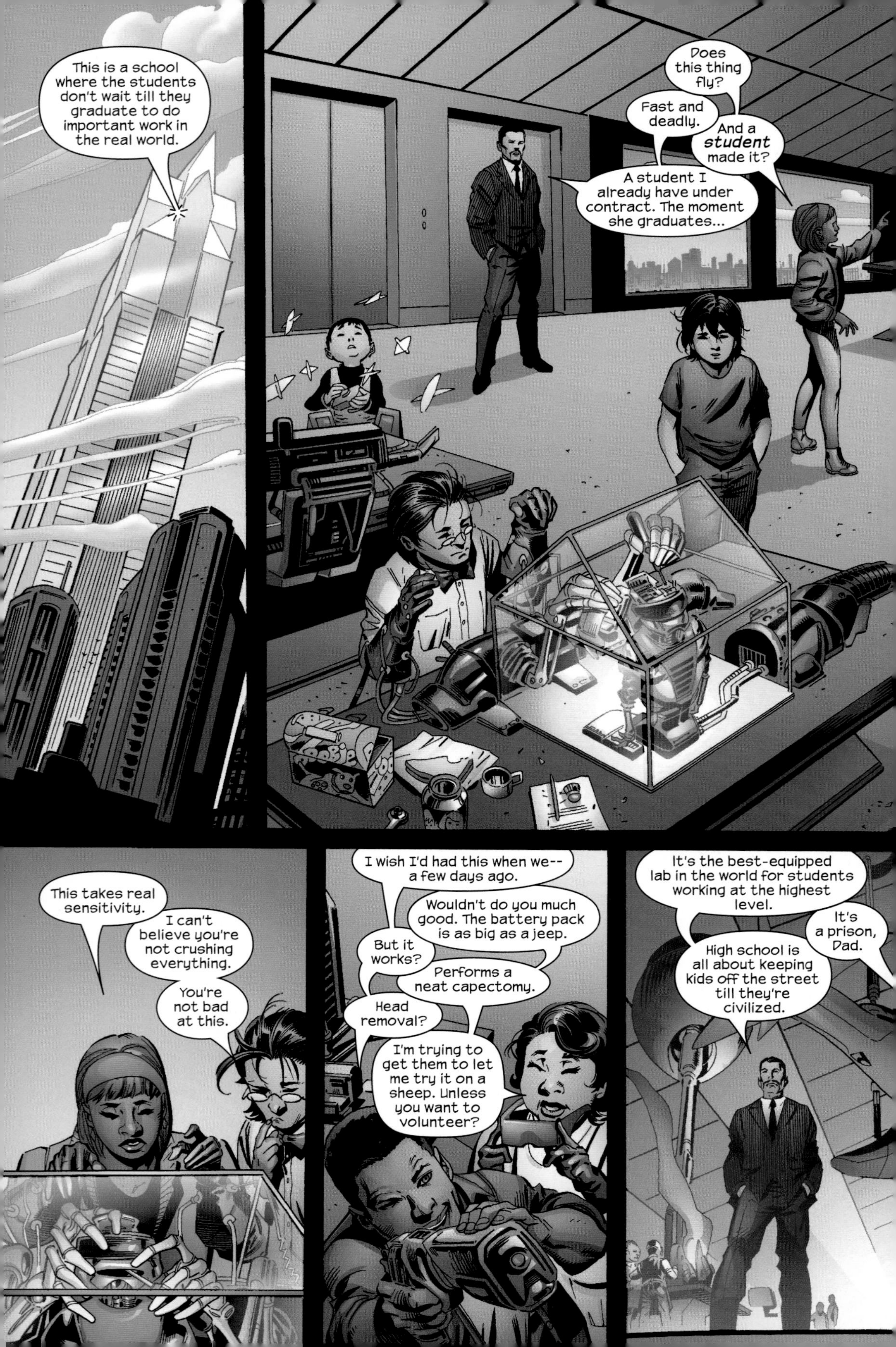
This is a school where the students don't wait till they graduate to do important work in the real world.
Does this thing fly?
Fast and deadly.
And a *student* made it?
A student I already have under contract. The moment she graduates...
This takes real sensitivity.
I can't believe you're not crushing everything.
You're not bad at this.
I wish I'd had this when we-- a few days ago.
Wouldn't do you much good. The battery pack is as big as a jeep.
But it works?
Performs a neat capectomy.
Head removal?
I'm trying to get them to let me try it on a sheep. Unless you want to volunteer?
It's the best-equipped lab in the world for students working at the highest level.
It's a prison, Dad.
High school is all about keeping kids off the street till they're civilized.

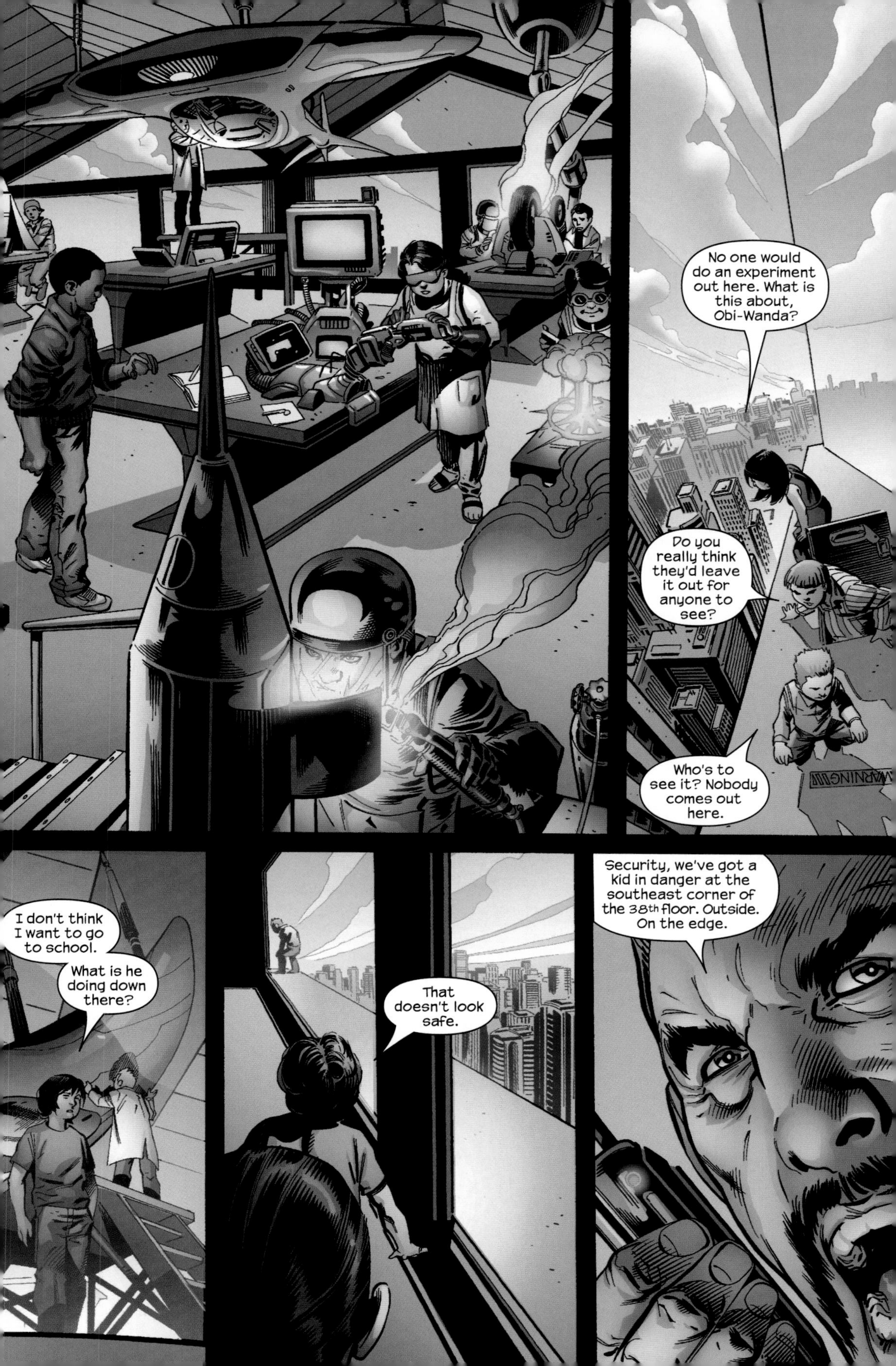

No one would do an experiment out here. What is this about, Obi-Wanda?
Do you really think they'd leave it out for anyone to see?
Who's to see it? Nobody comes out here.
I don't think I want to go to school.
What is he doing down there?
That doesn't look safe.
Security, we've got a kid in danger at the southeast corner of the 38th floor. Outside. On the edge.

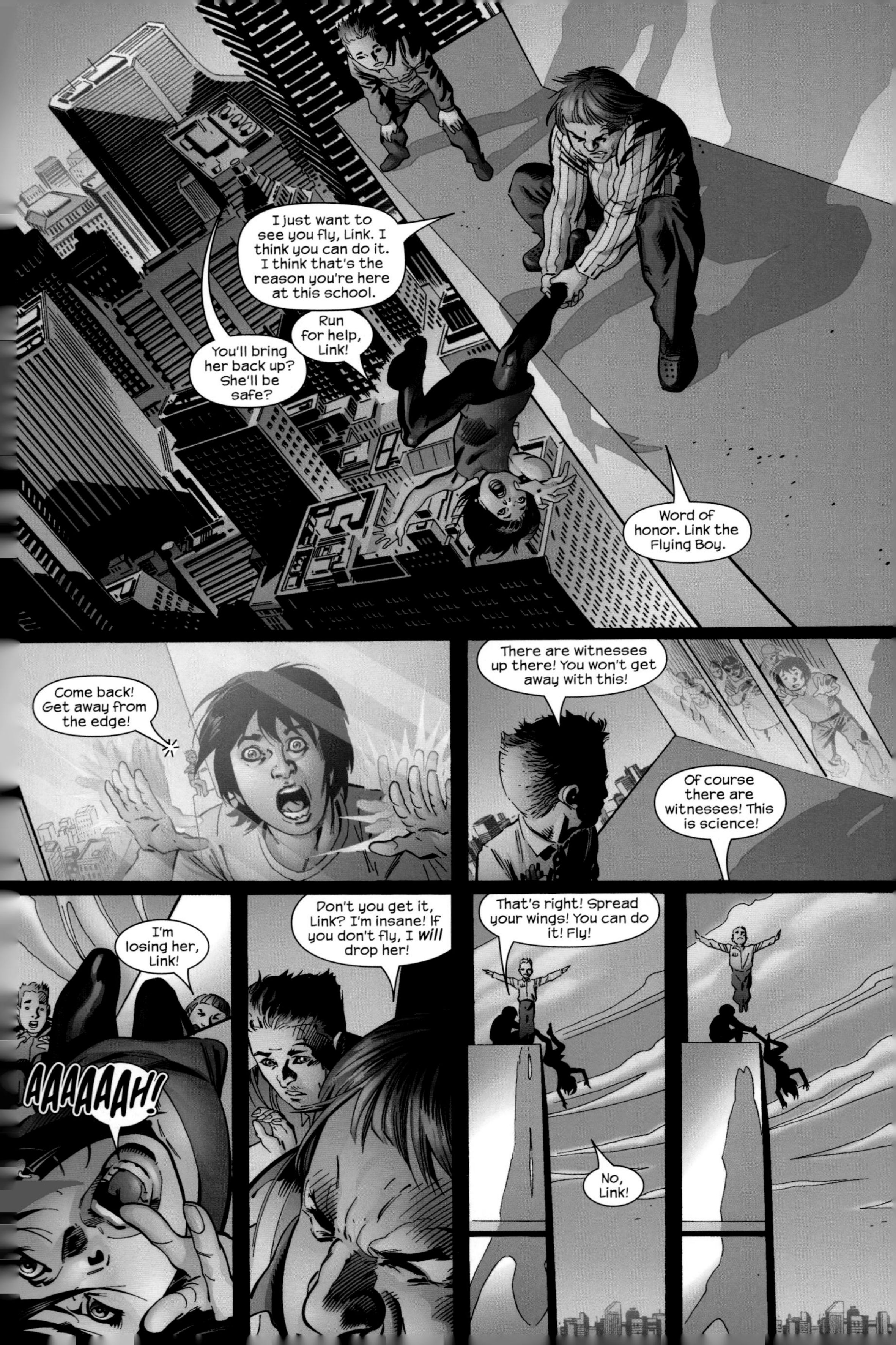
I just want to see you fly, Link. I think you can do it. I think that's the reason you're here at this school.
You'll bring her back up? She'll be safe?
Run for help, Link!
Word of honor. Link the Flying Boy.
Come back! Get away from the edge!
There are witnesses up there! You won't get away with this!
Of course there are witnesses! This is science!
I'm losing her, Link!
AAAAAAH!
Don't you get it, Link? I'm insane! If you don't fly, I *will* drop her!
That's right! Spread your wings! You can do it! Fly!
No, Link!

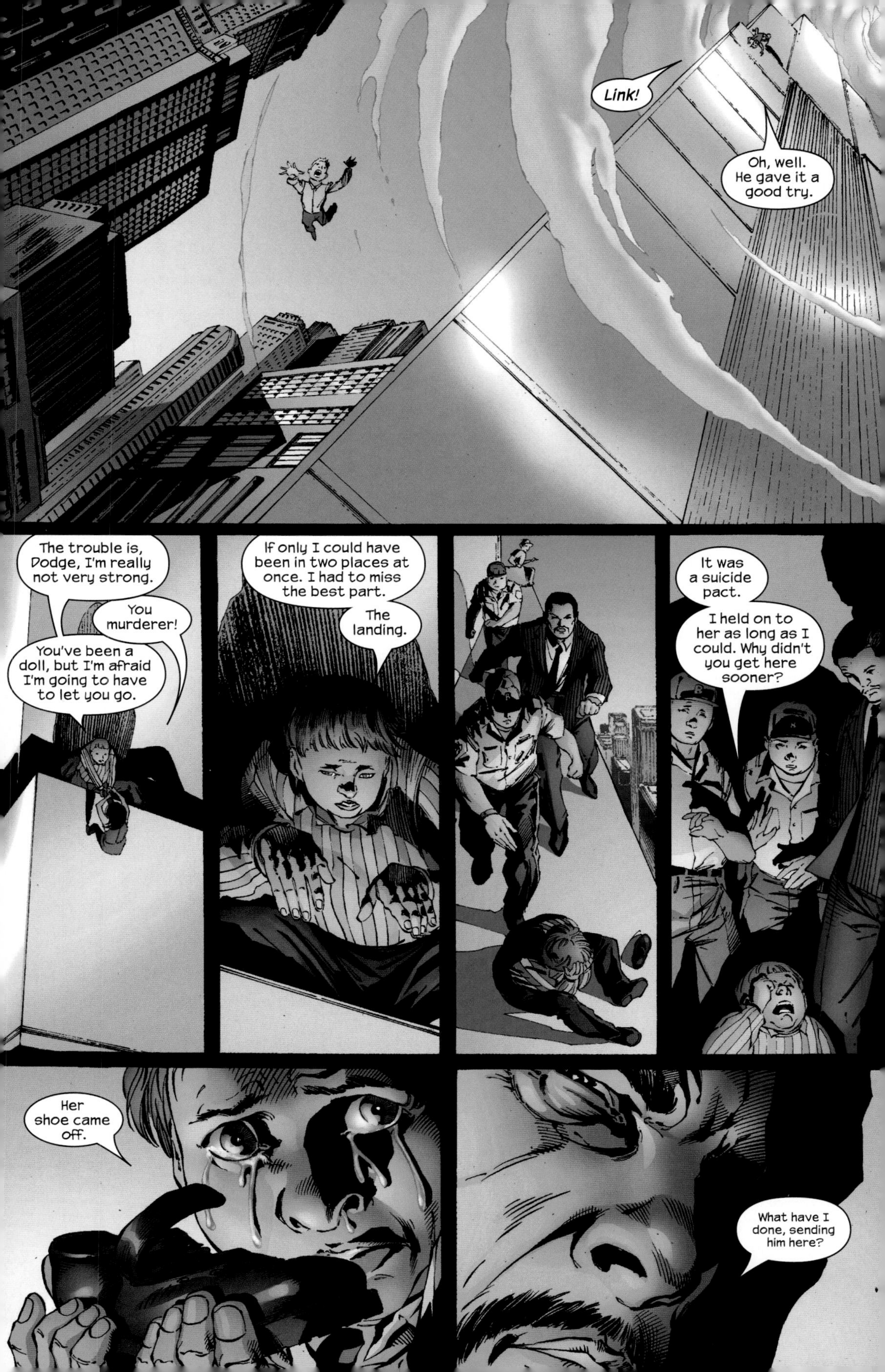
Link!
Oh, well. He gave it a good try.
The trouble is, Dodge, I'm really not very strong.
You murderer!
You've been a doll, but I'm afraid I'm going to have to let you go.
If only I could have been in two places at once. I had to miss the best part.
The landing.
It was a suicide pact.
I held on to her as long as I could. Why didn't you get here sooner?
Her shoe came off.
What have I done, sending him here?

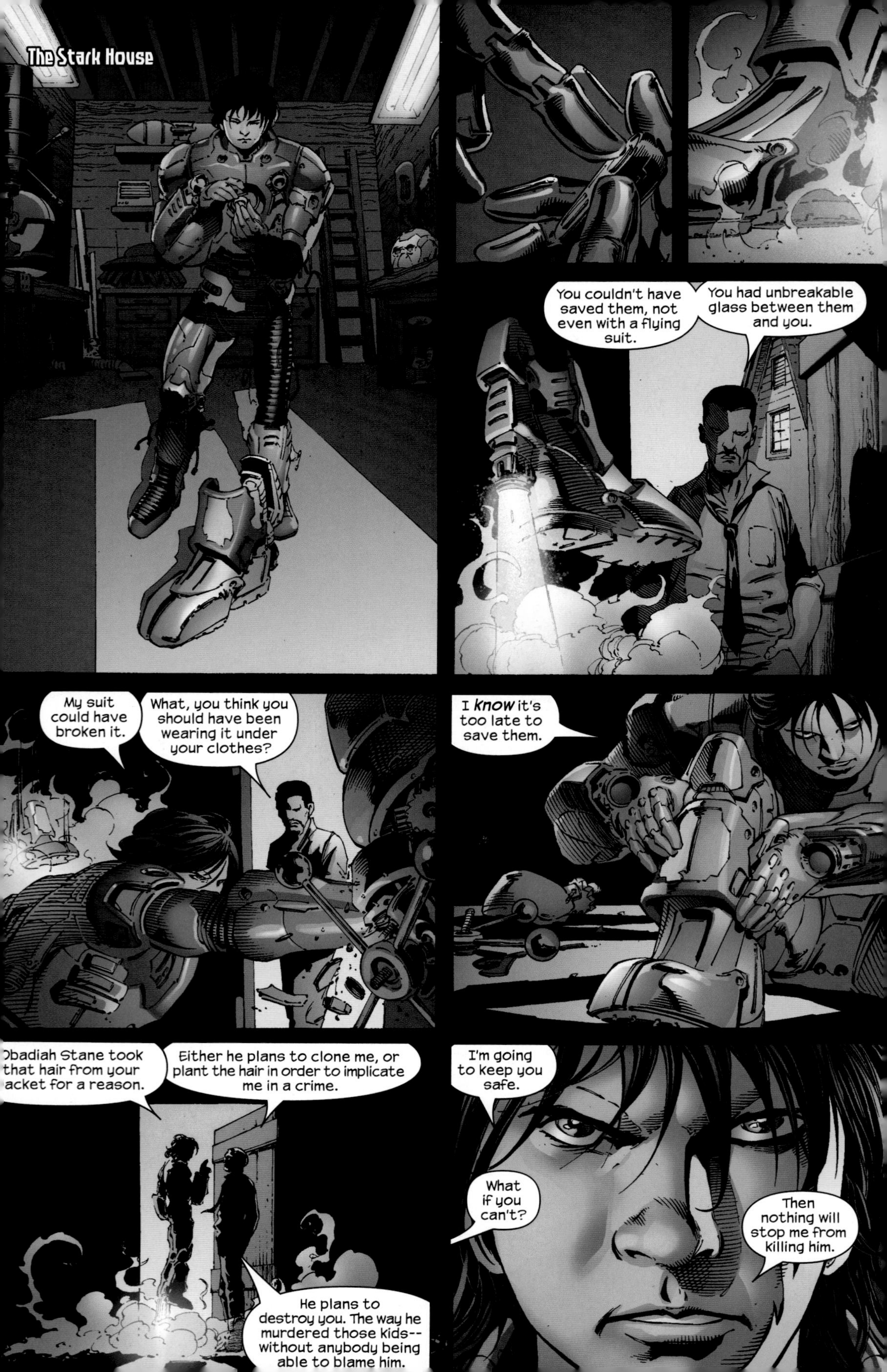
The Stark House
You couldn't have saved them, not even with a flying suit.
You had unbreakable glass between them and you.
My suit could have broken it.
What, you think you should have been wearing it under your clothes?
I *KNOW* it's too late to save them.
Obadiah Stane took that hair from your jacket for a reason.
Either he plans to clone me, or plant the hair in order to implicate me in a crime.
He plans to destroy you. The way he murdered those kids--without anybody being able to blame him.
I'm going to keep you safe.
What if you can't?
Then nothing will stop me from killing him.

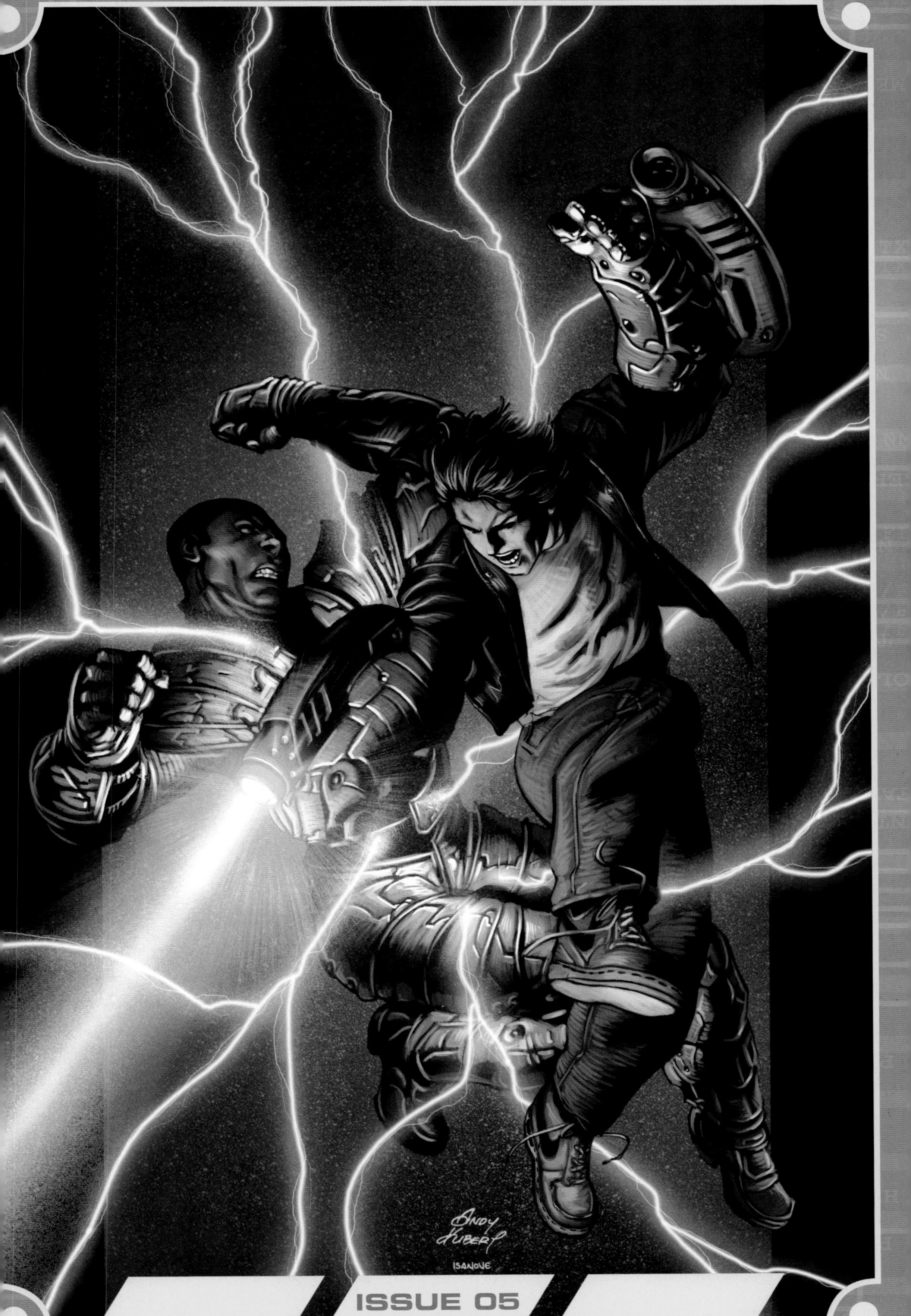
ANDY KUBERT
ISANOVE

ISSUE 05

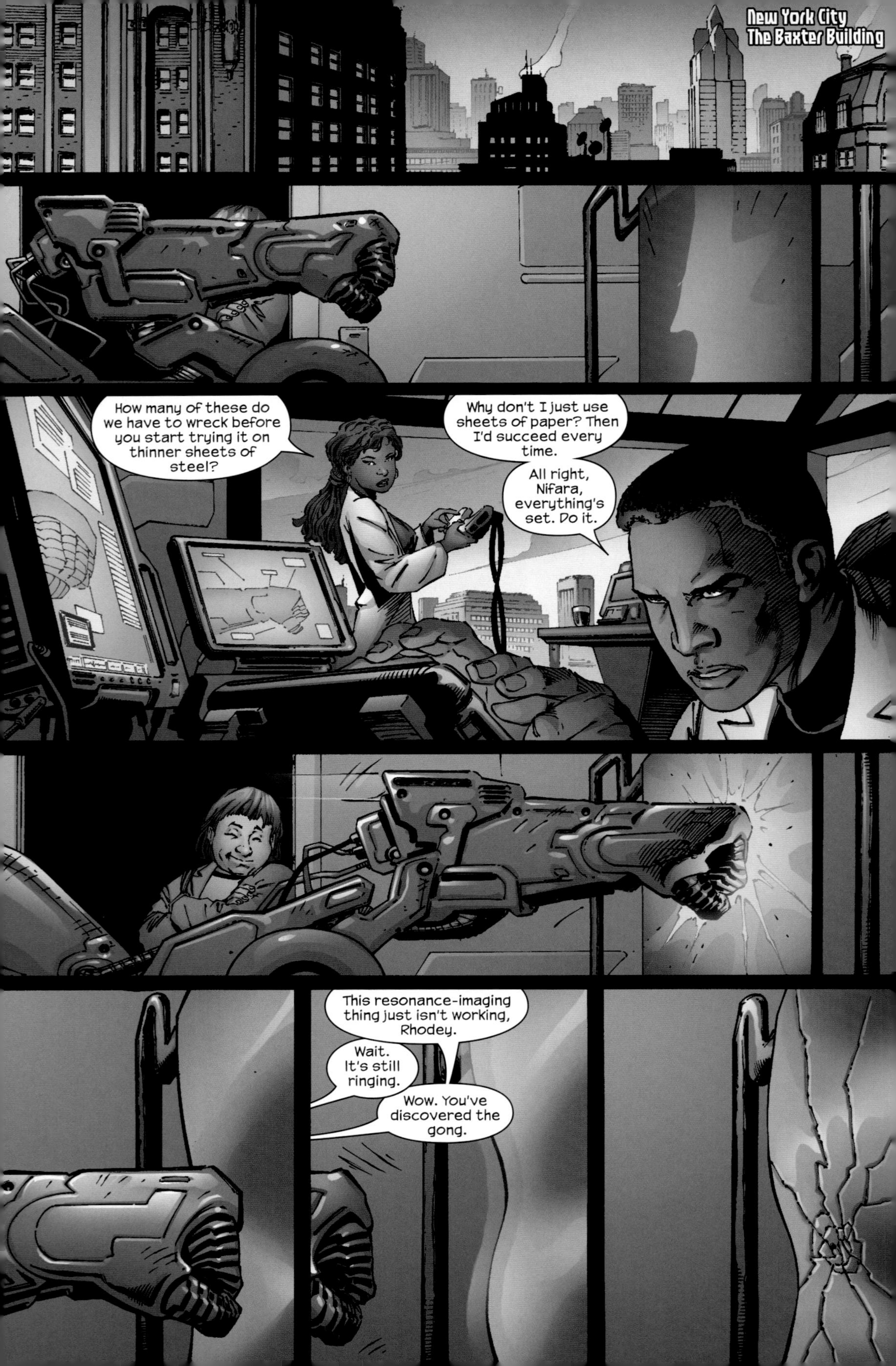
New York City
The Baxter Building
How many of these do we have to wreck before you start trying it on thinner sheets of steel?
Why don't I just use sheets of paper? Then I'd succeed every time.
All right, Nifara, everything's set. Do it.
This resonance-imaging thing just isn't working, Rhodey.
Wait. It's still ringing.
Wow. You've discovered the gong.

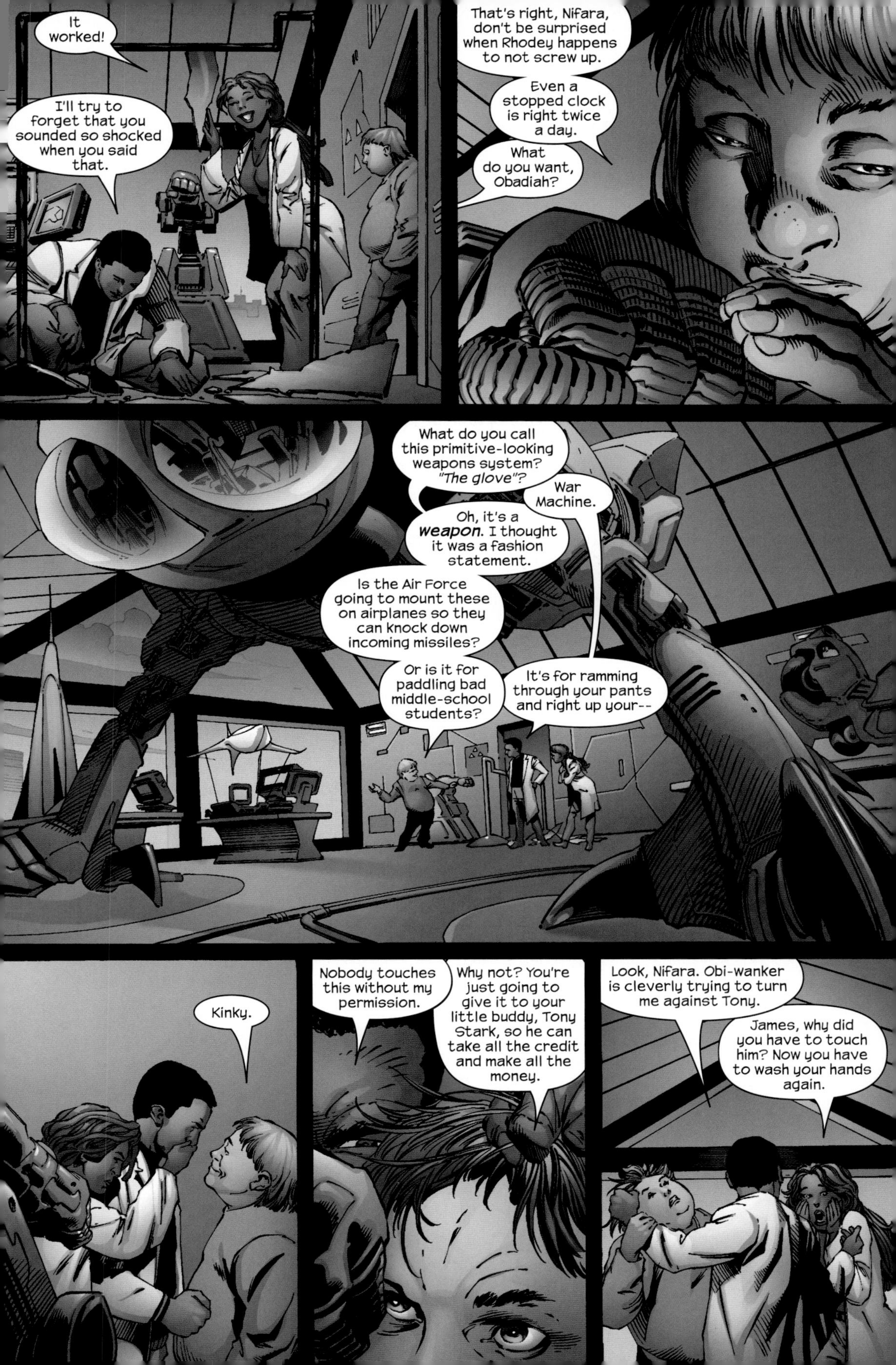
It worked!
I'll try to forget that you sounded so shocked when you said that.
That's right, Nifara, don't be surprised when Rhodey happens to not screw up.
Even a stopped clock is right twice a day.
What do you want, Obadiah?
What do you call this primitive-looking weapons system? *"The glove"*?
War Machine.
Oh, it's a ***weapon***. I thought it was a fashion statement.
Is the Air Force going to mount these on airplanes so they can knock down incoming missiles?
Or is it for paddling bad middle-school students?
It's for ramming through your pants and right up your--
Kinky.
Nobody touches this without my permission.
Why not? You're just going to give it to your little buddy, Tony Stark, so he can take all the credit and make all the money.
Look, Nifara. Obi-wanker is cleverly trying to turn me against Tony.
James, why did you have to touch him? Now you have to wash your hands again.

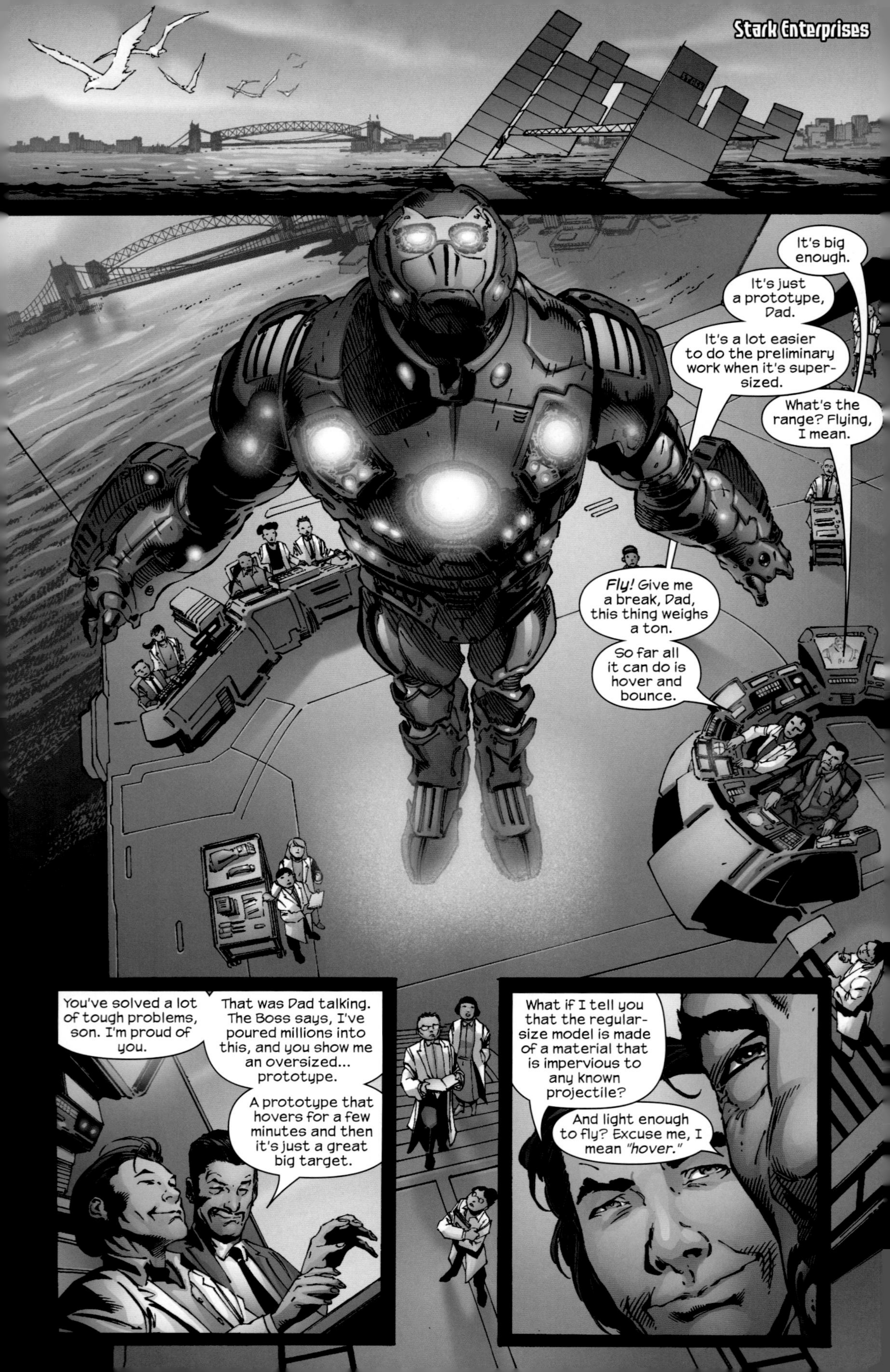
Stark Enterprises
It's big enough.
It's just a prototype, Dad.
It's a lot easier to do the preliminary work when it's supersized.
What's the range? Flying, I mean.
Fly! Give me a break, Dad, this thing weighs a ton.
So far all it can do is hover and bounce.
You've solved a lot of tough problems, son. I'm proud of you.
That was Dad talking. The Boss says, I've poured millions into this, and you show me an oversized... prototype.
A prototype that hovers for a few minutes and then it's just a great big target.
What if I tell you that the regular-size model is made of a material that is impervious to any known projectile?
And light enough to fly? Excuse me, I mean "hover."

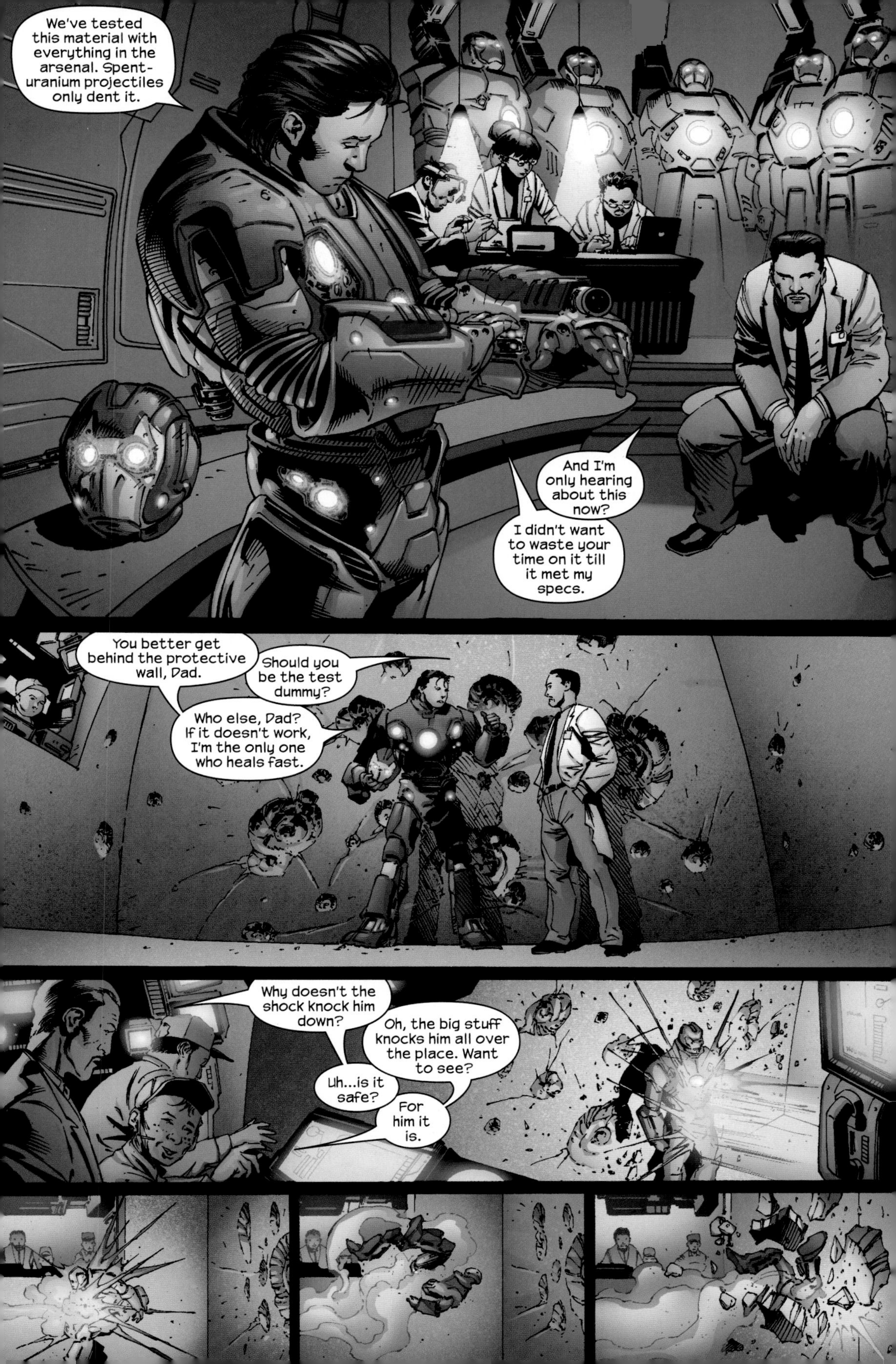

We've tested this material with everything in the arsenal. Spent-uranium projectiles only dent it.
And I'm only hearing about this now?
I didn't want to waste your time on it till it met my specs.
You better get behind the protective wall, Dad.
Should you be the test dummy?
Who else, Dad? If it doesn't work, I'm the only one who heals fast.
Why doesn't the shock knock him down?
Oh, the big stuff knocks him all over the place. Want to see?
Uh...is it safe?
For him it is.

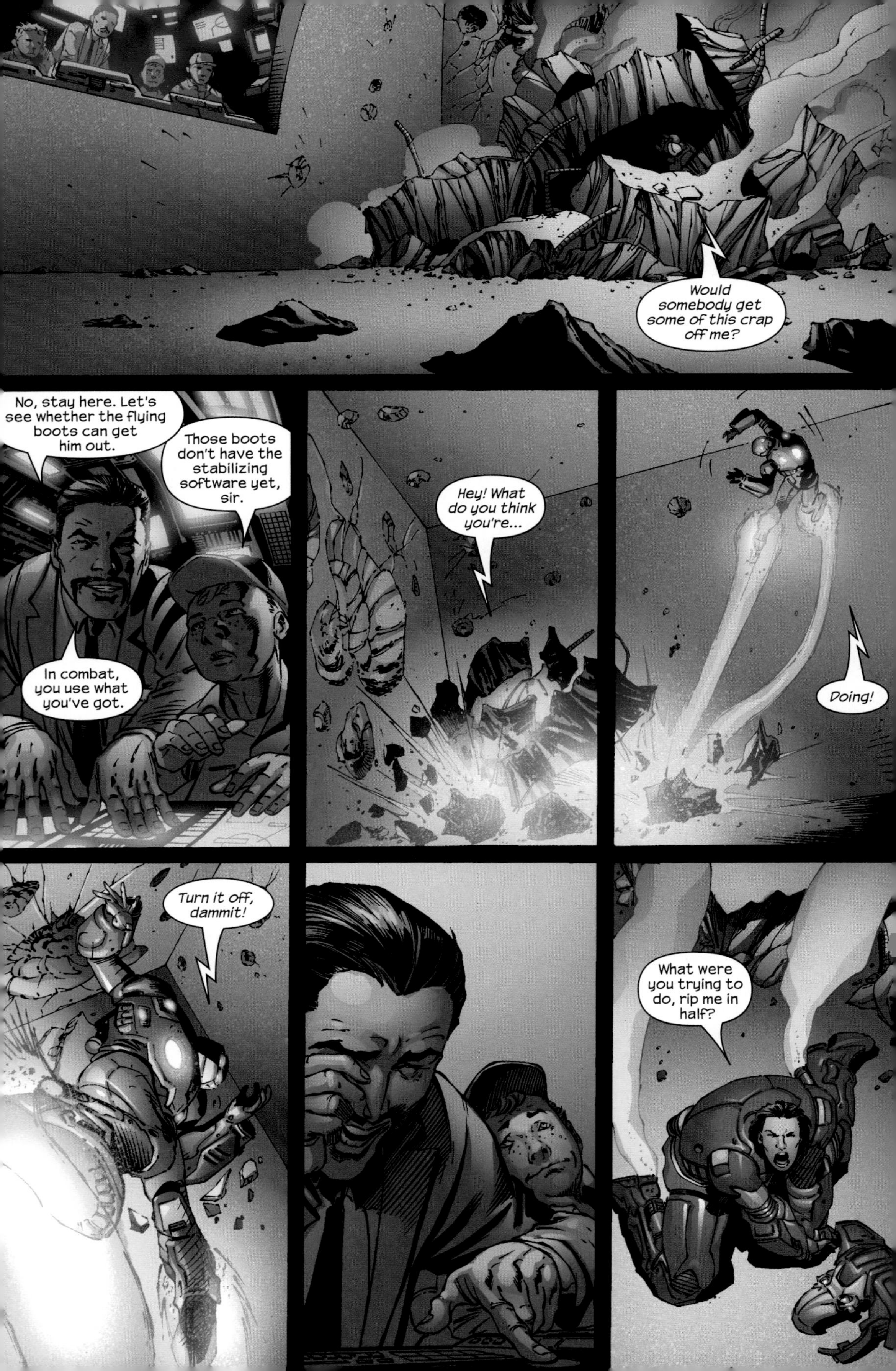
Would somebody get some of this crap off me?
No, stay here. Let's see whether the flying boots can get him out.
Those boots don't have the stabilizing software yet, sir.
In combat, you use what you've got.
Hey! What do you think you're...
Doing!
Turn it off, dammit!
What were you trying to do, rip me in half?

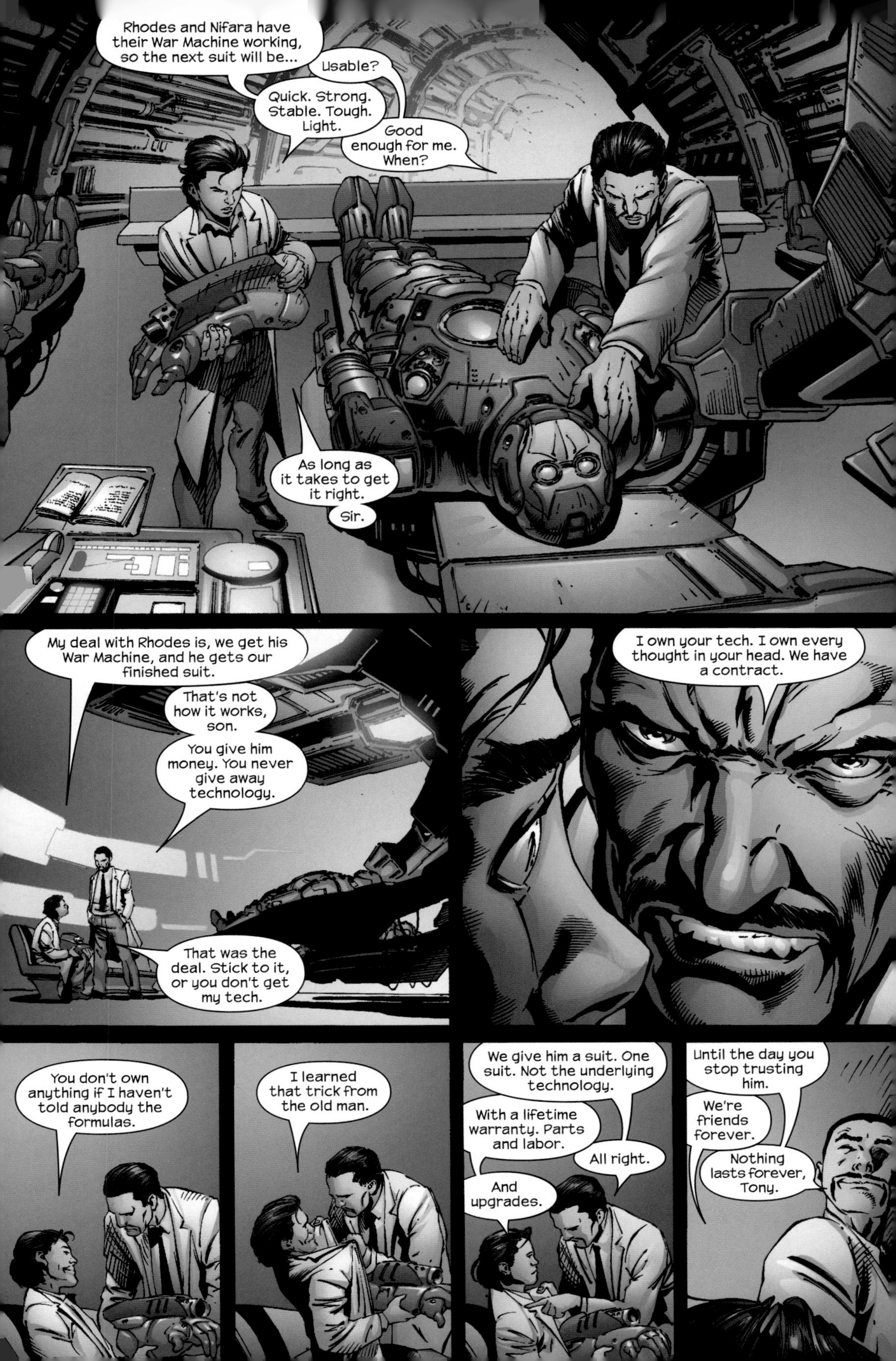
Rhodes and Nifara have their War Machine working, so the next suit will be...
Usable?
Quick. Strong. Stable. Tough. Light.
Good enough for me. When?
As long as it takes to get it right.
Sir.
My deal with Rhodes is, we get his War Machine, and he gets our finished suit.
That's not how it works, son.
You give him money. You never give away technology.
That was the deal. Stick to it, or you don't get my tech.
I own your tech. I own every thought in your head. We have a contract.
You don't own anything if I haven't told anybody the formulas.
I learned that trick from the old man.
We give him a suit. One suit. Not the underlying technology.
With a lifetime warranty. Parts and labor.
All right.
And upgrades.
Until the day you stop trusting him.
We're friends forever.
Nothing lasts forever, Tony.

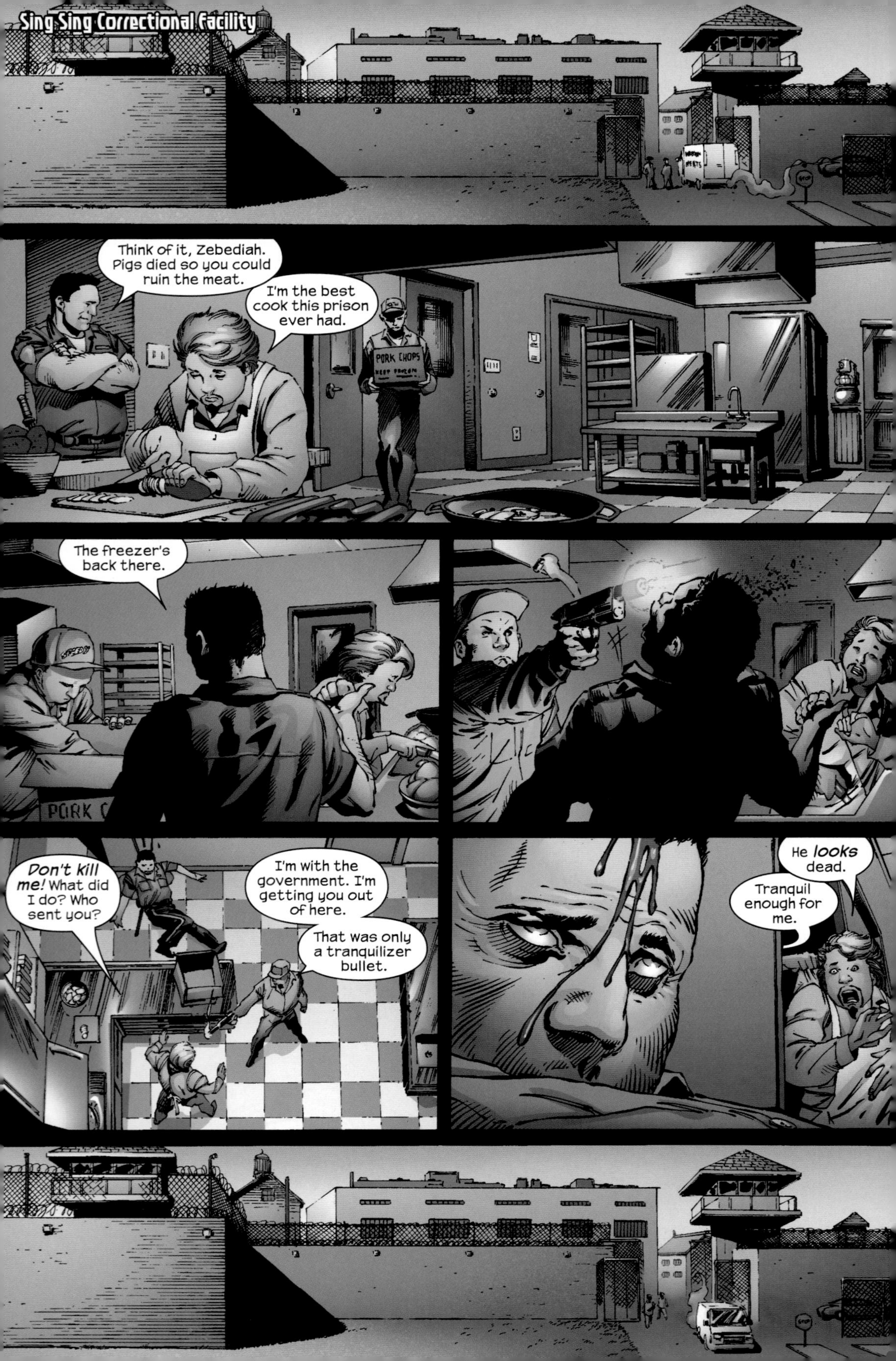

Sing Sing Correctional Facility
Think of it, Zebediah. Pigs died so you could ruin the meat.
I'm the best cook this prison ever had.
PORK CHOPS
The freezer's back there.
Don't kill me! What did I do? Who sent you?
I'm with the government. I'm getting you out of here.
That was only a tranquilizer bullet.
He looks dead.
Tranquil enough for me.

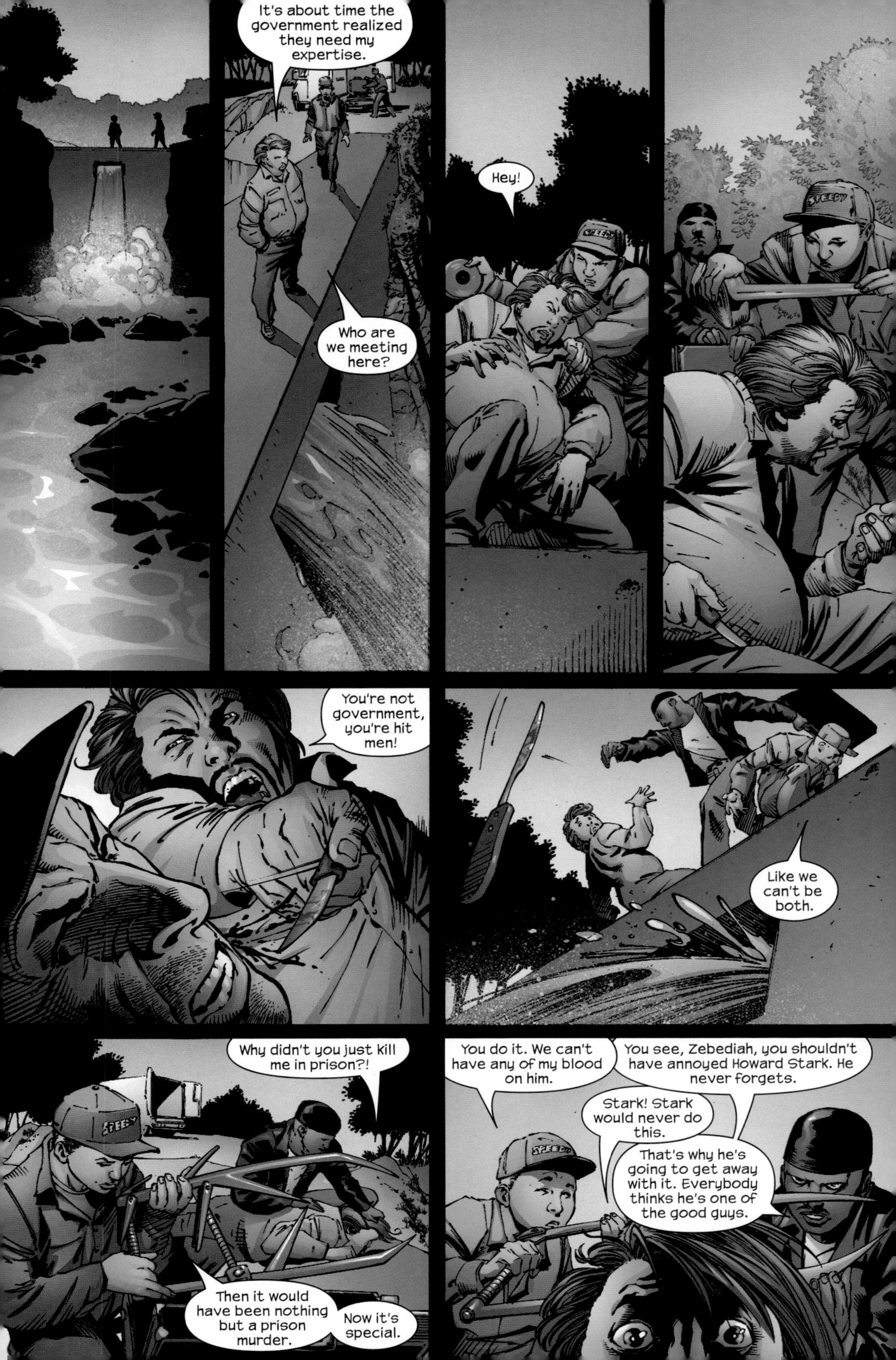
It's about time the government realized they need my expertise.
Who are we meeting here?
Hey!
SPEEDY
SPEEDY
You're not government, you're hit men!
Like we can't be both.
Why didn't you just kill me in prison?!
SPEEDY
Then it would have been nothing but a prison murder.
Now it's special.
You do it. We can't have any of my blood on him.
You see, Zebediah, you shouldn't have annoyed Howard Stark. He never forgets.
Stark! Stark would never do this.
That's why he's going to get away with it. Everybody thinks he's one of the good guys.
SPEEDY

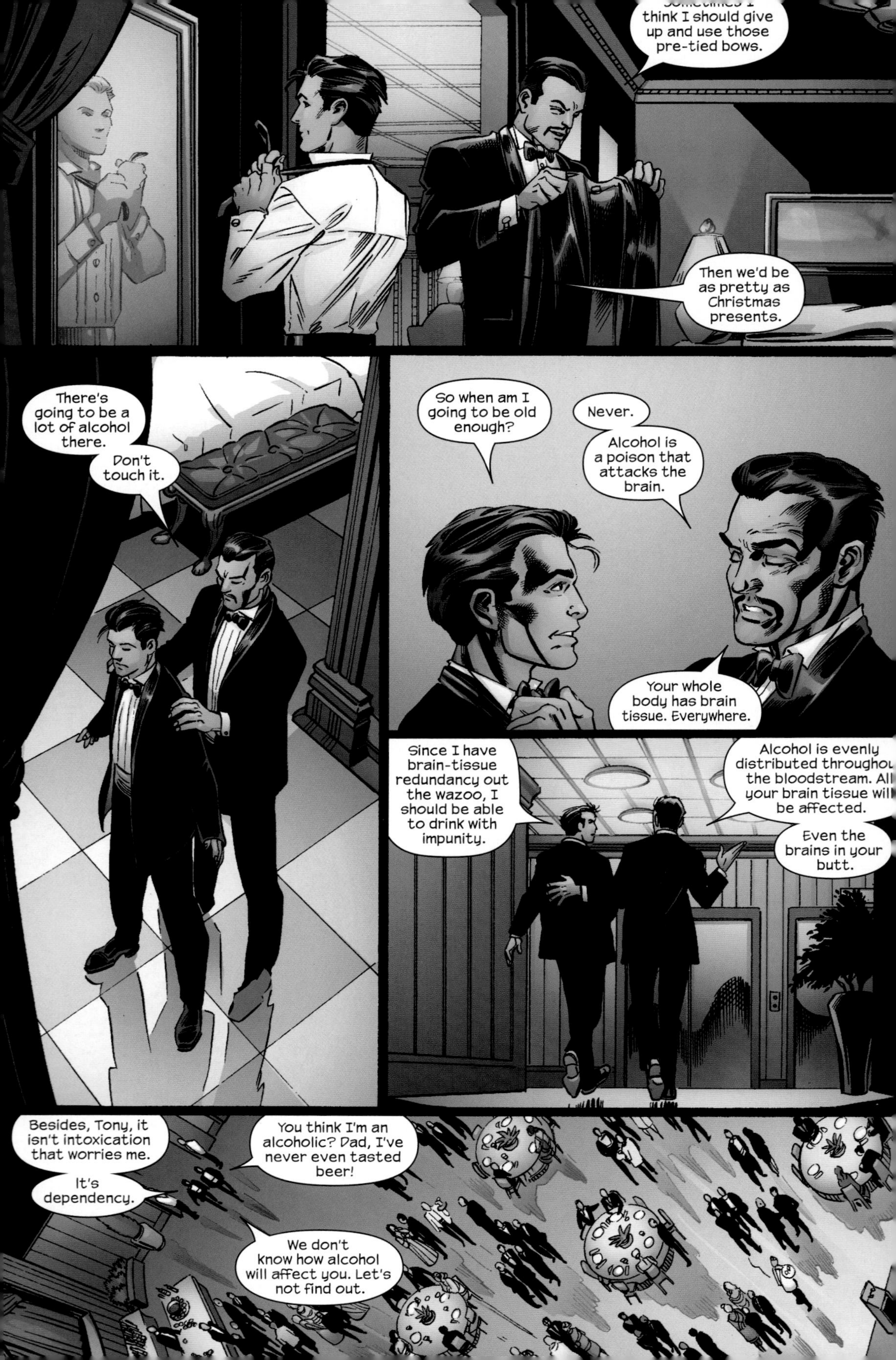
think I should give up and use those pre-tied bows.
Then we'd be as pretty as Christmas presents.
There's going to be a lot of alcohol there.
Don't touch it.
So when am I going to be old enough?
Never.
Alcohol is a poison that attacks the brain.
Your whole body has brain tissue. Everywhere.
Since I have brain-tissue redundancy out the wazoo, I should be able to drink with impunity.
Alcohol is evenly distributed throughou the bloodstream. All your brain tissue wil be affected.
Even the brains in your butt.
Besides, Tony, it isn't intoxication that worries me.
It's dependency.
You think I'm an alcoholic? Dad, I've never even tasted beer!
We don't know how alcohol will affect you. Let's not find out.

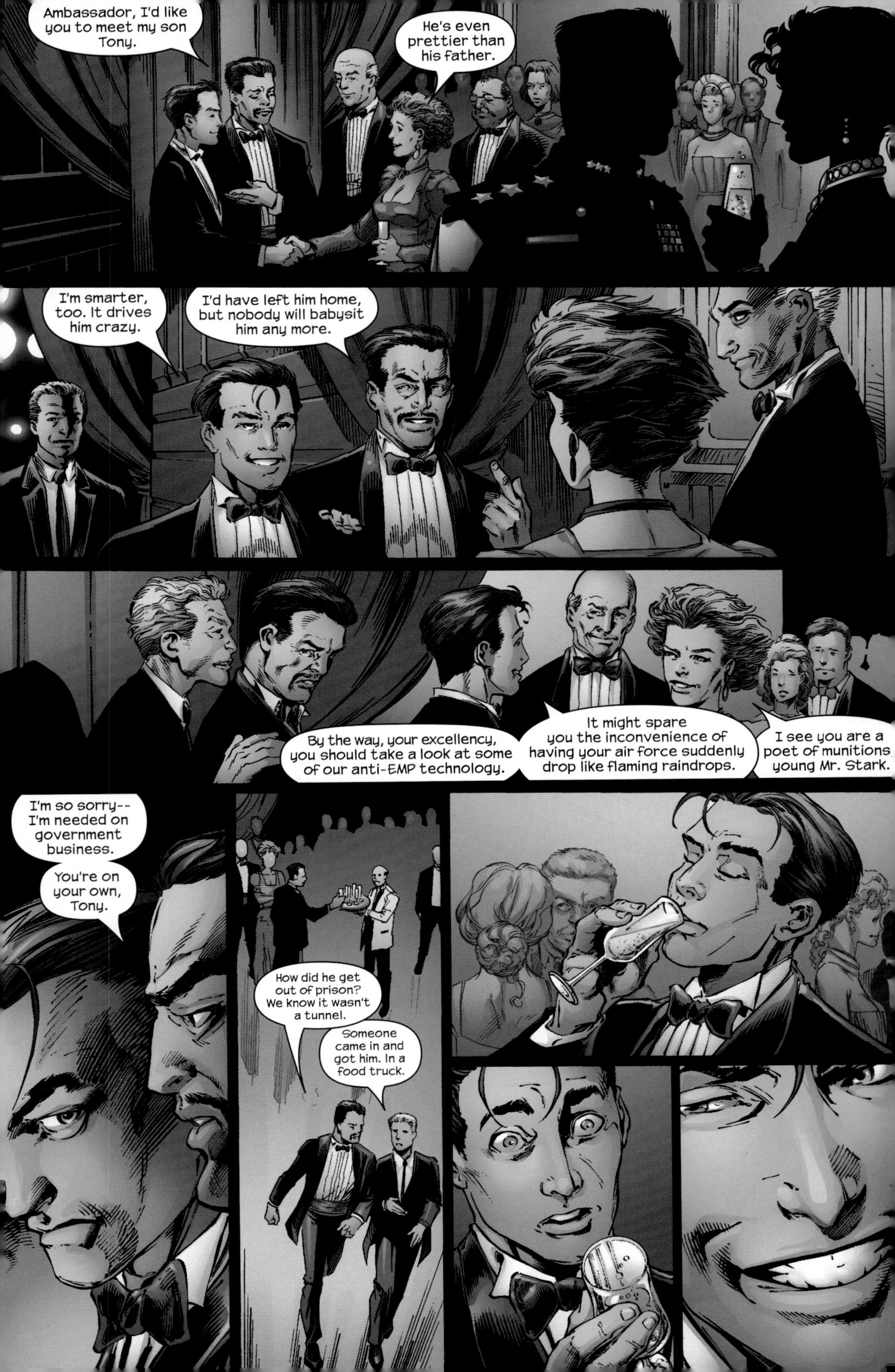

Ambassador, I'd like you to meet my son Tony.
He's even prettier than his father.
I'm smarter, too. It drives him crazy.
I'd have left him home, but nobody will babysit him any more.
By the way, your excellency, you should take a look at some of our anti-EMP technology.
It might spare you the inconvenience of having your air force suddenly drop like flaming raindrops.
I see you are a poet of munitions young Mr. Stark.
I'm so sorry-- I'm needed on government business.
You're on your own, Tony.
How did he get out of prison? We know it wasn't a tunnel.
Someone came in and got him. In a food truck.

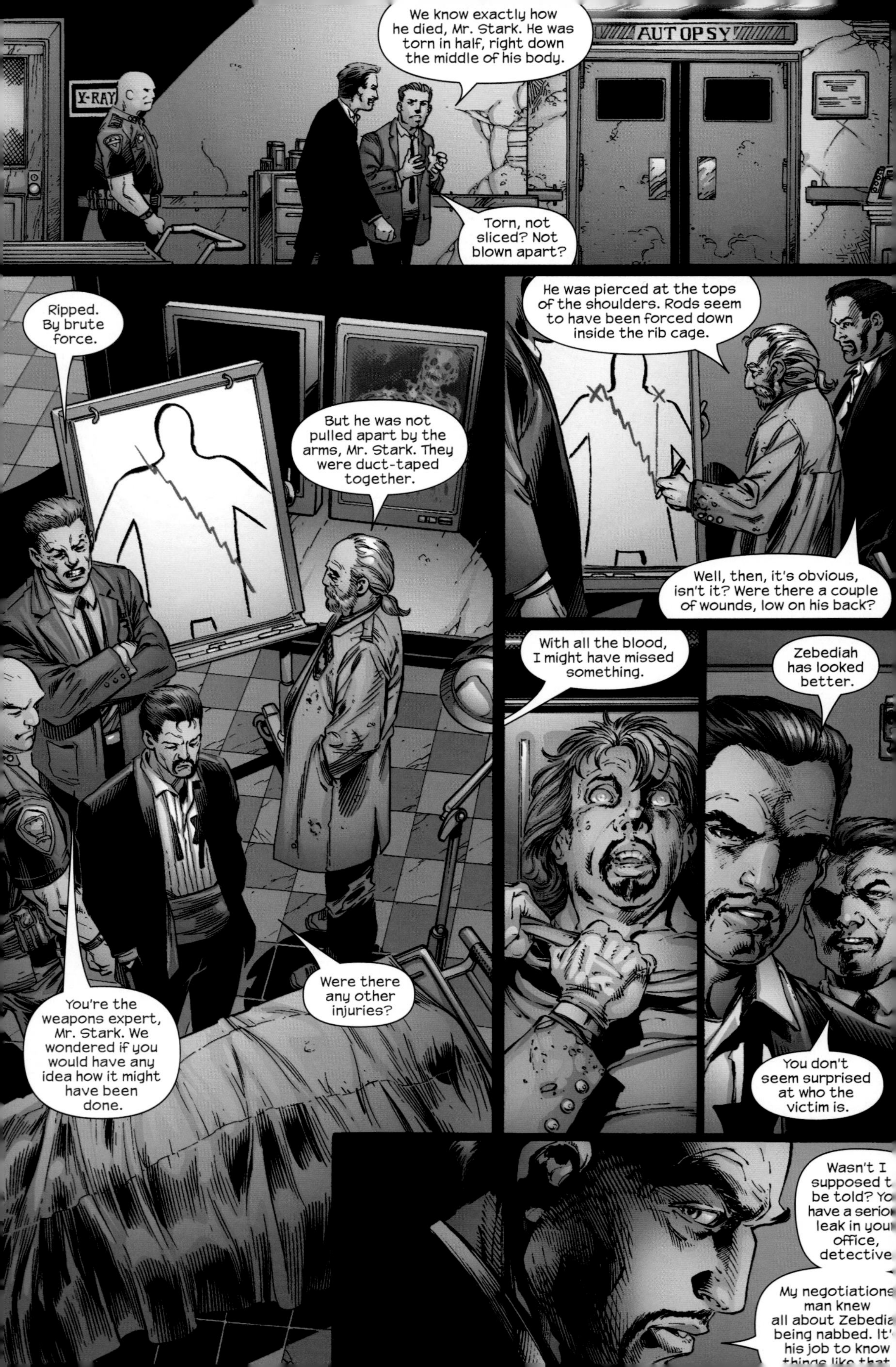

We know exactly how he died, Mr. Stark. He was torn in half, right down the middle of his body.
X-RAY
AUTOPSY
Torn, not sliced? Not blown apart?
Ripped. By brute force.
You're the weapons expert, Mr. Stark. We wondered if you would have any idea how it might have been done.
Were there any other injuries?
But he was not pulled apart by the arms, Mr. Stark. They were duct-taped together.
He was pierced at the tops of the shoulders. Rods seem to have been forced down inside the rib cage.
Well, then, it's obvious, isn't it? Were there a couple of wounds, low on his back?
With all the blood, I might have missed something.
Zebediah has looked better.
You don't seem surprised at who the victim is.
Wasn't I supposed t be told? Yo have a serio leak in you office, detective
My negotiations man knew all about Zebedia being nabbed. It' his job to know

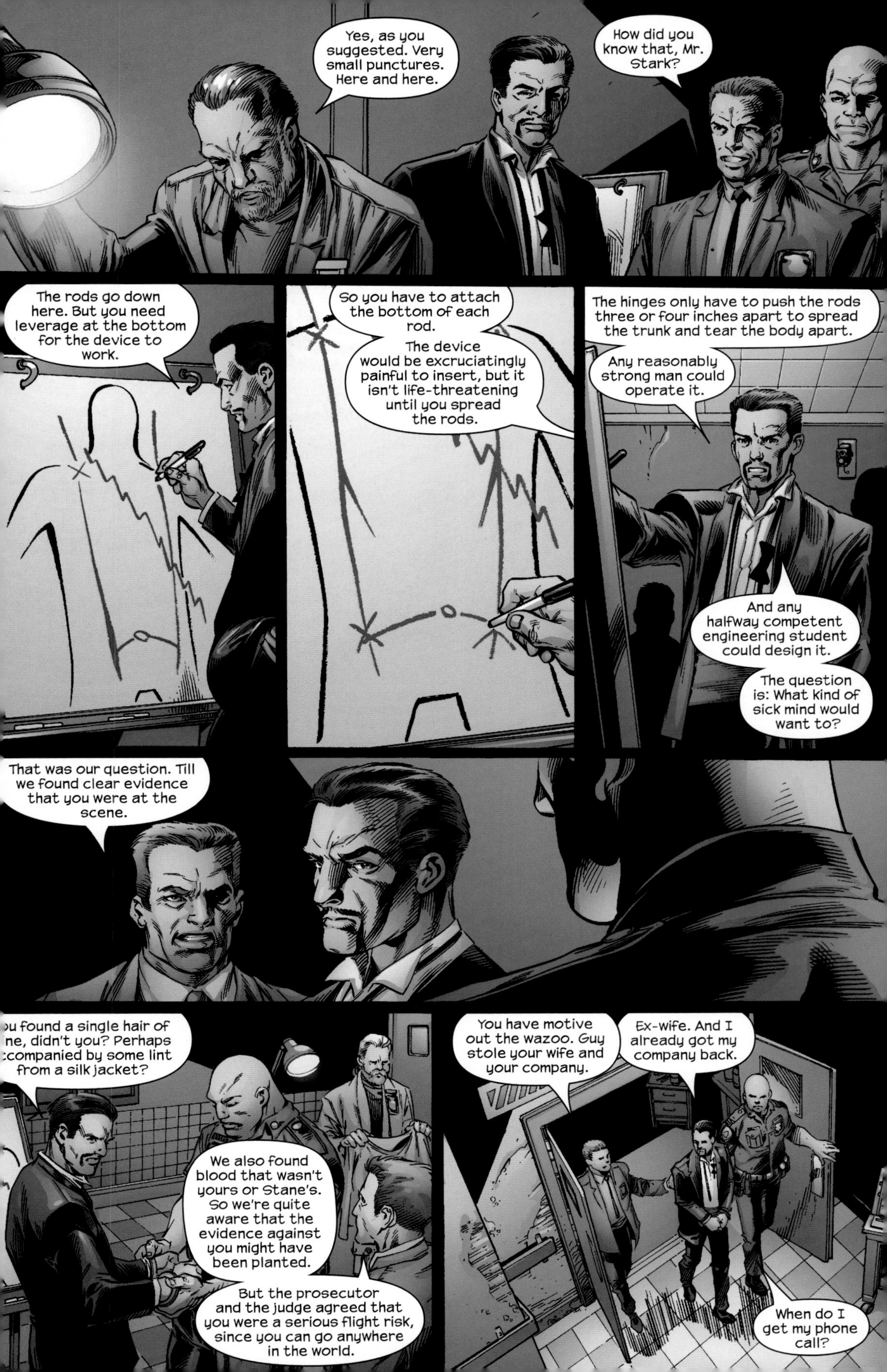
Yes, as you suggested. Very small punctures. Here and here.
How did you know that, Mr. Stark?
The rods go down here. But you need leverage at the bottom for the device to work.
So you have to attach the bottom of each rod.
The device would be excruciatingly painful to insert, but it isn't life-threatening until you spread the rods.
The hinges only have to push the rods three or four inches apart to spread the trunk and tear the body apart.
Any reasonably strong man could operate it.
And any halfway competent engineering student could design it.
The question is: What kind of sick mind would want to?
That was our question. Till we found clear evidence that you were at the scene.
u found a single hair of ne, didn't you? Perhaps ccompanied by some lint from a silk jacket?
We also found blood that wasn't yours or Stane's. So we're quite aware that the evidence against you might have been planted.
But the prosecutor and the judge agreed that you were a serious flight risk, since you can go anywhere in the world.
You have motive out the wazoo. Guy stole your wife and your company.
Ex-wife. And I already got my company back.
When do I get my phone call?

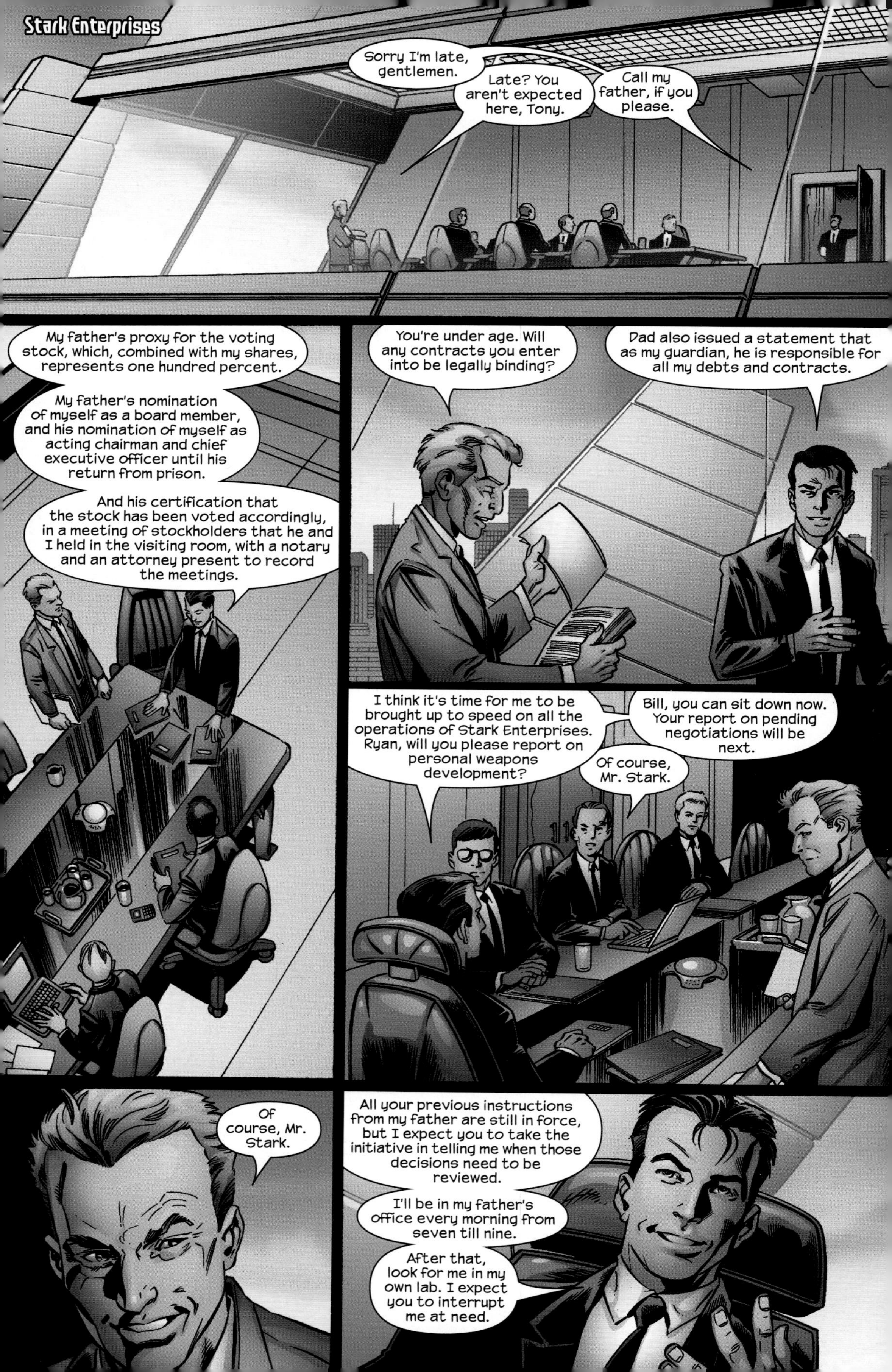

Stark Enterprises
Sorry I'm late, gentlemen.
Late? You aren't expected here, Tony.
Call my father, if you please.
My father's proxy for the voting stock, which, combined with my shares, represents one hundred percent.
My father's nomination of myself as a board member, and his nomination of myself as acting chairman and chief executive officer until his return from prison.
And his certification that the stock has been voted accordingly, in a meeting of stockholders that he and I held in the visiting room, with a notary and an attorney present to record the meetings.
You're under age. Will any contracts you enter into be legally binding?
Dad also issued a statement that as my guardian, he is responsible for all my debts and contracts.
I think it's time for me to be brought up to speed on all the operations of Stark Enterprises. Ryan, will you please report on personal weapons development?
Bill, you can sit down now. Your report on pending negotiations will be next.
Of course, Mr. Stark.
Of course, Mr. Stark.
All your previous instructions from my father are still in force, but I expect you to take the initiative in telling me when those decisions need to be reviewed.
I'll be in my father's office every morning from seven till nine.
After that, look for me in my own lab. I expect you to interrupt me at need.

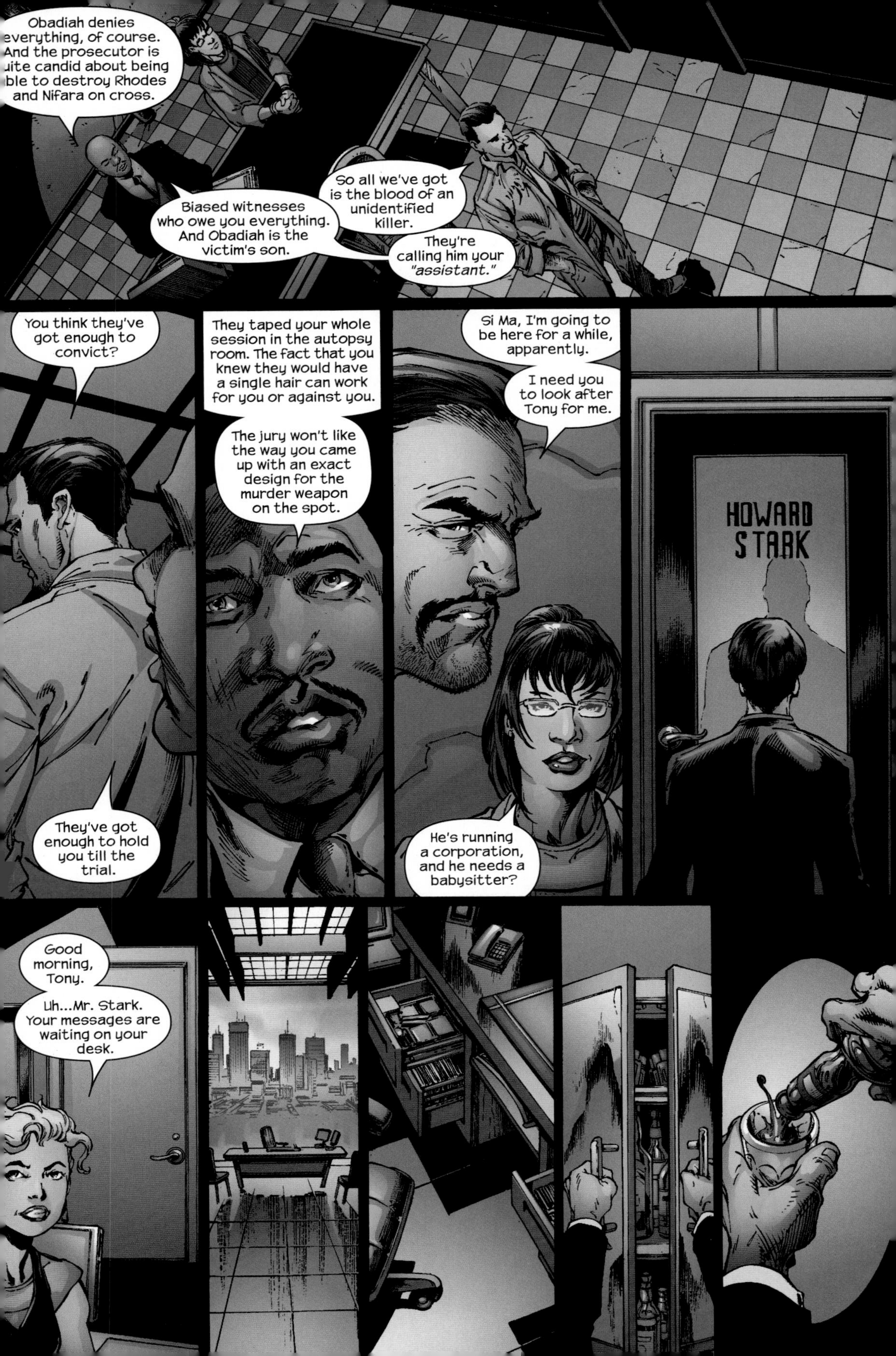

Obadiah denies everything, of course. And the prosecutor is uite candid about being ble to destroy Rhodes and Nifara on cross.
Biased witnesses who owe you everything. And Obadiah is the victim's son.
So all we've got is the blood of an unidentified killer.
They're calling him your "assistant."
You think they've got enough to convict?
They taped your whole session in the autopsy room. The fact that you knew they would have a single hair can work for you or against you.
The jury won't like the way you came up with an exact design for the murder weapon on the spot.
They've got enough to hold you till the trial.
Si Ma, I'm going to be here for a while, apparently.
I need you to look after Tony for me.
He's running a corporation, and he needs a babysitter?
HOWARD STARK
Good morning, Tony.
Uh...Mr. Stark. Your messages are waiting on your desk.

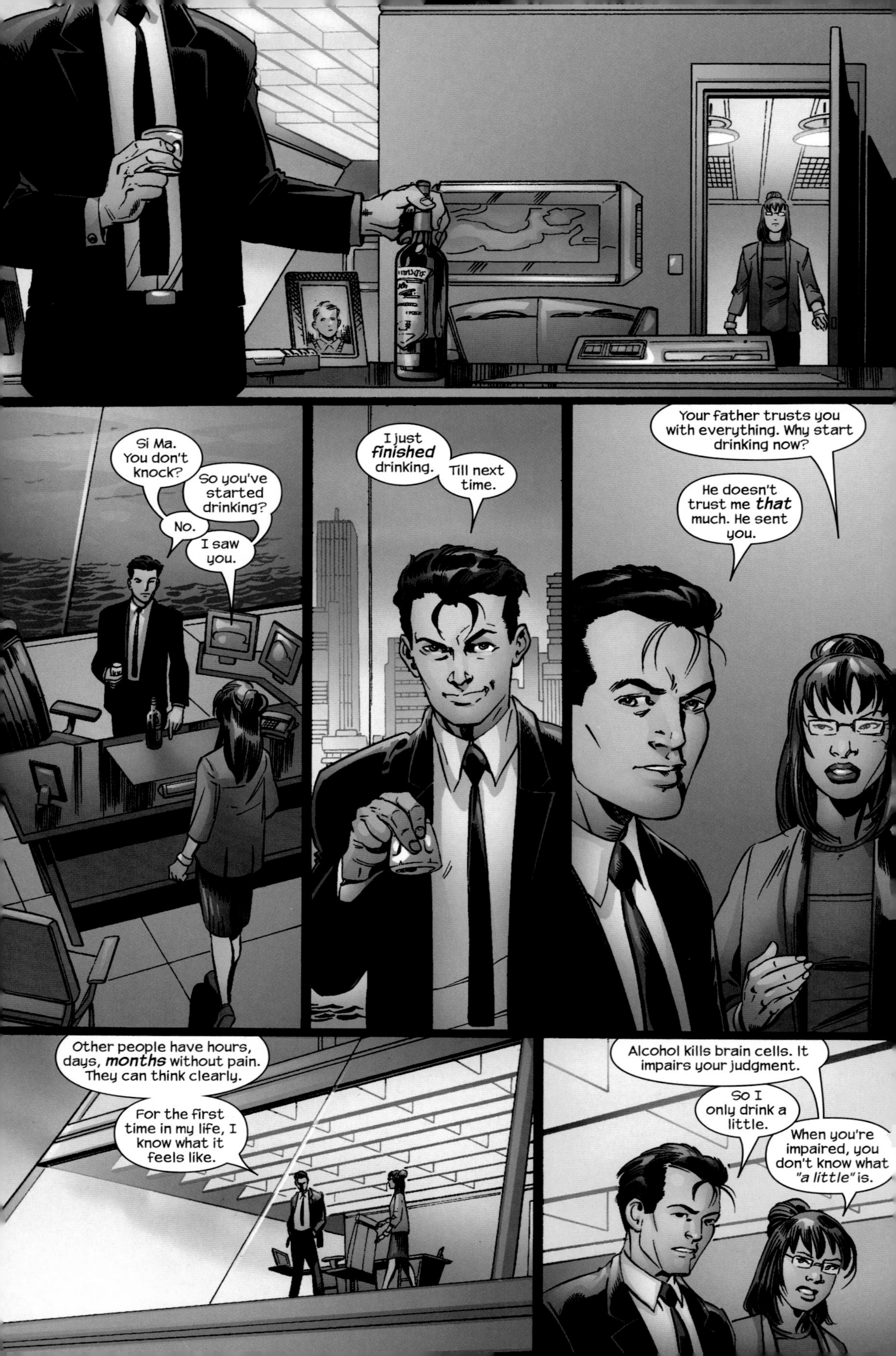
Si Ma. You don't knock?
So you've started drinking?
No.
I saw you.
I just *finished* drinking.
Till next time.
Your father trusts you with everything. Why start drinking now?
He doesn't trust me *that* much. He sent you.
Other people have hours, days, *months* without pain. They can think clearly.
For the first time in my life, I know what it feels like.
Alcohol kills brain cells. It impairs your judgment.
So I only drink a little.
When you're impaired, you don't know what *"a little"* is.

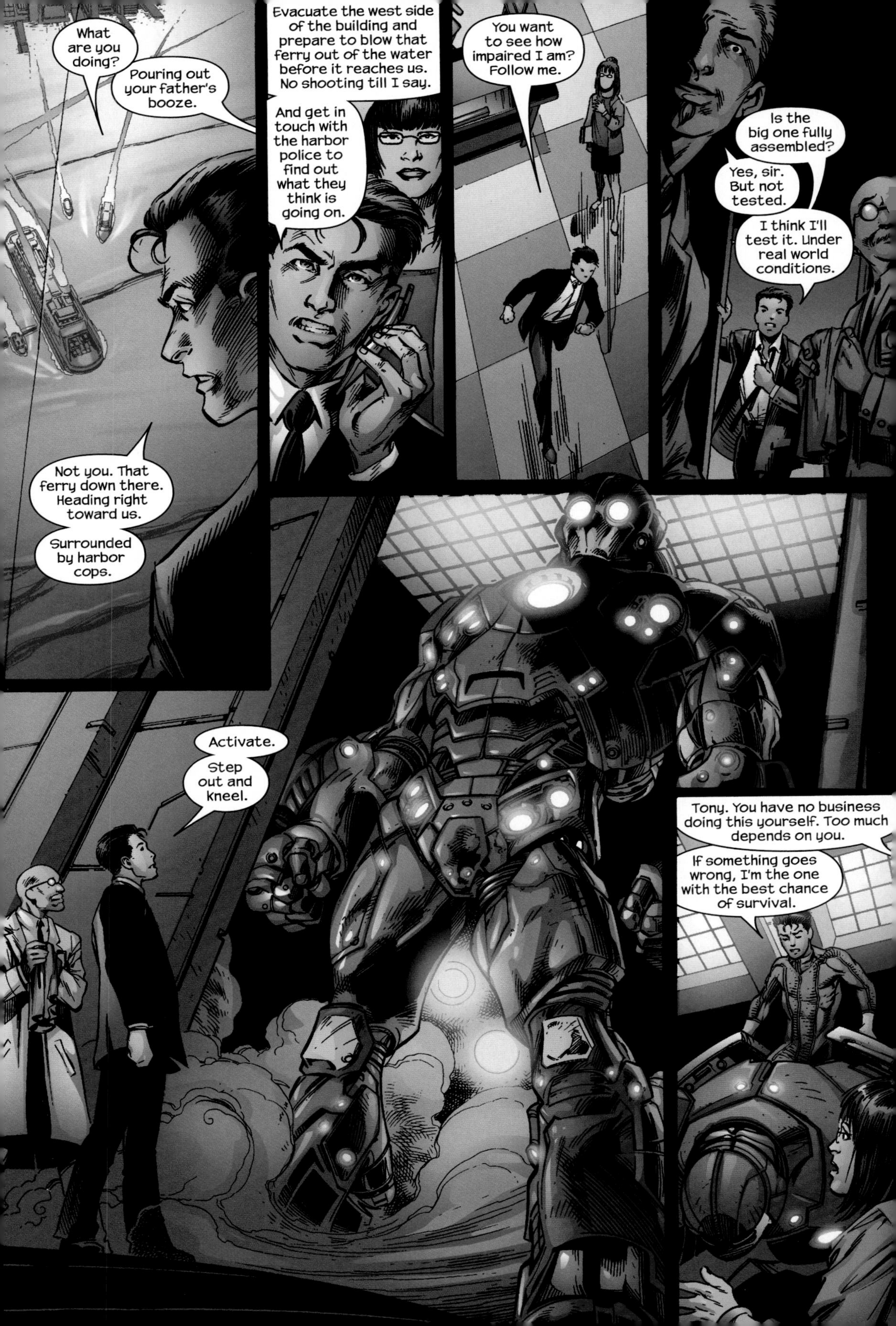
What are you doing?
Pouring out your father's booze.
Not you. That ferry down there. Heading right toward us.
Surrounded by harbor cops.
Evacuate the west side of the building and prepare to blow that ferry out of the water before it reaches us. No shooting till I say.
And get in touch with the harbor police to find out what they think is going on.
You want to see how impaired I am? Follow me.
Is the big one fully assembled?
Yes, sir. But not tested.
I think I'll test it. Under real world conditions.
Activate.
Step out and kneel.
Tony. You have no business doing this yourself. Too much depends on you.
If something goes wrong, I'm the one with the best chance of survival.

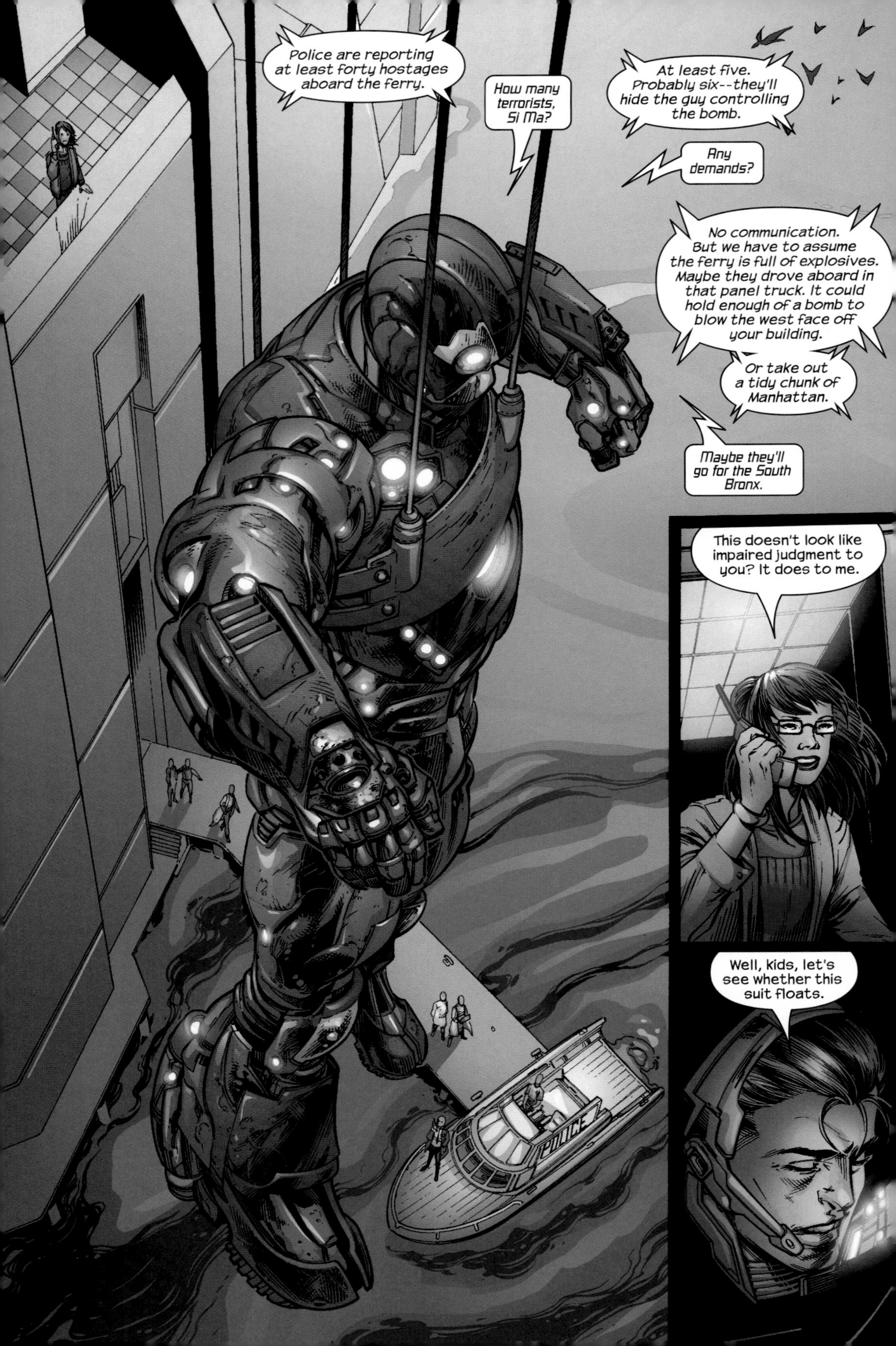
Police are reporting at least forty hostages aboard the ferry.
How many terrorists, Si Ma?
At least five. Probably six--they'll hide the guy controlling the bomb.
Any demands?
No communication. But we have to assume the ferry is full of explosives. Maybe they drove aboard in that panel truck. It could hold enough of a bomb to blow the west face off your building.
Or take out a tidy chunk of Manhattan.
Maybe they'll go for the South Bronx.
This doesn't look like impaired judgment to you? It does to me.
Well, kids, let's see whether this suit floats.
POLICE

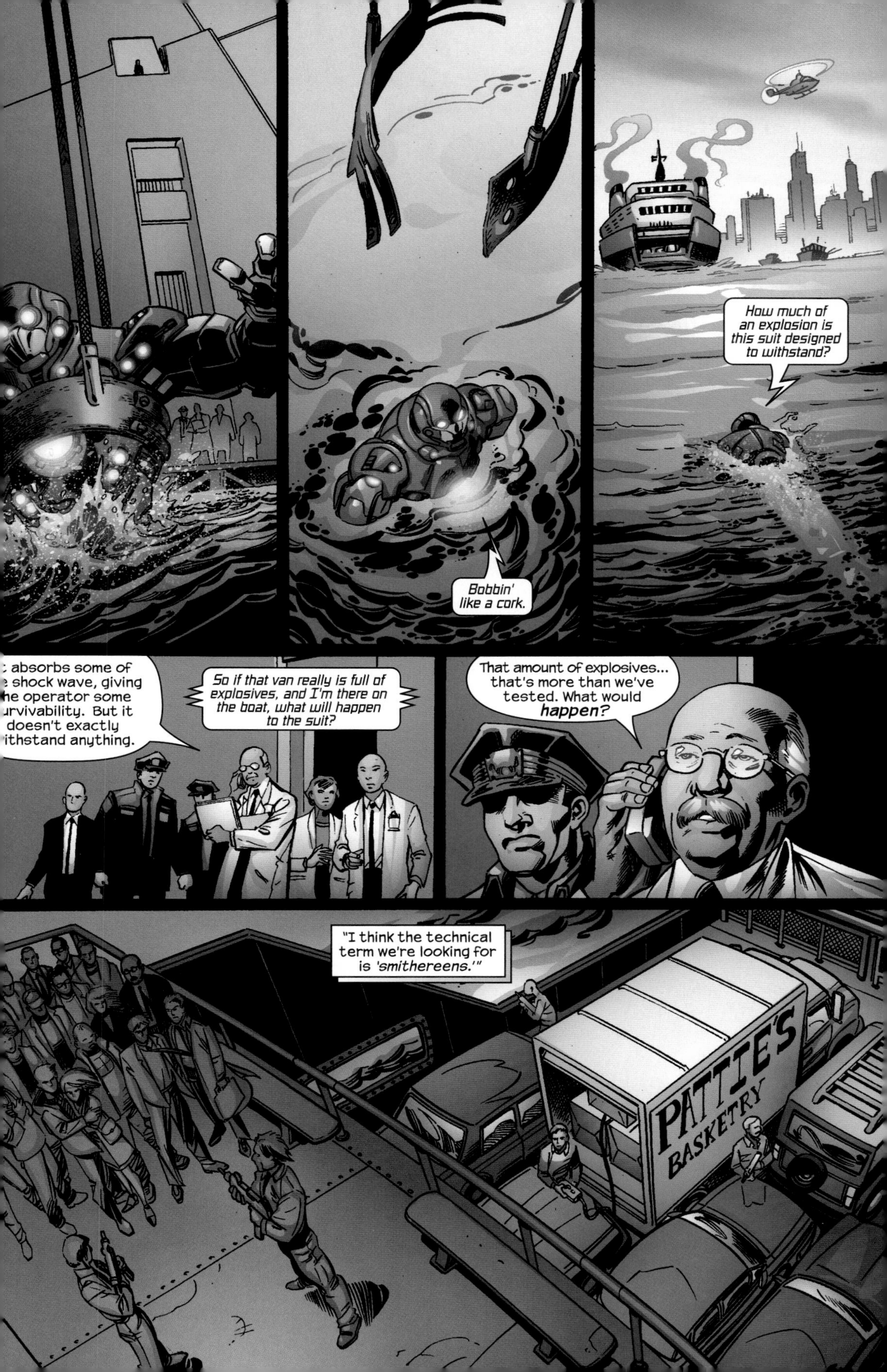
Bobbin' like a cork.
How much of an explosion is this suit designed to withstand?
absorbs some of shock wave, giving the operator some urvivability. But it doesn't exactly ithstand anything.
So if that van really is full of explosives, and I'm there on the boat, what will happen to the suit?
That amount of explosives... that's more than we've tested. What would happen?
"I think the technical term we're looking for is 'smithereens.'"
PATTIE'S BASKETRY

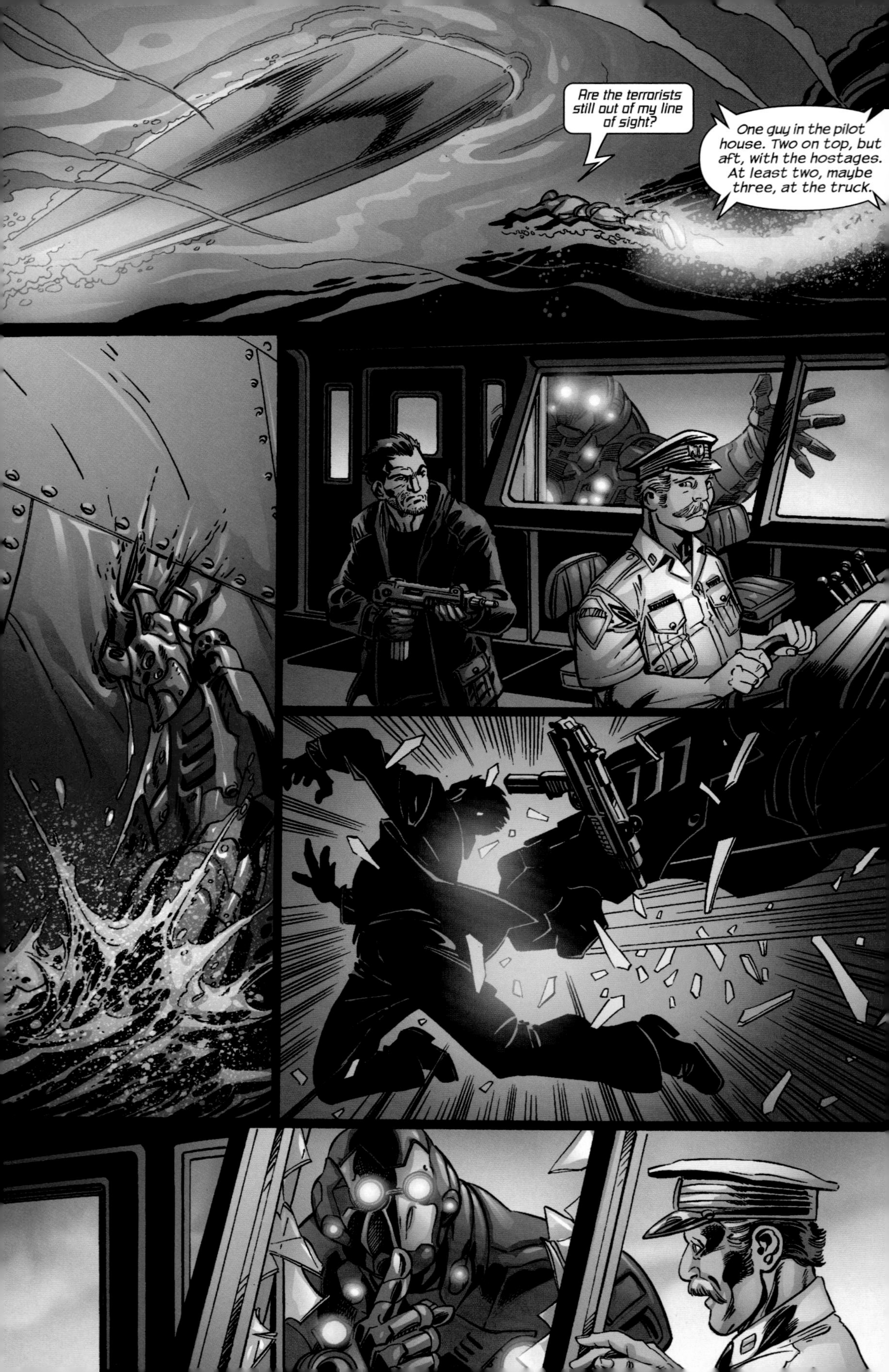
Are the terrorists still out of my line of sight?
One guy in the pilot house. Two on top, but aft, with the hostages. At least two, maybe three, at the truck.

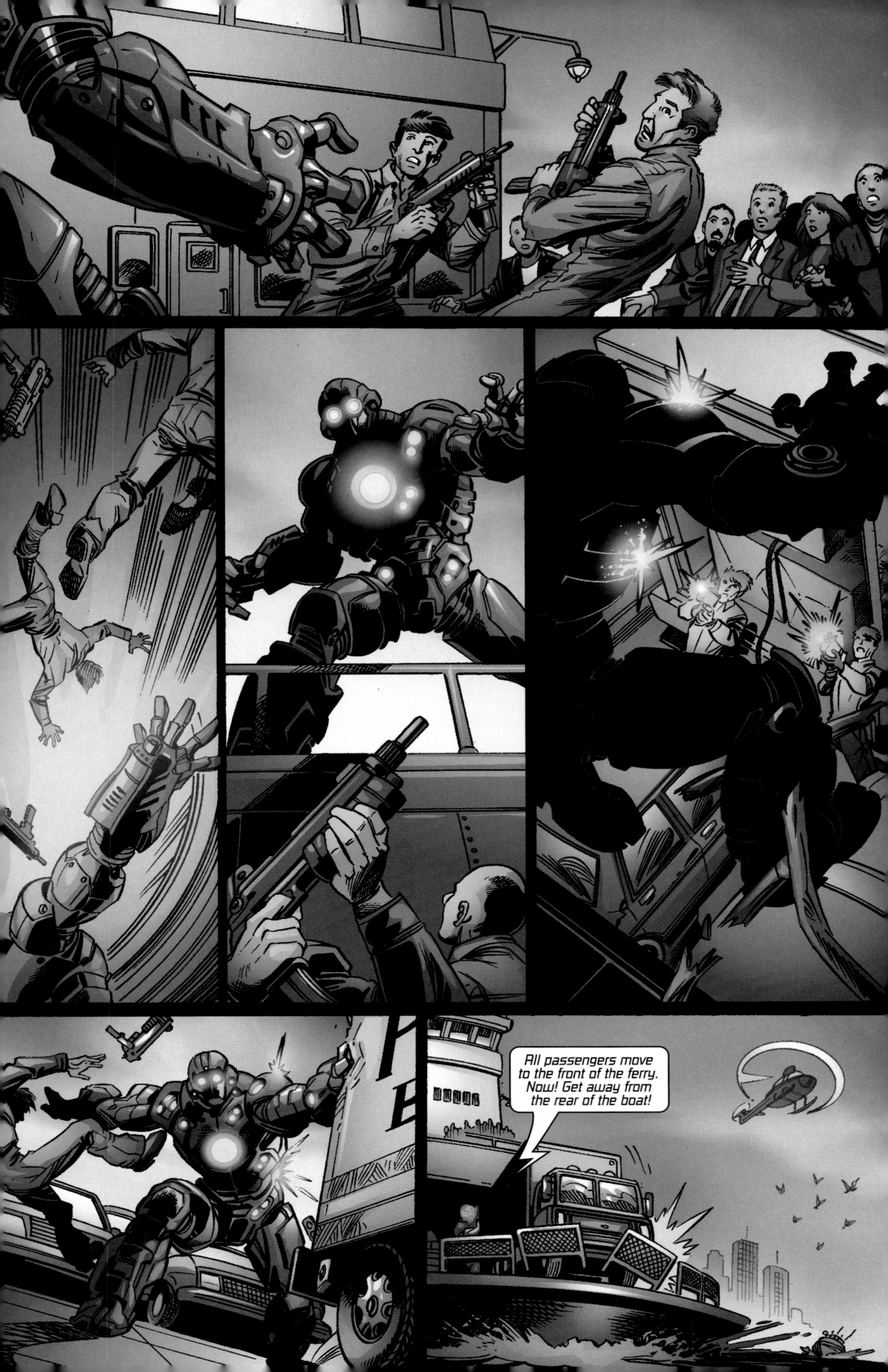
All passengers move to the front of the ferry. Now! Get away from the rear of the boat!

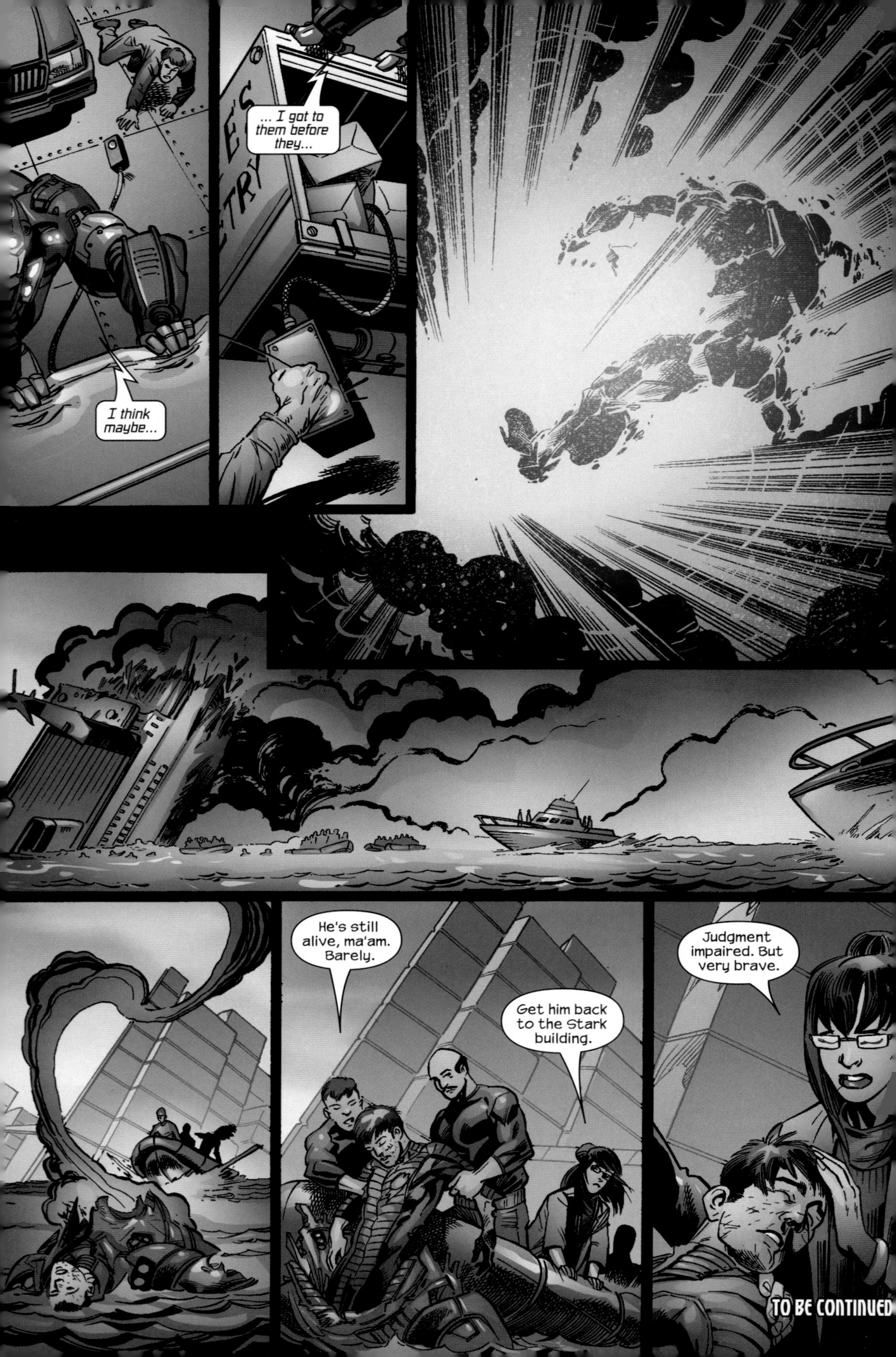
I think maybe...
... I got to them before they...
He's still alive, ma'am. Barely.
Get him back to the Stark building.
Judgment impaired. But very brave.
TO BE CONTINUED

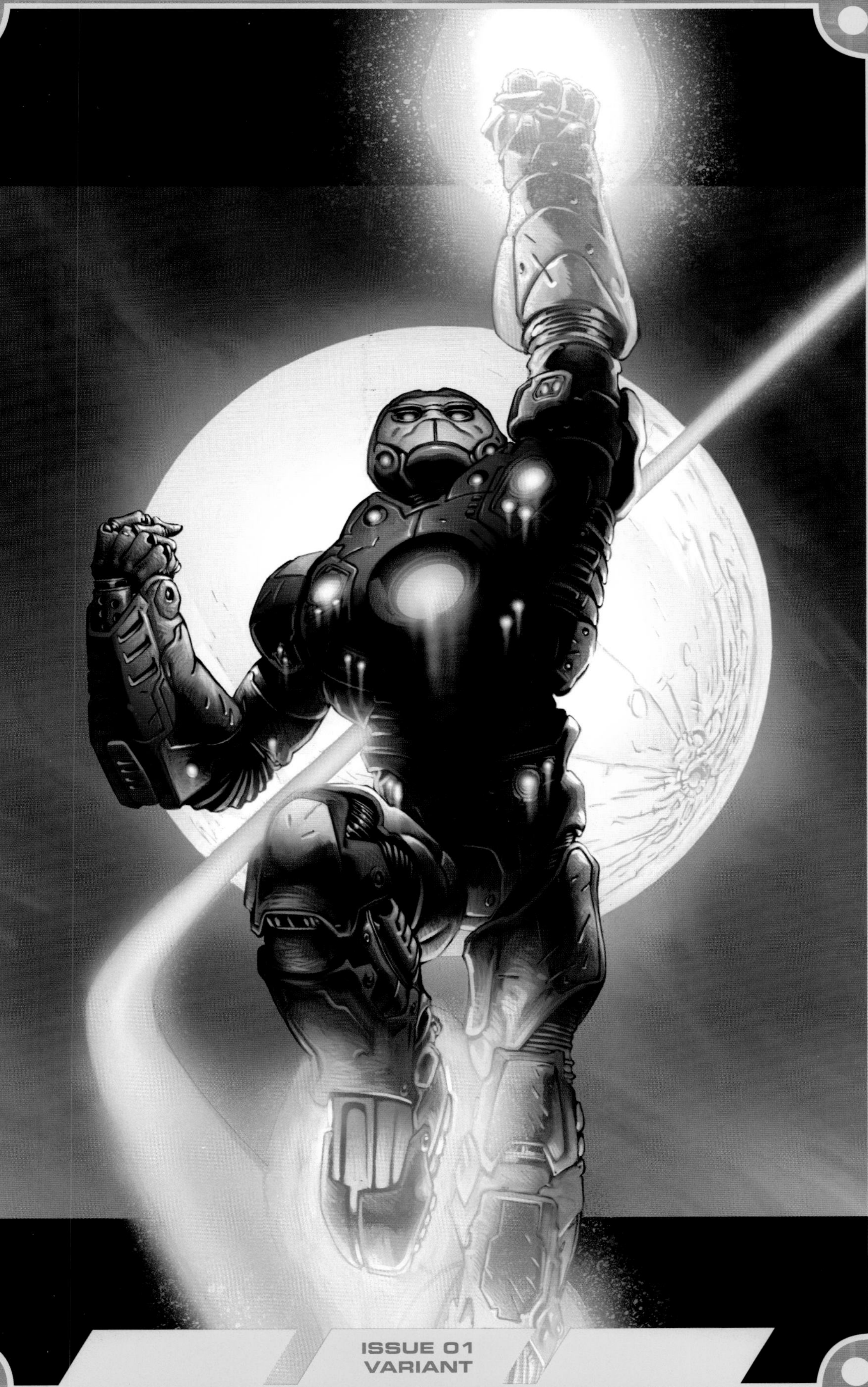

ISSUE 01
VARIANT

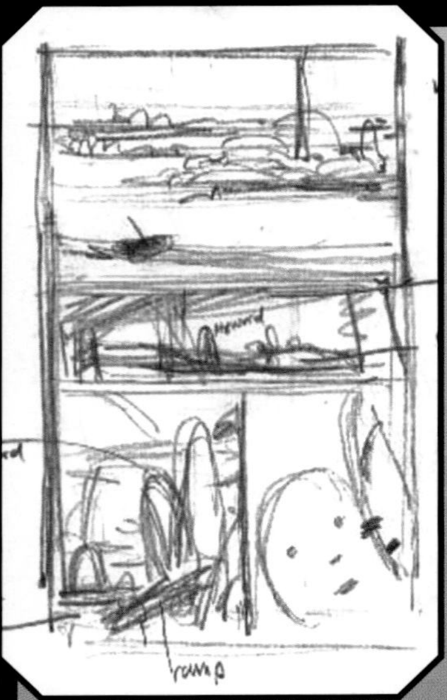
ramp

pg.1 thumbnail

ROUGH CUT: ULTIMATE IRON MAN #1 SCENE ONE

PAGE ONE

Pic 1; AERIAL VIEW: Long Island Sound between the Bronx and Queens. Rising out of the water is the Stark Defense Corporation plant. Domes on stilts, like tied-down bubbles. The domes are hardened for explosion containment, so there are no windows except in a single spire-like office tower in the middle. A fast launch is cutting across the water from Stark Pier in Queens to the plant.

CAPTION: Stark Defense Corporation Headquarters New York City

CAPTION 2: Years Ago...

Pic 2; The launch is at a landing platform among the stilts. HOWARD STARK, a tall wiry man in his forties, wearing a 1980s suit, reaches out to help MARIA CERRERA, a frail-looking Latina woman of thirty, make the leap onto the dock.

HOWARD: Dr. Cerrera, Welcome to Stark Defense Corp.

Pic 3; She stands a little too close to him, so that, tall as he is, she has her head thrown back to look up at him, and he's looking way down at her.

HOWARD: I'm Howard Stark.

MARIA: On TV you looked taller.

HOWARD: I've been losing height.

Pic 4; HOWARD'S POV: Maria gazes up at him. She may be wearing a business suit, but it doesn't hide that she's a woman.

MARIA: You had something to show me?

PAGE TWO

Pic 1; Inside a testing lab. A bare-chested young man is being sprayed by a female lab technician, Si Ma, with what looks like sky-blue paint. Howard and Maria are watching.

Pic 2; Howard is holding up an ice pick.

HOWARD: Here. Stick him with this.

Pic 3; Maria takes the ice pick, frowning.

MARIA: Stick him where?

HOWARD: Wherever.

Pic 4; Maria pushes it against the blue-painted man's arm.

HOWARD (OFF): Come on, put some weight behind it.

Pic 5; The ice pick goes part way in, the skin dimpling under the pressure.

HOWARD (OFF): Harder.

Pic 6; The ice pick is in his arm up to the handle. Maria looks at Blue Man.

MARIA: Doesn't that hurt?

Pic 7; Blue-painted man looks at her blandly.

BLUE MAN: Ouch.

Pic 8; Blue Man grins.

pg.2 thumbnail

PAGE THREE

Pic 1; Maria pulls out the ice pick. Only there's no shaft anymore. The metal looks more like a Brillo pad or a pom-pom — wiry twists of very thin metal going every which way.

Pic 2; Maria holds up the ice pick to show Howard.

MARIA: That blue stuff — it can do this to metal, and it doesn't hurt his skin?

HOWARD: Not for the first fifteen minutes.

Pic 3; Howard picks up a wooden baseball bat.

Pic 4; He rares back to let fly at Blue Man's chest.

BLUE MAN: I hate this part.

Pic 5; The bat connects with his chest.

Pic 6; Blue man flies backward.

HOWARD: Lift off!

pg.3 thumbnail

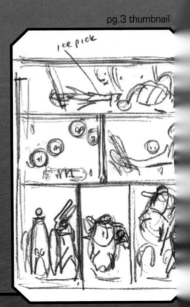

PAGE FOUR

Pic 1; Blue Man is sprawled on the floor.

Pic 2; The lab technician dips a sponge into a pan and wipes off the blue stuff, baring the skin on Blue Man's chest.

Pic 3; Maria kneels by him, examining him.

MARIA: Not even a bruise. What is that stuff?

BLUE MAN: Armor.

Pic 4; Howard helps Blue Man to his feet.

HOWARD: Go wash that off before it eats too much of your skin.

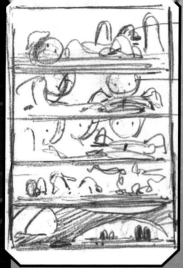

pg.4 thumbnail

Pic 5; As Blue Man and the lab technician leave, Maria and Howard watch.

MARIA: So that blue paste — it's alive?

PAGE FIVE

Pic 1; Howard inserts a cassette into a Betamax.

Pic 2; In a conference room, Howard and Maria watch a picture of swirling sky-blue microbes on the TV screen.

HOWARD: Bacteria. They live on the surface of the skin.

MARIA: Eating skin cells?

HOWARD: Only when they're hungry.

Pic 3; CLOSEUP of the microbes. Little tendrils link them together.

pg.5 thumbnail

HOWARD: Here's what happens when something hits them.

Pic 4; CLOSEUP of the microbes. They suddenly reorient and reshape themselves, long and thin now, and radiating outward from a center point.

HOWARD: They spread the shock of impact outward. The guy still flies across the room, but it's as if the bat were a big soft hand pushing him.

Pic 5; Maria gazes at the brillo-ended ice pick.

> **MARIA:** That still doesn't explain this.

Pic 6; Closeup of a single bacterium. Now we see that the tendrils are covered with tiny globules.

> **HOWARD:** Our bacterium has a parasite. Those little globules are like piranha, only instead of flesh, they eat metal.

> **MARIA:** Any metal?

> **HOWARD:** Not gold. But any metal that can oxidize.

PAGE SIX

Pic 1; Howard turns off the projector.

> **MARIA:** So you've reinvented armor.

> **HOWARD:** Still have a few problems.

Pic 2; Howard leads the way out of the conference room.

> **HOWARD:** It won't stop a bullet. Moving too fast.

Pic 3; Howard leads the way along an outside corridor, only a railing between them and the Long Island Sound far below.

> **HOWARD:** And after about three hours, it eats away all your skin.

Pic 4; Howard leans on the railing, looking out toward New York City in the distance, to the southwest. Maria is looking at Howard.

pg.6 thumbnail

> **MARIA:** So if you're attacked with ice picks and baseball bats...

> **HOWARD:** You're invulnerable. As long as you have soap and water close by.

Pic 5; Maria grins at him.

> **MARIA:** And it's such a lovely color.

> **HOWARD:** Sky blue. Goes with everything.

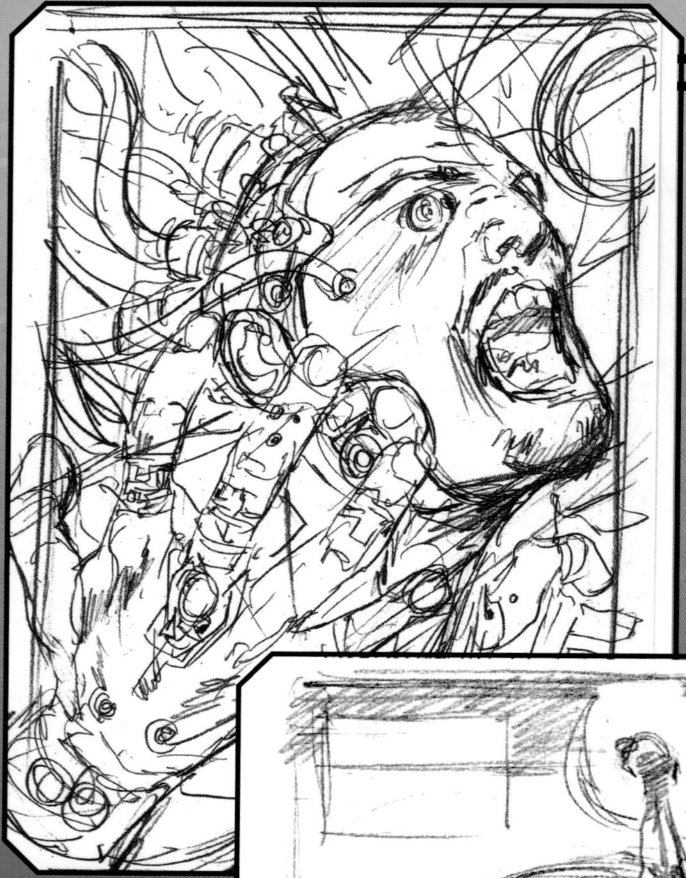

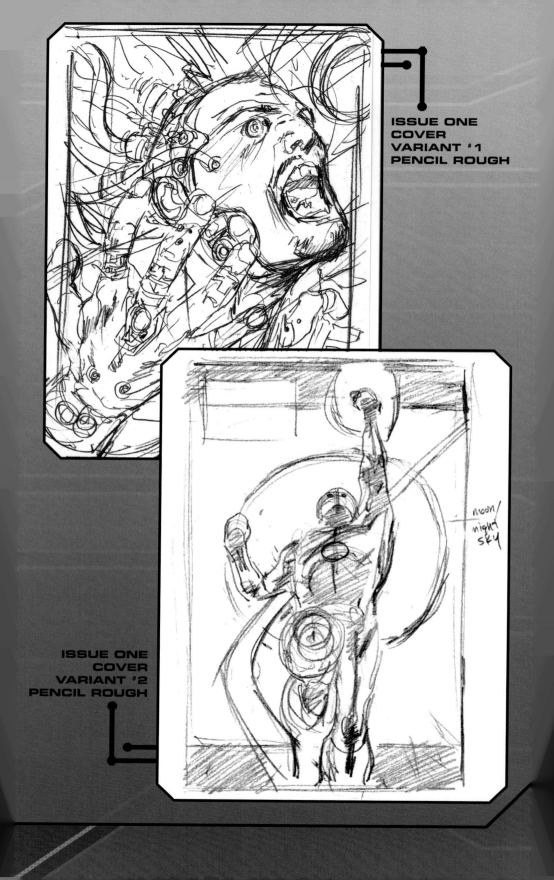

ISSUE ONE
COVER
VARIANT #1
PENCIL ROUGH

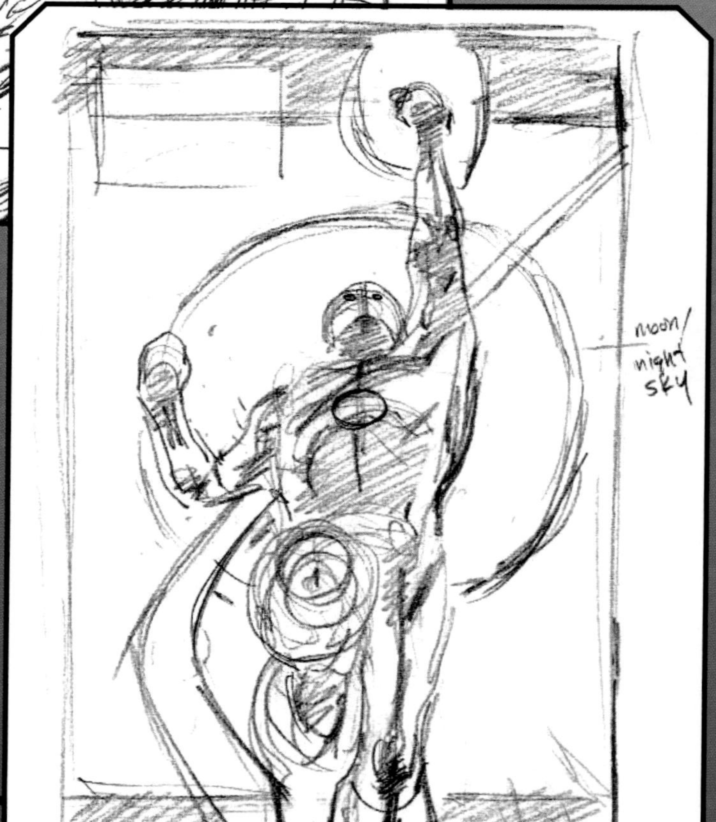
moon/
night
sky

ISSUE ONE
COVER
VARIANT #2
PENCIL ROUGH

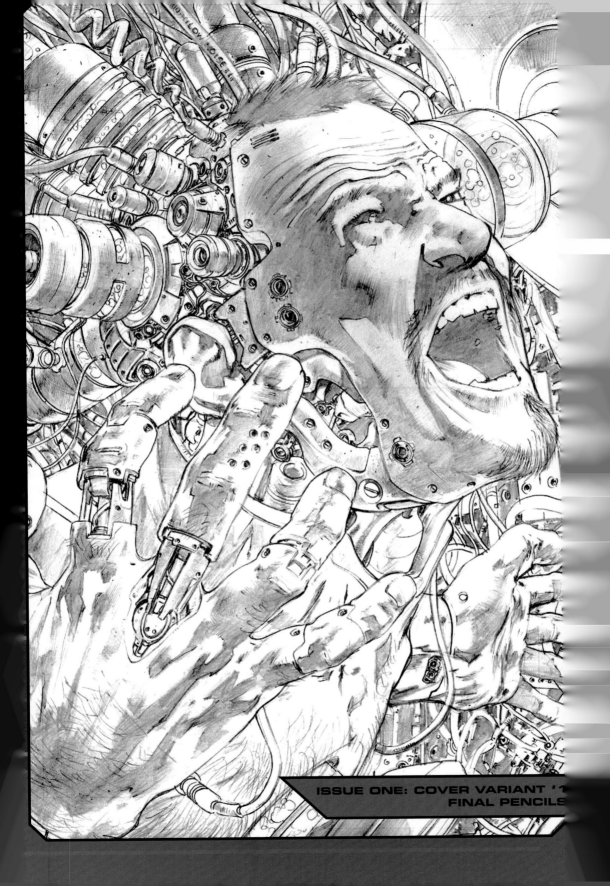

ISSUE ONE: COVER VARIANT '1
FINAL PENCILS

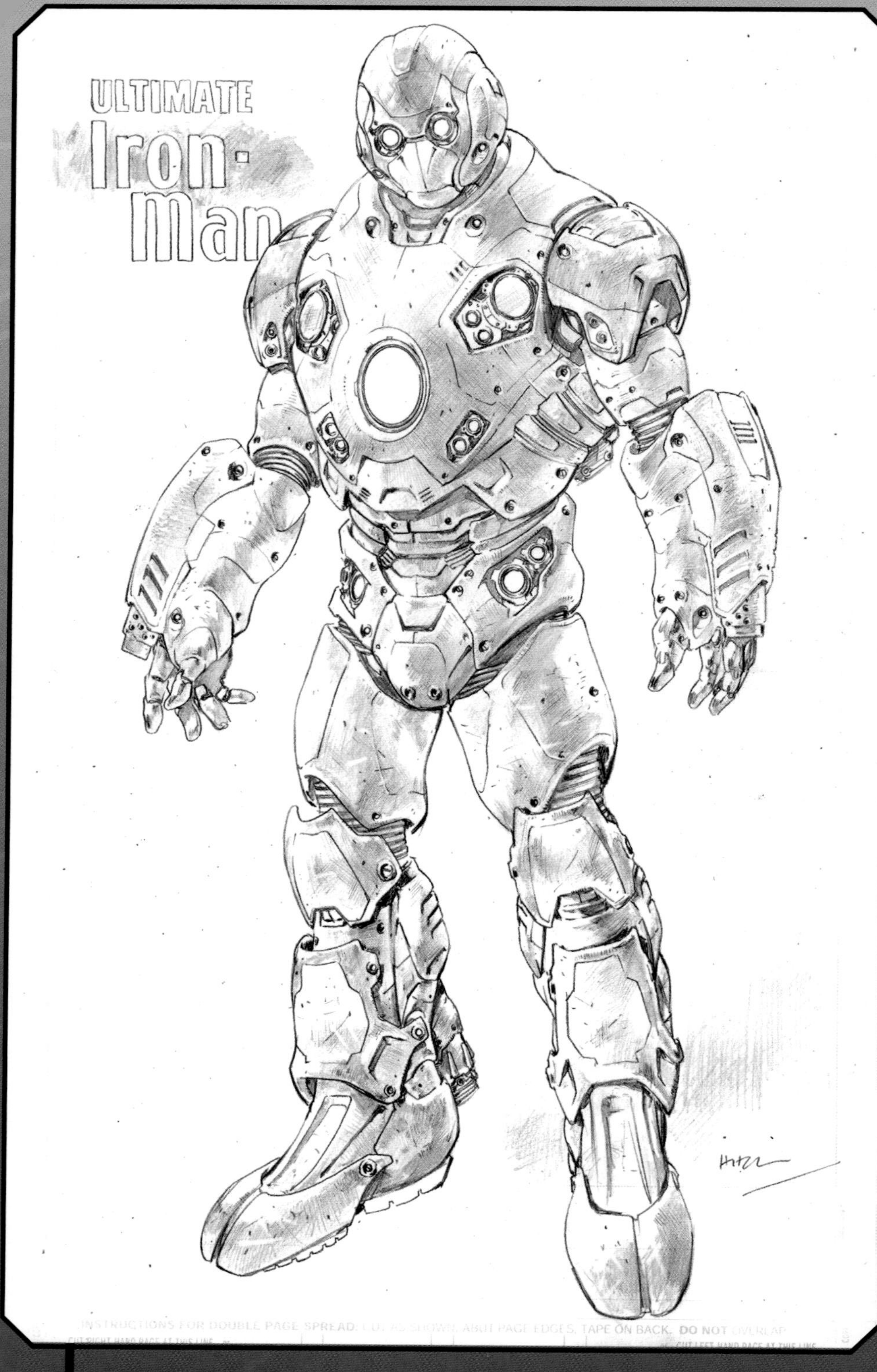
ULTIMATE
Iron-Man
INSTRUCTIONS FOR DOUBLE PAGE SPREAD: CUT AS SHOWN, ABUT PAGE EDGES, TAPE ON BACK. DO NOT OVERLAP
CUT RIGHT HAND PAGE AT THIS LINE
CUT LEFT HAND PAGE AT THIS LINE

IRON MAN
ARMOR CONCEPT

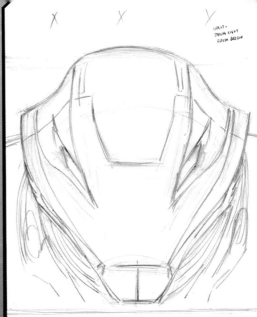

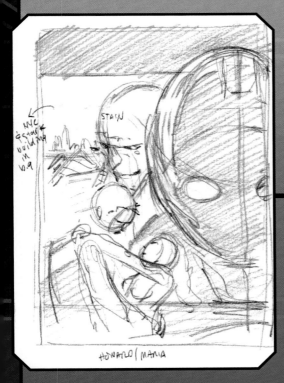

UNUSED COVER LAYOUTS

HOWARD / MARIA

Stane, howard, maria
STANE →
HOWARD EMBRACING MARIA
IRONMAN'S ARM SEEN THROUGH
NEW YORK CITY/ WATER IN B.G.

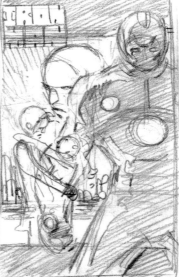

ISSUE #2 COVER PROCESS

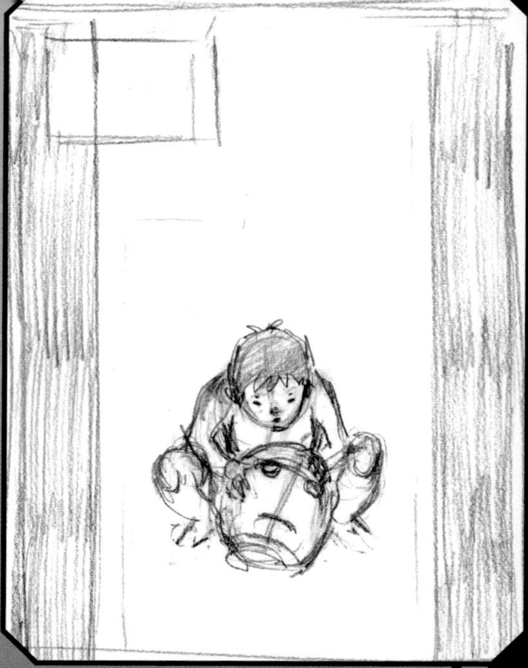

ORIGINAL THUMBNAIL

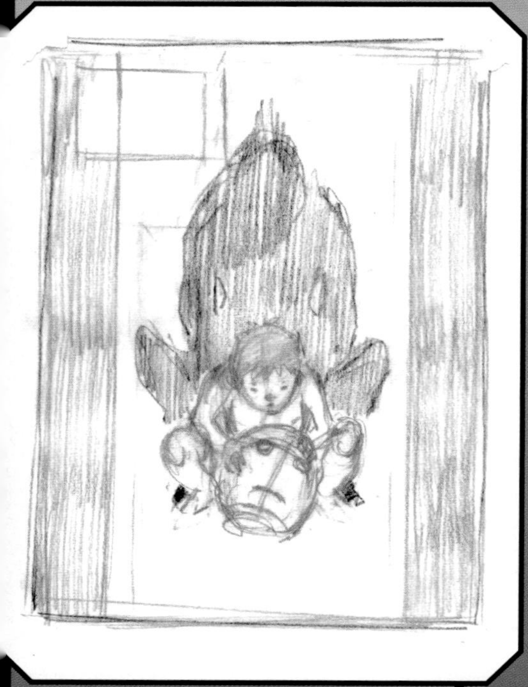

ORIGINAL THUMBNAIL

FINAL LAYOUT

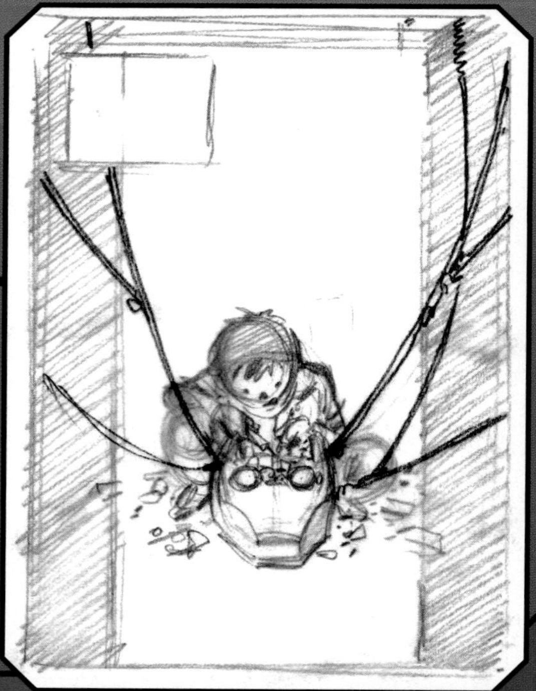

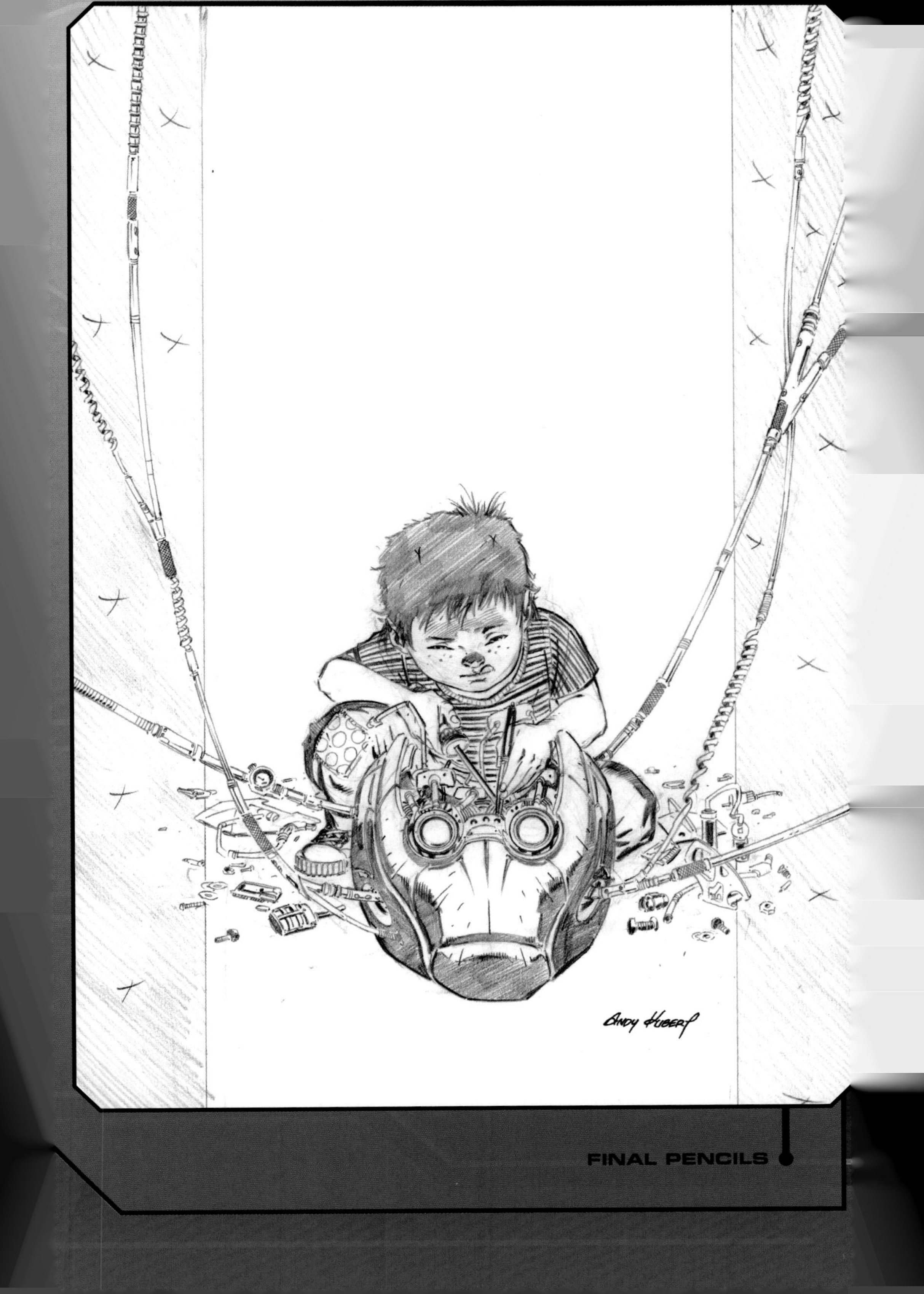
ANDY KUBERT

FINAL PENCILS

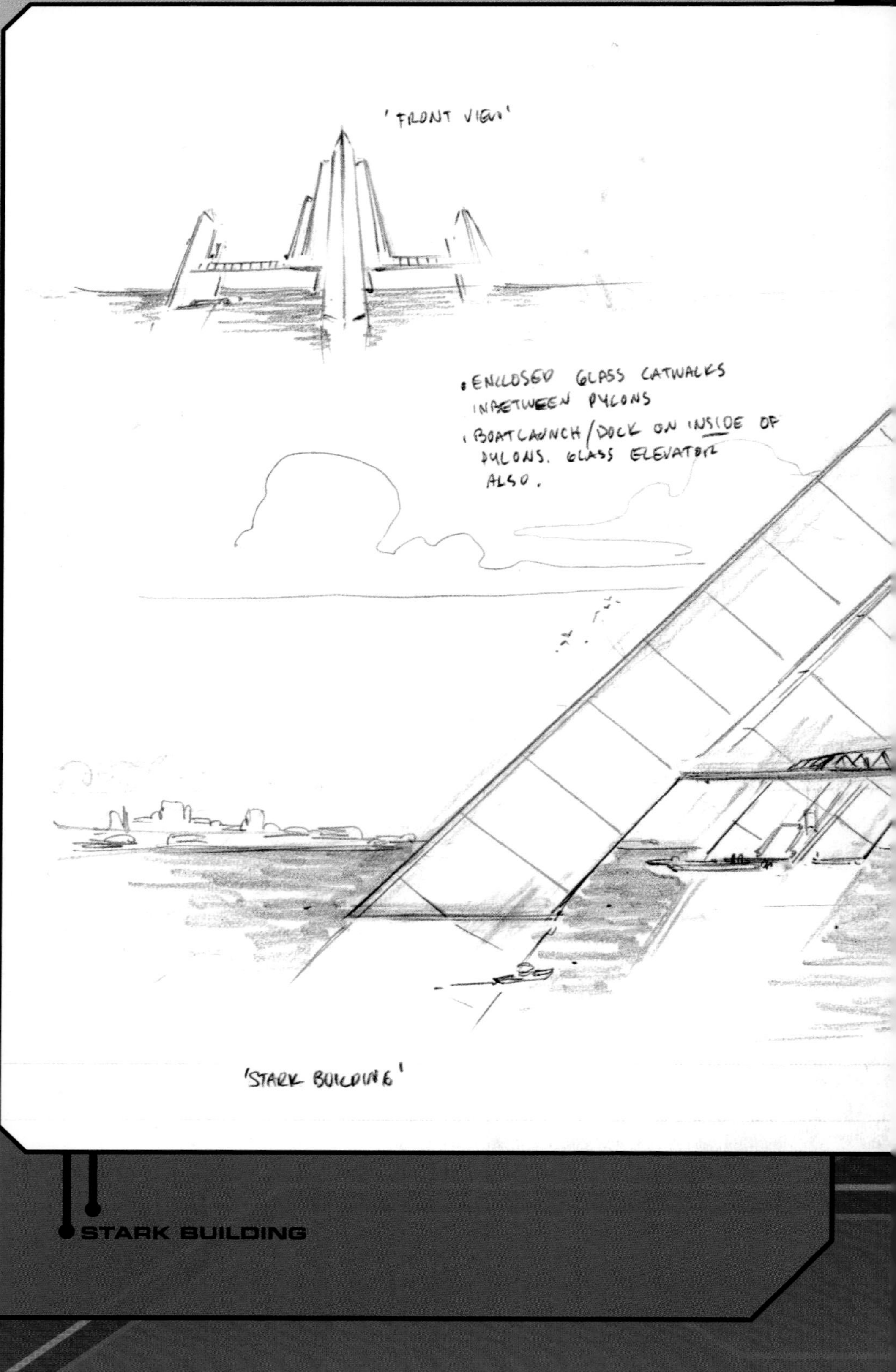
'FRONT VIEW'
•ENCLOSED GLASS CATWALKS INBETWEEN PYLONS
•BOATLAUNCH/DOCK ON INSIDE OF PYLONS. GLASS ELEVATOR ALSO.
'STARK BUILDING'

STARK BUILDING

¾ view

. VERY SHINY / YET OUTER CASING CAN WITHSTAND
       BLASTS.   ☐. 11/11/04

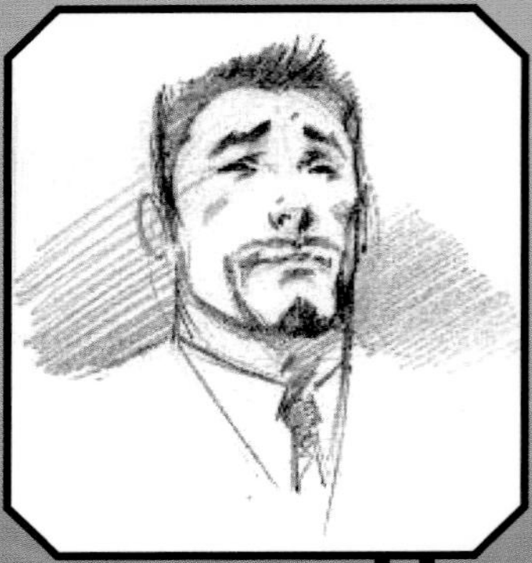

HOWARD
STARK

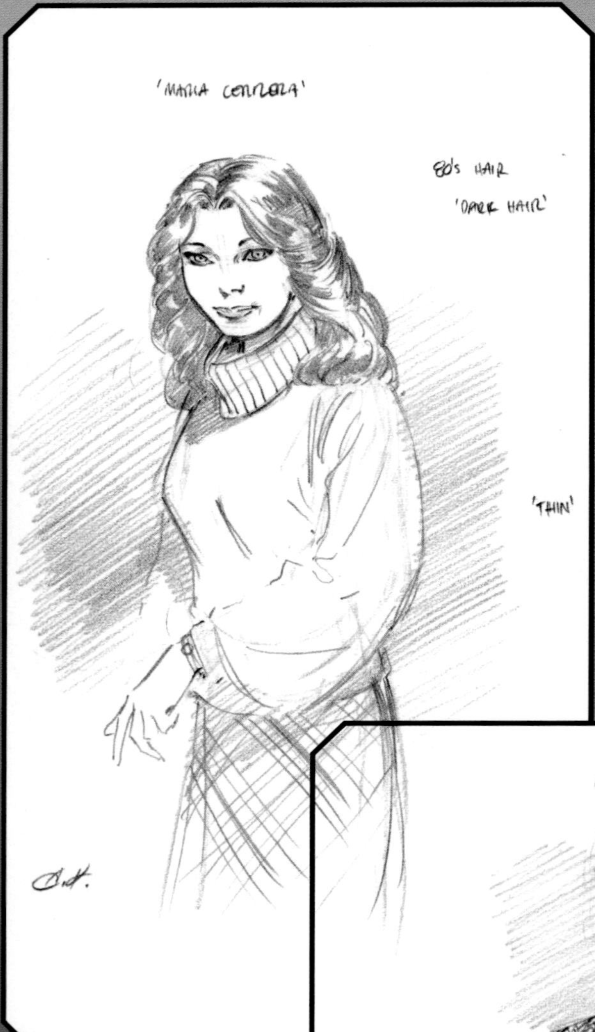
80's HAIR
'DARK HAIR'
'THIN'

ORIGINAL
CONCEPT ART
BY ANDY KUBERT

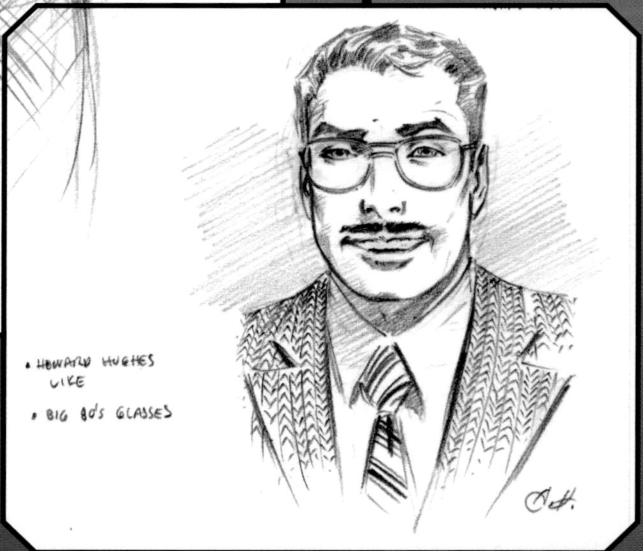
• HOWARD HUGHES LIKE
• BIG 80's GLASSES

MARIA
STARK

IRON MAN

HISTORY: Blessed and cursed with extraordinary genius, Tony Stark is the son of inventor and defense contractor Howard Stark, and geneticist Maria Stark. The Starks were developing a biological personal armor coating when a lab accident with a regenerative virus fatally infected Maria. The virus mutated her unborn child, Tony, growing additional neural tissue throughout his body which augmented his intelligence while causing chronic pain. Maria died, but Howard saved Tony by coating him in their bacterial bio-armor, which consumed ordinary skin but not Tony's constantly regenerating neural flesh. Business rival Zebediah Stane married Howard's scheming ex-wife Loni, with whom he stole Stark's company, and spent years trying to seize the bio-armor. As a teenager, Tony befriended fellow prep school student Jim Rhodes and began developing his own "Iron Man" armor technology. Becoming a wealthy celebrity and science prodigy, young Tony founded multi-billion dollar design and manufacturing corporation Stark International. He also became an infamous playboy, alcoholic, and womanizer, suffering from recurring depression and secretly learning he was dying from an inoperable brain tumor.

Later, Stark would claim he developed the armor. When he and his shifty cousin Morgan were taken hostage along with other civilians by Guatemalan guerrilla terrorists, their captors demanded Stark's technology in exchange for the hostages' freedom. They killed Morgan when Tony refused to cooperate. Pretending to acquiesce, Stark built makeshift armor and defeated the terrorists with it. Years later, Stark used new Iron Man armor to save the President from an assassination attempt, becoming a bigger celebrity than ever, but refusing to sell or mass-produce his armor technology. When Latverian ambassador Golog tried to steal Stark's "Irontech" with the covert approval of intelligence agency S.H.I.E.L.D., Stark fought off Golog's Mandroids with the aid of Spider-Man. Spurred by his

REAL NAME: Antonio "Tony" Stark
KNOWN ALIASES: Monopoly Man
IDENTITY: Publicly known
OCCUPATION: Inventor, CEO, U.S. government super-operative
CITIZENSHIP: U.S.A.
PLACE OF BIRTH: Unrevealed
KNOWN RELATIVES: Howard & Maria Cerrera Stark (parents, deceased), Morgan Stark (cousin, deceased), Antonio (uncle, deceased), uncle (name unrevealed, deceased)
GROUP AFFILIATION: Ultimates, Stark Industries
EDUCATION: Multiple scientific doctorates, studied at Harvard and MIT
FIRST APPEARANCE: Ultimate Marvel Team-Up #4 (2001)

tumor to make the most of his remaining days, Stark joined the Ultimates, a S.H.I.E.L.D.-sponsored superhero team. Forming an unlikely friendship with anti-corporate teammate Thor, Stark helped defeat the Hulk, the Chitauri and others. Dating teammate Natasha Romanov (Black Widow), Tony eventually proposed to her, creating new armor for her as an engagement gift; however, when a super-army conquered the team, Natasha suddenly attacked Tony, placing him — and their relationship — in jeopardy.

HEIGHT: (unarmored) 6'1", (armored) 7'
WEIGHT: (unarmored) 225 lbs., (armored) 2000 lbs.
EYES: Blue
HAIR: Black

ABILITIES AND ACCESSORIES: Tony Stark is a phenomenal scientific genius and inventor, thanks largely to his body-wide neural tissue, which enhances his intelligence and gives his body fantastic regenerative capacity. His bacterial bio-armor fits his body like a second skin, enhances his durability, and inhibits his chronic neurological pain. He is multilingual, has nearly total recall, and has a seemingly limitless capacity for multitasking. His Iron Man armor grants him tremendous superhuman strength and durability, enabling both supersonic flight and submersible travel, and houses repulsor rays, a uni-beam, mind-impairing "thought-scramblers," "light-negativity" devices allowing short-term invisibility, force field generators, a tracking system, communications tech and onboard computers. He can manually recharge his armor from outside sources or draw additional power from a network of dedicated satellites.

POWER GRID	1	2	3	4	5	6	7
INTELLIGENCE							
STRENGTH							
SPEED							
DURABILITY							
ENERGY PROJECTION							
FIGHTING SKILLS							

THE ULTIMATES

ACTIVE MEMBERS: Black Widow (Natasha Romanov), Captain America (Steve Rogers), Hawkeye (Clint Barton), Iron Man (Tony Stark), Quicksilver (Pietro Maximoff), Scarlet Witch (Wanda Maximoff), Wasp (Janet Pym)
FORMER MEMBERS: Giant-Man (Hank Pym), Hulk (Bruce Banner), Lieberman (deceased reservist), Thor (allegedly Thorlief Golman)
RESERVES: The Four Seasons, the Goliaths, Intangi-Girl, Owen, O'Donohue, Rocketman One (Dexter), Rocketman Two, Rocketman Three, Rusk, Son of Satan (Damien), Thunderbolt, unspecified others
BASE OF OPERATIONS: The Triskelion, Upper Bay, Manhattan
FIRST APPEARANCE: Ultimates #2 (2002)

HISTORY: The world's foremost superhuman strike force, the Ultimates trace their origins back to World War II super-operative Captain America (Steve Rogers), whom the U.S. government empowered in part to oppose the Nazis' secret extraterrestrial Chitauri allies. Rogers appeared to die while helping destroy the Chitauri/Nazi war effort, and U.S. scientists tried for decades to duplicate his powers. In recent years, the super-soldier program's lead scientist was geneticist Bruce Banner, reporting to General Ross, head of the S.H.I.E.L.D. intelligence agency. Later, new S.H.I.E.L.D. director Nick Fury pushed through a multi-billion expansion of the super-soldier program, though Banner's temporary transformation into the monstrous Hulk resulted in his demotion to deputy under new head scientists Hank and Janet Pym, who did double duty as size-changing super-operatives Giant-Man and Wasp. Altruistic armored billionaire inventor Tony Stark soon joined as Iron Man. Enigmatic left-wing powerhouse Thor refused membership at first, but Captain America himself was found alive and revived from a state of suspended animation to join the team. Together, Rogers, Stark and the Pyms became the Ultimates, headquartered in the high-tech Triskelion complex and backed by a huge support staff, a large conventional military force and black ops agents. Banner's semi-estranged girlfriend Betty Ross (daughter of General Ross) was hired as Director of Communications and helped make the new team into celebrities while making Bruce's life miserable. The depressed Banner finally snapped and transformed into the Hulk again, embarking on a destructive rampage stopped by the Ultimates with the aid of Thor, who began working with the team thereafter.

The Hulk's true identity was concealed from the public, and the Ultimates became beloved national heroes. The group soon expanded: intelligence veterans Hawkeye and Black Widow and mutant ex-terrorists Quicksilver and Scarlet Witch were promoted from the black ops division to the core team. Meanwhile, Hank Pym nearly killed his wife during a violent domestic dispute and was himself beaten into traction by Captain America, who later began dating the Wasp. Pym's former assistant Dr. Eamonn Brankin became the new scientific head of the program. Despite losing Giant-Man, the Ultimates saved the world from a Chitauri plot with the unwitting aid of the Hulk and became bigger icons than ever. They went on to apprehend Kraven, Electro, Luther Manning, the X-Men and Norman Osborn's "Six." Later allied with the European Super-Solider Initiative, the Ultimates became more controversial as they began operating in foreign territory, notably the Middle East. Thor quit, and a traitor within the group outed Banner as the Hulk. Seemingly executed for the Hulk's crimes, Banner secretly survived with the aid of Hank Pym, who was soon fired from the Ultimates altogether. Meanwhile, apparently exposed as a madman, Thor was brutally arrested by the team. The global community grew wary as the Ultimates developed many more superagents as their reserves, and anti-Ultimates sentiment accelerated when the team stripped a small "rogue" Middle Eastern nation of its nuclear capability. The traitor within the Ultimates responded by murdering Hawkeye's family, framing Captain America for the crime, and helping a foreign super-army invade America. Assisted by Hank Pym, this foreign force destroyed the Triskelion and occupied major American cities, slaughtering the reserves and capturing the remaining Ultimates in the process.